The Arab Spring

THE ARAB SPRING

*Change and Resistance
in the Middle East*

Edited by

MARK L. HAAS
Duquesne University

and

DAVID W. LESCH
Trinity University

WESTVIEW
PRESS

A MEMBER OF THE PERSEUS BOOKS GROUP

Westview Press was founded in 1975 in Boulder, Colorado, by notable publisher and intellectual Fred Praeger. Westview Press continues to publish scholarly titles and high-quality undergraduate-and graduate-level textbooks in core social science disciplines. With books developed, written, and edited with the needs of serious nonfiction readers, professors, and students in mind, Westview Press honors its long history of publishing books that matter.

Westview Press books are available at special discounts for bulk purchases in the United States by corporations, institutions, and other organizations. For more information, please contact the Special Markets Department at the Perseus Books Group, 2300 Chestnut Street, Suite 200, Philadelphia, PA 19103, or call (800) 810-4145, ext. 5000, or e-mail special.markets@perseusbooks.com.

Designed by Linda Mark
Text set in 11.5 Adobe Jenson Pro

Library of Congress Cataloging-in-Publication Data

The Arab Spring : change and resistance in the Middle East / edited by Mark L. Haas, David W. Lesch.
    p. cm.
   Includes bibliographical references and index.
    ISBN 978-0-8133-4819-3 (pbk. : alk. paper) — ISBN 978-0-8133-4820-9 (e-book)
1. Arab Spring, 2010– 2.   Arab countries—Politics and government—21st century.
3.   Revolutions—Arab countries—History—21st century. 4.   Arab countries—History—21st century.   I. Haas, Mark L. II. Lesch, David W.
   JQ1850.A91A77 2012
   909'.097492708312—dc23
                                                                2012028568
10 9 8 7 6 5 4 3 2 1

Mark dedicates the book to his aunt Trudy and uncle John, for a lifetime of love, support, and interest in his work and well-being. He cannot thank them enough for all they have done.

David dedicates this book to his wife, Judy Dunlap, for her unswerving support, energy, and love, without which tasks such as this would be impossible.

Contents

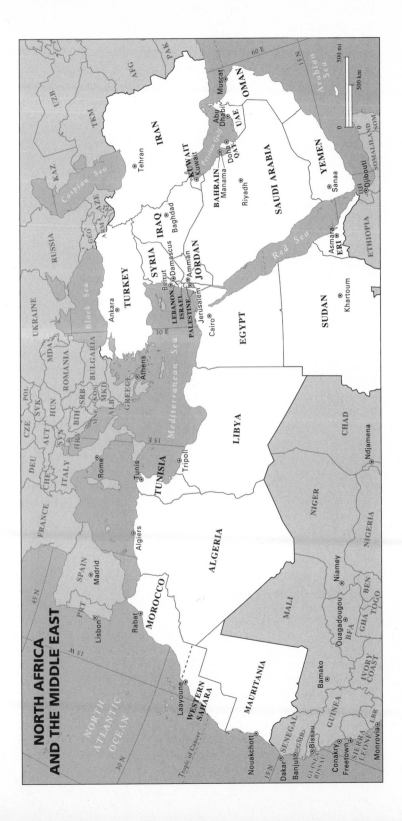

NORTH AFRICA
AND THE MIDDLE EAST

Preface

WRITING OR COMMENTING on current or recent events in the Middle East is a hazardous business. The fluidity of the moment and the different outcomes of a particular course of events, frequently resting on the whim of individuals, often make predicting anything an exercise in futility—or a book risking being partially outdated before it is even published. Who would have guessed that a twenty-something fruit vendor in Tunisia, by lighting himself on fire in late 2010 in abject frustration and anger at his lot in life, would unleash a torrent of protest that may rewrite the landscape of the Middle East? Sometimes, however, such is the importance of a series of events that they demand coverage and examination in the short term. This is the case with the so-called Arab Spring that engulfed the region—and riveted the world—beginning in late 2010 and continuing throughout all of 2011 and well into 2012. Although the ultimate impact of the uprisings of the Arab Spring may not become truly apparent for a generation, attempting to understand the origins of the uprisings, the actual course of events in particular countries directly and indirectly hit by the Arab Spring, and the regional and international responses is necessary in order to acquire a level of comprehension that will allow us to track and give meaning to all this history and politics in the making.

The editors of this volume selected the countries and topics to be examined. Anyone who has ever edited a volume such at this, however, understands that sometimes the topics chosen depend upon who is or is not available and who can or cannot complete their chapters in the requisite amount of time—which was very short in this case in order to quickly react to what has happened in the Middle East. Additionally, we are, as always, mindful of page counts—and thus of the price of a book—in order to make this volume affordable. We are very happy with the final tally of topics and pages. We believe that it was necessary to paint a broad picture of the Middle East in order to account for the interplay between actors and states at the domestic, regional, and international levels. As such, we have chapters on Arab countries that gave rise to the term "Arab Spring" as well as chapters examining regional and international players that have become deeply involved in the Arab Spring and/or deeply affected by it. We think this will be particularly useful for the interested general public and in the classroom for students attempting to understand the short- and long-term causes of the Arab Spring itself as well as the complex matrix of the Middle East that often reverberates well beyond its geographical limits. This book should act as an in-depth introduction to the Arab Spring and/or a supplementary reader for courses on modern Middle East history, politics, and international relations.

The editors first and foremost want to thank the contributors, whose expertise and dedication to their work are recognized and much appreciated. They had a small window of time in which to write their chapters, and they all answered the bell. It is quite the compilation of well-known specialists in their respective fields, so we feel particularly fortunate to have gathered such as esteemed group on short notice. We also want to thank Westview Press for their professional and efficient handling of the process, particularly Kelsey Mitchell, Priscilla McGeehon, and Collin Tracy. When we approached editors at Westview Press with the idea of this volume, they instantly saw the value of it and acted accordingly in an expeditious fashion in order to get this volume out in a timely manner. Most importantly, the editors want to profusely thank their families, without whose support none of this would be possible. Finally, we hope that the Arab Spring and its aftermath, which have thus far resulted in so much change—or at least the potential for it—in a way that has been at one and the same time hopeful and foreboding but also very disruptive, often at the cost of thousands of lives, may ultimately bring peace, freedom, and prosperity to peoples who deserve it no less than anyone else.

A Note on the Text

ONE OF THE CHALLENGES of compiling an edited volume is ensuring stylistic and spelling consistency among chapters written by different contributors. In particular, many authors have used their own system of transliteration. We generally retained each author's style except for names, places, and terms that appear throughout the text. In these cases, we selected one variation of spelling, which is often the more recognizable version rather than a strict transliteration: for example, Assad rather than Asad; Hussein rather than Husayn; and Gadafi rather than Qadhdhafi, Kaddafi, Qaddafi, or numerous other transliterations of the name of the former Libyan leader.

Also, as is the case with every other region on earth, Middle East history, politics, and even geography are subject to many different interpretations depending upon who is doing the talking or writing. As such, wars, events, and places are often referred to in sometimes drastically different ways. Even the term "Arab Spring," as pointed out in the Introduction and in several other chapters, is not at all universally accepted and is something of a misnomer. As a historical example, the 1973 Arab-Israeli War (the most neutral and objective of all appellations for the event) has been called the October War, the Ramadan War, the War of Liberation, and the Yom Kippur War. In the few cases such as this one, authors sometimes employ one particular reference; however, the reader should be aware that oftentimes there are other references as well that have meaning to different populations, and for the most part this has been pointed out by the authors and/or editors.

Introduction

MARK L. HAAS AND DAVID W. LESCH

THE SO-CALLED ARAB SPRING unexpectedly erupted in late 2010 and early 2011. It was characterized in the beginning by huge and largely peaceful popular protests in a number of Arab countries against long-standing entrenched regimes. It began in Tunisia, where a young man trying to eke out a living as a street vendor engaged in an act of defiance against the government borne of frustration and disillusionment over the socioeconomic malaise and political repression in his country. He lit himself on fire. Little did he know that he would light a fire across the region. Soon mass protests forced the Tunisian president to leave office. In neighboring Egypt, also suffering from many of the same systemic maladies, throngs of protesters gathered at Tahrir Square in the center of Cairo, eventually forcing President Husni Mubarak from power. Protests sprang up elsewhere in the Arab world from the Persian Gulf to North Africa, most spectacularly leading to the death of Libyan President Muammar al-Gadafi following a campaign of armed popular resistance supported militarily by NATO and the Arab League. Then the regime in Syria, which many had thought would weather the storm of the Arab Spring, began to encounter mass protests. The regime in Damascus, however, unleashed a brutal crackdown against the opposition, displaying a resiliency that confounded the prognostications that it, too, would soon fall.

All the while, countries in and outside of the Middle East, such as Iran, Israel, Turkey, the United States, and Russia, that have a significant stake in what the Arab Spring means in terms of their own interests and objectives, look on in fascination and confusion as to how to respond to the tremendous

changes occurring before their eyes. Debates in both academic and policymaking circles about the meaning, consequences, and likely outcomes of the mass
protests abound. Indeed, the very name "Arab Spring" is controversial. As a
number of the contributors to this volume point out, this term is something
of a misnomer. Just ask the protesters in Syria in the spring of 2011 or 2012
fighting against a brutal crackdown ordered by a repressive regime if they feel
like they are in an "Arab Spring." You will likely get laughed at or punched in
the mouth. However, we employ the term in the title of this volume primarily
for recognition purposes, because rightly or wrongly and more so than not,
most of what this volume addresses is known as the Arab Spring.

Beyond the matter of labeling, the events of 2010 through 2012 create a
host of questions that have major implications for regional and global politics.
Were the uprisings a spontaneous combustion caused by the unique confluence
of factors that produced a "perfect storm" of dissatisfaction and dissent? Or
were there important historical antecedents, of which the Arab Spring is only
the latest, albeit most dramatic, manifestation? Or both? Will the Arab Spring
auger in a period of democratic development and prosperity? Will it lead to a
period of retrenchment as status quo forces fight back and find ways to effectively remain in power? Has the Arab Spring simply cleared the road for
Islamist parties, long suppressed across the region, to take power? If so, what
will this mean for domestic and international politics?

This volume attempts to answer these and other key questions by examining
specific countries directly or indirectly affected by the Arab Spring. It collects
an impressive array of leading experts in the field who are noted specialists on
the countries and/or issues on which they write. It is intended to introduce
and explain the Arab Spring for the interested general public as well as students
and scholars of the Middle East in a way that will help them understand how
all of this came about and what might happen in the near- and long-term future
of the region.

THE ORIGINS OF THE PROTESTS
AND THEIR KEY CONSEQUENCES

The mass demonstrations throughout the Arab world beginning in 2010
took most analysts by surprise. The Middle East and North Africa seemed
to be an important exception to what prominent political scientist Samuel
Huntington labeled the "third wave" of democratization that swept across

much of Eastern Europe, Latin America, and Asia after the end of the cold war.[1] Analysts consistently ranked the Arab states as the least free in the world, and few in 2010 were predicting that this situation was likely to change any time soon.

Soviet leader Leon Trotsky reportedly asserted that revolution is impossible until it is inevitable.[2] The logic underlying this statement applies to the Arab Spring. In retrospect, it is clear that there were very powerful forces pushing people across the Arab world to revolt, and that some authoritarian governments had feet of clay: they were not nearly as invulnerable to popular protests as widely believed.[3] Perhaps most importantly, states in the Middle East and North Africa have more "youth bulges"—which are a disproportionate number of young people in a particular state—than any other regions in the world. Throughout the entire Middle East and North Africa, roughly one out of every three people is between the ages of ten and twenty-four.[4] Youth bulges are particularly pronounced in those countries that experienced the most widespread and powerful protests during the Arab Spring. In Tunisia, more than 42 percent of the population is under twenty-five. This number is 48 percent in Libya, 51 percent in Egypt, and 57 percent in Syria.[5]

Youth bulges, as numerous studies have documented, frequently create highly combustible social and political environments. Large numbers of young people are much more likely than other demographic cohorts to act on their grievances to try to rectify them, even if this requires large-scale protests and even violence.[6] Arab youth certainly had pressing grievances against their governments, including the systematic denial of basic rights, massive governmental corruption, extreme levels of unemployment, widespread poverty, and steady increases in the cost of living. There was also a general hopelessness that none of these conditions would improve without revolutionary political change. Youth bulges and widespread dissatisfaction with the political status quo, combined with the socioeconomic challenges created by the 2008 global financial crisis, were critical to the creation of the Arab Spring protests.

Systemic, powerful incentives pushing populations to rebellion does not mean, however, that revolutions will succeed. The Arab Spring uprisings demonstrate major variations in outcomes. Tunisian and Egyptian protesters were able to topple their governments, Libyan rebels did so only with significant foreign militarily aid, demonstrators in Bahrain and Syria have thus far been unsuccessful in their efforts, and protests in Saudi Arabia barely got off the ground. A number of factors account for these differences. The chapters in this volume highlight some of the most important. When a state's military largely comprises ethnic and/or religious minorities (as is the case, for example, in Syria—see Chapter 4), there is an increased likelihood that military personnel will remain loyal to the regime, even if this loyalty requires firing on fellow citizens engaged in political protests. Minority groups will fear that the creation of a more democratic regime will result in their ouster from power or even their persecution. These fears create powerful incentives to do whatever it takes to remain in positions of influence. Large revenue streams that are controlled by the government—such as are created by Saudi Arabia's massive oil wealth—further tip the balance in favor of the political status quo. Resources allow governments to maintain patronage systems (including for the military) to help ensure loyalty and assuage some popular grievances. As long as repressive governments are able to continue vast financial support systems, and especially when their militaries remain willing to brutally crush dissent, it will be very difficult for revolutionary forces to achieve their objectives.

Conversely, when governments do not control large resource-based wealth (as is the case in Syria and Egypt) that can maintain patronage systems and buy off protesters, or when states possess professional militaries whose leaders and personnel are drawn from the dominant ethnic and religious groups in a society (as is the case in Tunisia and Egypt), revolutionary forces are advantaged. In the latter scenario, militaries can reasonably anticipate that they will remain in power even after a regime change. The incentives for militaries to support current governments to the bitter end against popular protests are, as a result, much lower in these instances.[7]

Even in those cases, such as Tunisia, Egypt, and Libya, in which protesters were able to topple dictatorial governments, the creation of stable democratic regimes in their place is far from guaranteed. Unfortunately, the same factors that spurred the protests in the first place are likely to work against such political transitions. Youth bulges and high levels of youth unemployment will continue to create highly unstable and violence-prone environments. Moreover, the pernicious effects of authoritarianism, even after the dictator has been overthrown, are likely to continue to plague new governments. Authoritarian regimes that crushed independent sources of power, thereby preventing the creation of a thriving civil society, inhibited widespread respect for democratic principles and political pluralism, and prevented the creation of democratic institutions and leaders, often greatly handicap future efforts at state building, sometimes for generations. One 2005 study found that of sixty-seven countries trying to transition from authoritarian regimes, roughly only half were judged to be "free" a generation after the transition began.[8]

Perhaps the most interesting issue for postauthoritarian societies in the Middle East and North Africa concerns the relationship between Islam and democracy, and especially between Islam and liberal democracy. Although populists, democracy activists, and liberals appeared to lead the uprisings in early 2011, these groups have been less successful in creating effective, cohesive parties that can challenge in competitive elections either the old elite or, especially, Islamists. Political mobilization for mass demonstrations is one thing; effective campaigning is another. Given this current reality, there is little doubt that Islamist parties, because of their superior political organization, will be the most powerful actors in the new regimes, at least in the short run. Islamists believe that the prescriptions in the Quran and the traditions of the Prophet Muhammad should have important political effects. These parties have already dominated in elections held in Tunisia and Egypt after the Arab Spring began. Islamists' victories mean that the separation between religion and politics will not be as great as is the norm in Western liberal democracies.

It is a mistake, however, to paint all Islamist parties with the same brush, as is frequently done in popular outlets in the West. Indeed, in many ways the most important domestic battles in postauthoritarian societies in the wake of the Arab Spring will not be between Islamists and secular liberals, but among different types of Islamists. Three broad varieties of Islamist leaders are likely to vie for power: hard-liners (or ideological conservatives), pragmatic conservatives, and liberal Islamists.[9] Hard-line Islamists believe that a primary objective of government is the regulation of personal virtue based on a narrow and literal interpretation of the Quran and the traditions of the Prophet. This position most often requires that religious authorities have important input into political decisionmaking and also that there be limits on popular sovereignty. To hard-line Islamists, majoritarian preferences should not take precedence over sharia, or Islamic law. Hard-liners also tend not to support equal rights for all groups, especially women and religious minorities. Leaders of the Egyptian hard-line Islamists known as Salafis, for example, have demanded "strict prohibitions against interest-bearing loans, alcohol and 'fornication,' with traditional Islamic corporal punishment like stoning for adultery." One leader of this party, Sheik Abd al-Monam al-Shahat, expressed in a public debate his understanding of the priority of Islamic law over all else as follows: "I want to say: citizenship restricted by Islamic Shariah, freedom restricted by

Islamic Shariah, equality restricted by Islamic Shariah. Shariah is obligatory, not just the principles—freedom and justice and all that."[10]

Pragmatic conservatives share with their hard-line brethren the objectives of creating a state based on Islamic law. This goal, however, is subordinate to more pragmatic considerations, including creating modern, dynamic economies and fostering political stability based on widespread participation and engagement. The *New York Times* summarizes this position by examining the Egyptian Muslim Brotherhood's 2011 platform for parliamentary elections: "Unlike the Salafis, [the Muslim Brotherhood] has not proposed to regulate the content of arts or entertainment, women's work or dress, or even the religious content of public education. In fact, the party's platform calls for smaller government to limit corruption and liberalize the economy."[11]

Liberal Islamists, like other Islamists, ground their political prescriptions in Islamic principles and tenets. The *content* of these prescriptions is, however, largely liberal. Many liberal Islamists, including leaders of the Ennahda Party in Tunisia and the Justice and Development Party in Turkey (see also Chapter 2, where Bruce Rutherford argues that key Egyptian parties, including the Muslim Brotherhood, are dedicated to important liberalizing objectives) assert that God gave individuals free will, which makes religious compulsion immoral. Similarly, because humans' interpretations of the Quran and God's will are always imperfect, pluralism, tolerance, democracy, separation of powers, the protection of minority rights, and an evolving interpretation of scripture are all necessities.

The domestic future of new regimes created in the wake of the Arab Spring uprisings is likely to vary widely depending on which of these varieties of Islamists dominates. The tension between democracy, especially liberal democracy that respects minority rights and protects political pluralism, is great for hard-line Islamists, but not nearly as much for pragmatic conservatives and, particularly, liberal Islamists. Indeed, the preferred political institutions for liberal Islamists are likely to be quite similar to those found in Western democracies, even if the ideological foundations and justifications for these preferences are different. The forces for liberalization will obviously be even stronger the more power secular liberals possess. Such individuals were instrumental in creating and sustaining the protests that ultimately toppled authoritarian governments. Their challenge will be organizing in such a way that allows them to compete against well-established Islamist parties in competitive political processes.

The international implications resulting from the Arab Spring are just as unsettled as the domestic ones. Will, for example, a new Egyptian regime reject its peace treaty with Israel? If the Assad government in Syria is overthrown, will this mark the end of the Syrian-Iranian alliance, which has been one of the longest-lasting alignments in modern Middle Eastern politics? Will the Arab Spring, ironically, significantly increase the regional influence of two non-Arab states, Turkey and Iran, whose leaders are claiming to be exemplars for political change based on their particular legitimating principles and ideological beliefs? Will the political changes created by the uprisings be a net detriment to American interests in the region as some pro-U.S. autocracies are overthrown, or will they potentially be a net benefit if more liberal regimes are created? Will Russia continue to position itself as a counter to U.S. interests in the Middle East in a way that is reminiscent of the superpower cold war?

As these questions indicate, the uprisings create both major threats and opportunities for foreign powers' interests. The dominant risk for foreign countries is that regime change will switch an allied state (e.g., America's alliance with Egypt, or Iran's alliance with Syria) into a neutral or even an enemy. From the perspective of Western states in particular, the destabilization created by the Arab Spring revolts and even the spread of democratic regimes could threaten energy supplies, increase international terrorism, and empower Islamist groups through elections. This last danger, though, assumes that all Islamist groups are intrinsically hostile to the West, which is not a settled point. Just as different varieties of Islamist groups are likely to pursue very different domestic agendas depending on the specific content of their ideological beliefs, these same parties are likely to perceive Western countries in different ways for analogous reasons.[12]

Although the potential risks created by the Arab Spring for foreign powers are considerable, so, too, are the potential benefits. To begin with, alterations in others' alliance portfolios due to regime changes are a double-edged sword for foreign countries. One's own state could lose a key ally, but one's enemy could lose an even more vital partner (e.g., it could be argued that losing Syria as an ally if the Assad regime falls would be a greater blow to Iran than losing Egypt as an ally in the aftermath of Mubarak's ouster would be to the United States).

Also important to states' security is the fact that the Arab Spring uprisings create an opportunity for states to better protect their interests with neighboring countries through enhanced "soft power," which is influence based on the power of persuasion and the attractiveness of one's principles. As noted above, both Turkish and Iranian leaders are touting themselves as ideological models for postauthoritarian regimes in order to increase their influence in these countries (see Chapters 8 and 7, respectively, for much greater detail on this point), and the United States, Russia, and the European powers are making similar efforts. In a related move, Saudi leaders are pushing to tighten and expand cooperation among conservative monarchies as a bulwark against revolution, including advocating that the Gulf Cooperation Council become a more cohesive political and economic federation, while also expanding the group's membership to include Jordan and Morocco.[13]

Given the risks and opportunities for foreign countries created by the Arab Spring uprisings, it is no wonder that outsiders have not only been watching events closely, but also frequently intervening in various ways on the side of either the existing governments or the revolutionaries. Saudi Arabia sent troops into Bahrain in 2011 (at the request of Bahrain's monarch) to quell domestic unrest while supporting the opposition to the Syrian regime, the NATO powers bombed Libyan forces in support of the rebels, Turkey has provided increasing support of demonstrators against the Assad regime, and Iran has provided significant material and intelligence aid to help the Syrian government crush these same protesters. The decisions by foreign powers to intervene or not, and on which side of the struggle if they do, are a product of a complex interplay of material, ideological, and humanitarian interests that must be understood on a case-by-case basis. These issues are central to the analysis of many of the book's chapters, especially those on Iran, Russia, the United States, and Turkey.

THE ORGANIZATION AND CONTENT OF THE BOOK

The book is divided into two main sections. Julia Clancy-Smith (Tunisia), Bruce K. Rutherford (Egypt), Mary-Jane Deeb (Libya), and David W. Lesch (Syria) begin the volume by examining the Arab countries hit most dramatically by the Arab Spring. These chapters appear in the order in which the protests occurred. Although the political upheavals in these states shared some important characteristics, the causes and course of the uprisings as well as regime responses and actions by external actors were different, some ending fairly cleanly (at least at first) with the removal of the authoritarian leader, others continuing with the dictatorial regime tenaciously fighting back to remain in power.

These four case studies are followed by chapters by Steve A. Yetiv and Curtis R. Ryan, who analyze developments in Saudi Arabia and Jordan, respectively. The central focus of these chapters is to explore why these countries, at least for the present time, were able to escape large-scale revolutionary pressures. Apprehending variations in outcomes in those states that witnessed massive uprisings, as well as why some countries have not experienced such protests, is critical to both prediction and prescription. Almost all analysts and policymakers were caught off guard by the Arab Spring. Correctly understanding the sources, successes, and failures of these protests will not only reduce the likelihood of similar surprises in the future, but also, perhaps, help to shape outcomes toward desired ends.

The book's second section explores the policies of non-Arab states that have major interests at stake in the uprisings. Reza Marashi and Trita Parsi (Iran), Mark L. Haas (Turkey), Ilan Peleg (Israel), Robert O. Freedman (Russia), and Jeremy Pressman (United States) examine the threats and opportunities that the Arab Spring protests created for these outside powers, as well as these states' responses to the revolts. All five of these countries sometimes supported and sometimes opposed particular uprisings, though the dominant tendency in favor of revolution or reaction varied considerably among them. The chapters in this section highlight how the Arab demonstrations affected the material and ideological interests of the non-Arab powers, and how the latter tried to protect and even advance both sets of interests in the wake of the protests. James L. Gelvin concludes the volume with an analysis of some of the common themes of the Arab Spring, as well as an examination of some of the myths and common misinterpretations of these uprisings.

Only time will tell if the Arab Spring will mark the beginning of a "fourth wave" of democratization that will allow North Africa and the Middle East to share in the dominant regime type of much of the world, or if this region will experience the continuation of authoritarianism and the widespread denial of individuals' basic rights. Understanding the forces that have led to this revolutionary era and how Arab and non-Arab states have responded to it is, however, the first step in accurately predicting the region's likely political trajectory. It is to precisely these fundamental objectives that this volume is dedicated.

NOTES

1. Samuel Huntington, *The Third Wave: Democratization in the Late Twentieth Century* (Norman: University of Oklahoma Press, 1991).

2. Bruce Crumley, "Tunisia Pushes Out Its Strongman: Could Other Arab Countries Follow?," *Time* online, January 14, 2011, http://www.time.com/time/world/article/0,8599,2042541,00.html.

3. On this last point, see Jack A. Goldstone, "Understanding the Revolutions of 2011," *Foreign Affairs* 90, 3 (May-June 2011): 8–16.

4. Antonello Cabras, "The Implications of the Youth Bulge in Middle East and North African Populations," NATO Parliamentary Assembly, November 20, 2010, http://www.nato-pa.int/Default.asp?SHORTCUT=2342.

5. United Nations, *World Population Prospects: The 2010 Revision* (New York: United Nations Population Division, 2011), http://esa.un.org/unpd/wpp/unpp/panel_indicators.htm.

6. See, for example, Henrik Urdal, "A Clash of Generations? Youth Bulges and Political Violence," *International Studies Quarterly* 50, 3 (September 2006): 607–629.

7. For similar analysis, see F. Gregory Gause III, "Why Middle East Studies Missed the Arab Spring," *Foreign Affairs* 90, 4 (July-August 2011): 81–90.

8. Cited in "People's Revolutions Don't Guarantee Democracy," Reuters, February 13, 2011.

9. Anthony Shadid and David D. Kirkpatrick, "Activists in Arab World Vie to Define Islamic State," *New York Times*, September 21, 2011; Carrie Rosefsky Wickham, "The Muslim Brotherhood After Mubarak," *Foreign Affairs* online, February 3, 2011, http://www.foreignaffairs.com/articles/67348/carrie-rosefsky-wickham/the-muslim-brotherhood-after-mubarak.

10. Both quotes in David D. Kirkpatrick, "Egypt's Vote Puts Emphasis on Split over Religious Rule," *New York Times*, December 11, 2011.

11. Ibid. See also Wickham, "Muslim Brotherhood."

12. For in-depth analysis supporting this claim, see Mark L. Haas, *The Clash of Ideologies: Middle Eastern Politics and American Security* (New York: Oxford University Press, 2012).

13. Mehran Kamrava, "The Arab Spring and the Saudi-Led Counterrevolution," *Orbis* 56, 1 (Winter 2012): 96–104; Kareem Fahim and David D. Kirkpatrick, "Saudi Arabia Seeks Union of Monarchies in Region," *New York Times*, May 14, 2012.

PART I

Spring in the Arab World

1

From Sidi Bou Zid to Sidi Bou Said: A *Longue Durée* Approach to the Tunisian Revolutions

JULIA CLANCY-SMITH

PRELUDES

IN 1982–1983, I FOUND MYSELF once again residing in Tunisia, this time for research on my doctoral dissertation in history. Because we lived in the coastal suburbs but worked in the National Archives, then housed in the Dar el-Bey in the madina (or medina, "old city"), we spent long periods of time each day on the only highway linking Sidi Bou Said with downtown Tunis negotiating fearsome traffic jams. Big, tough-looking traffic cops riding enormous motorcycles periodically imposed order. We could not help noticing that young men stationed along the La Marsa road often pelted with rocks the expensive, obviously imported cars coming from toney seaside villages to the capital. In fact, it became a frequent occurrence whose targets of individual and collective anger appeared carefully selected; the projectiles were aimed at fellow Tunisians, not foreigners.

The previous years had been difficult for many but not all classes. While increased labor migration to Europe and Arab oil countries had pumped remittances into a stagnant economy, domestic wage earners, particularly in agriculture and small businesses, experienced scant improvement in livelihoods. The increasingly globalized liberal economy brought new social expectations and disparities, as concretized by lavish Mediterranean villas mushrooming in places such as Sidi Bou Said and Carthage. By then high-end as well as mass international tourism, mainly from Europe, had taken off, furnishing much-needed hard currency and employment but fueling socioreligious and cultural discontents. In response to growing public disillusionment with the broken promises of political freedom and representative party politics, lawyers, academics, and journalists had formed a local Tunisian section of the international organization the International League for Human Rights in 1977, the first such chapter in the Arab world. Unionized workers' grievances mounted, and the Union Générale des Travailleurs Tunisiens (General Union of Tunisian Workers, or UGTT), the largest and oldest labor organization, chafed under the growing authoritarianism of Tunisia's single party, the Parti Socialiste Dusturien (Dustur Socialist Party, or PSD), and President Habib Bourguiba's (1956–1987) regime.[1] Labor activism was a political force to be reckoned with because of its deep historical roots. The UGTT's predecessor, the Confédération Générale des Travailleurs Tunisiens (General Confederation of Tunisian Workers), had been created in 1924 during the French Protectorate and at that time constituted the second oldest native labor union in all of Africa. In January 1978, the UGTT and its leadership openly broke with the now "president for life" and his elite inner circle, which controlled the country. In the context of a countrywide strike, unequivocal demands were made for political pluralism and democracy as well as for economic reforms ensuring greater social equality. "Black Thursday" (January 1978), as the day of the strike came to be known, unleashed demonstrations across Tunisia that turned into fierce clashes, but state repression proved even more violent. Habib Achour, the respected head of the UGTT, was imprisoned, along with countless other activists.[2]

But things only got worse in the early 1980s. Windfall oil revenues dropped off, and Tunisia, still an agrarian-based economy, was beset by poor harvests due to unfavorable climatic conditions. In the same period, fortress Europe began shutting ever more firmly its doors to North Africans of whatever educational background or social class searching for a secure livelihood through expatriation. Government and public debt ballooned. Internal austerity measures in 1983 collided with International Monetary Fund (IMF) and World Bank (WB) pressures for an end to state subsidies on basic foodstuffs in exchange for international loans. For many social groups, food insecurity increased to intolerable levels when the price of bread and other staples doubled. It came as no surprise when, the next year, in January 1984, a series of disturbances erupted throughout the country. And a hitherto unthinkable event occurred—Bourguiba's car was stoned in a symbolic act "indicative of 1984 the depth of frustration and rage among the poorest and most afflicted Tunisians."[3] The resulting repression was nothing short of draconian; the social pact among Bourguiba, the state-controlled single party (the PSD), and Tunisian citizens that had been concluded long before independence in 1956 was unraveling. The food subsidies were restored, but the president for life would be removed from power four years later in a bloodless (allegedly constitutionally valid) "medical" coup. Zine al-Abidine Ben Ali (born 1936) became president for twenty-four years.[4]

By then under- and unemployment grievously affected specific regions of the country—notably the interior—and particular social demographics; young men between the ages of eighteen and twenty-five were most likely to be deprived of adequate means to earn a living that would permit them to marry and establish their own households. The media and most social activists characterized the events of 1984 as "bread riots," a misleading label that downgrades the socio-ideological substance of civic mass action—and its many histories—to a story about mere subsistence. It was during the 1980s that the Islamist party, the Harakat al-Ittijah al-Islami (Islamic Tendency Movement), later renamed al-Nahda or Ennahda (Rebirth or Renaissance), became politically active, advocating for the needs of the most underprivileged.[5] But in 1985 the party also demanded a national referendum on the 1956 Personal Status Code (PSC), part of a state-driven secularization of society, which had conferred equal rights in law upon Tunisian women.[6] As the Islamists argued, the PSC not only violated Islamic principles, notably the religious-sanctioned existence of different, though complementary, spheres for man and woman, but also promoted female equality in the job force, which had deprived men of employment.[7]

Similar patterns of boom-and-bust capitalism, dissent, and repression recurred. The phosphate mining zones around the city of Gafsa, where an industrial labor force had emerged before independence, constituted an ongoing source of worker unrest.[8] Moreover, a local theater of protest had crystallized there by the 1970s, if not before; productions lampooned and derided elites in the political center, harkening back to the colonial era when the nationalist party, the New Constitution Party formed in the 1930s, used theater to communicate anti-French grievances to the populace.[9] Two long-term trends had proven successful: family planning first tentatively introduced under the Protectorate by a Tunisian Muslim woman, Tawhida ben Shaykh (who had earned a medical degree from the School of Medicine in Paris in 1936 but subsequently been denied a physician's position in a French colonial hospital), and modern education for both girls and boys. In 1991, universal education for all children became compulsory by law, although by then spectacular results had already been achieved in Tunisia relative to other Arab or African nations: 85 percent of school-age boys were enrolled and 70 percent of girls.[10] But education, too, created inevitable discontents: employment consonant with degrees of schooling for graduates proved elusive, and educational institutions on the coast were almost always better endowed than those in the interior.

Then came the global economic crash in 2008, which contributed significantly to growing mass civic action first in the interior, where unemployment had climbed to unbearable levels, and then in the capital. However, unusual and unsettling features had materialized when compared to the past. While corruption characterizes all states to varying degrees, the systemic corruption of the Ben Ali regime was breathtaking in its shameless audacity and sheer scale, as revealed by WikiLeaks (see below for more details). On December 17, 2010, a young man who scrambled to earn a living as a street vendor in Sidi Bou Zid set himself on fire to draw national attention to the plight of under- and unemployed youth. Badly burned, he was eventually transported to a hospital in Tunis, where he died on January 4, 2011. While Muhammad Bouazizi's sacrificial act of self-immolation in December 2010 provided the trigger for collective nationwide action, this was not the first case of political suicide. A number of young people had killed themselves before 2010 in order to draw attention to the plight of youth, poverty, and lack of life opportunity, which together created a pervasive sense of hopelessness. Indeed, that a "culture of suicide" had developed among the country's most marginalized youth by the turn of the millennium was utterly shocking to Tunisian society.[11] Important historical continuities remained, however. The visibility and audibility of the economic and cultural rift between the disadvantaged interior and the urban, cosmopolitan Mediterranean coast could no longer be concealed, much less denied.

The spatial coordinates of what transpired after Bouazizi set himself on fire in his hometown are key to the geography and ethnography of the revolutions in progress. Local teachers in Sidi Bou Zid transported Bouazizi to Tunis for medical treatment in the country's burn center. Ben Ali's decision a few days later to visit the terminally injured young man in the hospital for a media moment proved fatal to the president because this calculated act of self-interest betrayed the deplorable social and political autism of the autocracy in its terminal stages. The despot was himself absurdly on display, although he failed to even realize it because he had been seduced by his own power. Thus came the fall of Tunisia's second dictator.[12] On January 14, 2011, Ben Ali and his entourage fled the country, at first seeking refuge in France and subsequently finding haven in Saudi Arabia.

It is tempting to see the causes for the Tunisian Revolutions in the growing social injustices, disjunctures, and asymmetries of the previous four decades, all of which undoubtedly played a major role in the timing and nature of the protests.[13] For the historian, however, the story is much deeper and more complicated; many of the processes at work, directly or indirectly, boasted longer historical pedigrees, stretching not only to the early years of independence but also to the colonial and even precolonial periods.

This chapter argues for a *longue durée* approach to the so-called Arab Spring—or, better, the "Maghrib Spring"—particularly when explaining the Tunisian *Revolutions*. It employs the plural because once sufficient time has elapsed to allow for objective, serene historical research—outside the daily hubbub of attention-grabbing headlines—we may well find that several, or even numerous, social movements converged. This insistence on the deep past grows from my historical training but also from a concern with the perceptible tendency in the current literature and media coverage toward "presentism"— the tendency to seek causation and meaning in the very recent past.[14] Moreover, the distressing deficit of historical knowledge about the Maghrib has meant that astonishing errors have been committed to print. For example, one major fiction incubated by ignorance was the claim that 2010–2011 witnessed the Arab world's *first modern* revolutions.[15] Directly related, analysts constantly invoke as causes for the current upheavals, which are not new to the twenty-first century, the youth "bulge," globalization, and the impact of novel social media technologies, so critical for communication and mobilization. But diverse social media for collective protest and action have always existed, and globalization was already apparent by the nineteenth century.[16]

This chapter investigates the recent democratic uprisings in relationship to traditions of militant mass action directed against several kinds of states stretching back to the colonial and precolonial periods. In part, it adopts not only a long-term historical view but also an environmental perspective to understand the trans-Mediterranean, indeed global, transformations that produced the coastalization occurring in the early twenty-first century. I posit that the socioeconomic and cultural rupture between the Tunisian (or North African) coastal zones and the interiors illustrates larger worldwide reconfigurations of resources, human and otherwise.[17] This chapter also probes the historical currency of present-day political targets and spaces, notably the symbolic significance of the Mediterranean villa and the critical realms of women and education. And it examines some of the transnational repercussions of the Tunisian Revolutions, which inspired protests in Egypt, the rest of the Maghrib, the Middle East, and elsewhere in the world.[18] To grapple with this problem, we must keep in mind that national histories have always been constructed in transnational contexts and circumstances and that ruptures and continuities exist in continuous, yet contingent, dialogue and tension.[19] In short, my contribution raises the following question: How and to what degree did historically older moments of radical transformation inform and shape the emergent—because unfinished—sociopolitical order in today's Tunisia?

COASTALIZATION: INTERIORS, COASTS, AND FLOATING HINTERLANDS

The photos of protesters holding up baguettes that appeared in early 2011 could easily have been misinterpreted by an uninformed international media to mean that mainly economic grievances and household security were principally at stake. However, Tunisians quickly dispelled that myth-in-the-making by explaining that the brandished baguettes meant quite the opposite—that they could not be "bought off" as the Ben Ali regime had hoped (along with international financial interests and institutions, such as the WB and IMF) by bread alone and a middle-class existence, one sorely undermined by more than a decade of stupendous venality on the part of President Ben Ali, his family, and allies that filled the coffers of foreign banks. Another related message was that Tunisians were prepared to "live on bread and water alone" but that they refused to live any longer with the Ben Ali regime.[20] Indeed, after 1987 corruption had gone from "artisanal" to industrial as transnational corporate economic and financial liberalism opened up vast opportunities for methodical fraud. Yet the food subsidies had largely remained in place for bread, oil, and couscous and were critical to urban populations living beyond the margins of rising middle-class prosperity and, above all, to rural society.

In a sense, the revolutions could have broken out anywhere in the country, but they erupted in a place that seemed of no great importance to the outside world. Until recently, Sidi Bou Zid had attracted little attention and even fewer tourists—apart from World War II buffs. The scene of a critical military engagement pitting German Panzer divisions against U.S. forces in February 1943, the "Battle of Sidi Bou Zid" constituted the opening act in fierce Axis-Allied struggles over the Kasserine Pass. However, in the decades that followed, the region and others like it had been badly bruised by the abortive forced collectivization of agriculture instituted from 1964 until 1973 under Bourguiba's minister of planning, Ahmad Ben Salah. By then, farm exports largely to European markets did not cover even 50 percent of the cost of imported food.[21] After 1974, state planners abandoned socialized agriculture for free-market strategies, although Tunisia's economy had been progressively integrated, often at a disadvantage, into world market forces at least since the nineteenth century.[22]

Water, an increasingly scarce resource worldwide but especially in the North African interior, and above all in Tunisia, where the tourist industry siphons off large quantities, became even more precious to local farmers with the 1987 removal of Bourguiba. After Ben Ali's wife and in-laws embarked on a national pillage-cum-privatization campaign with substantial support from foreign corporations, aquifers in the Sidi Bou Zid governorate were targeted for expropriation. By then, parts of the region had come to depend upon a more or less thriving food processing and citrus export economy and on local water sources—as well as on world markets. The construction of a pipeline extracting water from the governorate for distribution in the large industrial city of Sfax as well as imposition of the Hayet Water Company only fanned social anger. In a maneuver seen worldwide, where global resources are currently being privatized, the Trabelsi clan created a bottled water enterprise that ultimately forced local growers and families to buy their own water back from Hayet.[23] This lined the already well-lined pockets of the clan, threatening the arid region's future water supplies and the agrarian economy on which social relations depend.[24] The ultimate irony—and a cruel one at that—was the company name, Hayet, which in Arabic means "life"; its slick branding smacks of Madison Avenue–type marketing devices.

But it had not always been that way; North Africa had been an exporter of foodstuffs, principally grains and olive oil, for centuries. Indeed, Tunisian factory laborers, colonial soldiers, and farmers had greatly aided the war effort in Europe and the Mediterranean during both world wars. Nevertheless, agriculture and the peasantry have not fared well since the colonial period. During the Protectorate (1881–1956), rural society suffered from benign neglect or more disruptive, calculated strategies of forced land seizures, which resulted in the consolidation of large agribusinesses, inevitably owned by Europeans, and the creation of a rural proletariat. By the eve of the 1930s Depression, more than 25 percent of the Tunisian population was under the age of twenty-five, the mixed blessing of modern public health measures. Thus, a youth "bulge" existed long before the early twenty-first century. In response to the Great Depression and strident demands for independence from Tunisian nationalists, the colonial regime shored up export crops by subsidizing wheat production but did next to nothing for the Sahil's olive growers, whose ancient crop provided sustenance, directly or indirectly, for one-third of the Tunisian population. One of the anomalies of French economic imperialism in the Maghrib was the expansion of viticulture and the colonial wine industry, which competed with France's domestic production; European-owned estates favored the more lucrative, and highly subsidized, viticulture sector. The shift from mixed subsistence farming into market-oriented agriculture focused on a crop that the Muslim population did not consume (alcohol consumption is forbidden by Islam) and undermined the traditional rural economy. This in turn encouraged rural-to-urban migrations by former cultivators; from Casablanca to Tunis *bidonvilles*, or shantytowns, sprang up to house, however indecently, the rural immigrants. These processes, at work across French North Africa, also endangered local food supplies, unleashing cycles of shortages and even famine.[25] But the growing malaise of the agricultural sector and the North African interior has longer historical roots.

Progressively from the late eighteenth century on, and rapidly during the succeeding centuries, coastal cities, elites, and economic interests turned their back on Tunisia's interior and its people, places such as Sidi Bou Zid, Kasserine, and Tala. One key indicator of this tendency was that by the nineteenth century the princes of the Husaynid dynasty (1705–1956) no longer took wives from among the big tribal confederations in the interior but preferred Circassian, Georgian, and even Italian spouses. Due to the growing importance of transnational exchanges and communication, Tunisia's Mediterranean provinces were ever more firmly, if disadvantageously, enmeshed in European, transsea, and transatlantic/global circuits. The shifting hinterland for the Tunis–Cap Bon area was no longer the interior but instead became Malta, Sicily, and Marseille even before 1881. Geographers now note with alarm the global coastalization of human societies and power.

But this phenomenon, readily perceived in North Africa and the Mediterranean rim, has much earlier antecedents in the mid-eighteenth century, with the waning of the "Little Ice Age."[26]

That growing divergence between coast and interior was unmistakable during an 1864 revolt, the largest rebellion in modern Tunisian history. Multiple factors can be invoked for this rebellion, but the two major elements were abusive taxation of the peasantry and state-driven centralization and modernization. The rebellion began in the regions between Le Kef and al-Qayrawan but spread to the coastal cities, where it was brutally crushed by the political center, the Husaynid dynasty, which stirred up local rivalries, cunningly doled out bribes, and promised government employment to less enthusiastic rebels, mainly local elites. Its consequences proved historically monumental. With the revolt's suppression in 1866, the 1861 constitution (the first in the Arab world) was suspended, the Ottoman Empire belatedly recognized the Husaynids' hereditary right to rule in return for acknowledging Istanbul's supremacy, and the nineteenth century's version of IMF bankers and pashas declared the state bankrupt by 1869 and instituted structural adjustments in the guise of the International Finance Commission, which was controlled by France, Great Britain, and Italy.[27] Both the Sahil and the interior were devastated; however, their shared enmity toward Tunis, urban notables, and the dynasty concealed profound antagonisms that divided (and still do) the two economic and cultural sectors. In 1881, the French army stationed in eastern Algeria invaded after another border incident provided a pretext for adding Tunisia to France's rapidly expanding empire, which provoked three years of armed resistance, once again in the Tunisian south and along the borders.

Some scholars argue that the 1864 revolt and opposition to France's 1881 invasion constituted the last moments in modern Tunisian history when the peoples of the south and border areas engaged in concerted political action—until the recent revolutions. But this is historically inaccurate. Between 1955 and 1956, Bourguiba, in exile for extended periods of time, nearly lost control of the New Constitution Party in its negotiations with France over the terms of independence. Tunisian anticolonial guerrilla fighters, *fallaqa*, who supported Salah Ben Yusuf, the in-country secretary general of the party, continued fighting against France in the interior in a rebellion that represented the interests of the people there. This constituted a serious challenge to Bourguiba's claims to be the sole nationalist leader. Dismayed by Ben Yusuf's sizeable popular following and support, Bourguiba enlisted the French army and police in quashing the rebellion, driving its leader to Cairo (where he was assassinated in 1961), and killing or imprisoning most of his armed followers.[28]

Today, 80 percent of current national production is concentrated in coastal areas from Bizerte to Sfax. The provinces of the southwest and center-west, home to 40 percent of the total population of more than 10 million, can claim only 20 percent of GDP. And two of the greatest ecological threats to the Mediterranean rim—fossil fuels and tourism—have converged upon Tunisia with great force.[29] The historical processes of coastalization, its local impact and social fallout, relate directly to the different symbols of oppression chosen by many of the protesters.

FROM SIDI BOU SAID TO SIDI BOU ZID: POLITICAL TARGETS AND SYMBOLS

The rapid-fire spread of revolt overwhelmed initial facts on the ground. But for the inhabitants of Sidi Bou Zid, the truth of what happened mattered.[30] Eventually, they demanded that local officials open an investigation into the highly contested versions of what transpired to establish an accurate account. While initial reports claimed that Bouazizi had a college degree, the investigation found that he had been forced to drop out of high school in order to help his economically struggling family. Regardless of the "facts," the country and many parts of the Arab world, and particularly its youth, had found a national hero and martyr. However, by the time the official report was issued, the townspeople had lost control of their own story, and perhaps their own history. Culturally and economically distant from the "tourist gold coast," Sidi Bou Zid has yet to enjoy the fruits of its catalyst role in the Arab Spring. One of the town's trade unionists remarked that much of the misery of daily life hasn't changed since Ben Ali's departure. A local lawyer noted that the emblems of the revolution have been hijacked.[31]

THE POLITICS OF MEDITERRANEAN VILLAS

The historical weight of the Mediterranean villa in Tunisian collective memory is undeniable; its origins can be traced to the medieval Hafsid period, if not before. After Bouazizi's family decided to leave their hometown, rumors in Sidi Bou Zid had it that they were in Tunis in a Mediterranean villa. This rumor might appear unimportant to outsiders, but not when interpreted through a long-term historical lens. In the pre-1881 era, French or foreign-owned communications systems, such as telegraph lines connecting Tunisia to French Algeria, and later the railway, were repeatedly attacked by dissident groups. During the post–World War I colonial period, rural gendarmes, European agribusiness estates, and Protectorate offices and officials were assailed. But the Mediterranean palaces owed by the Husaynids, once architectural expressions of power, privilege, and notability, came to be associated with subservience to outside rule. The La Marsa Convention, signed in 1883 at the bey's palace by the sea, established the military, financial, and institutional framework of the Protectorate.

One of Bourguiba's first acts after deposing the dynasty in 1957 was to demolish with dynamite and backhoes as many of the Husaynid-owned seaside palaces and gardens in La Marsa as possible in an effort to erase historical memory.[32] Fifty-four years later, the Mediterranean villas and palaces sited on parcels of prime real estate that had been seized by Ben Ali and the Trabelsi clan were sacked and burned by protesters. Much of the illegally acquired land had either been *mulk al-dawla* (state properties) or privately owned family properties confiscated for their view of the Mediterranean. The super-Walmart-size palace in Sidi Dhrif, close to Sidi Bou Said, stands vacant. Now the looted and trashed Mediterranean palaces and villas have been transformed into political shrines, pilgrimage sites where crowds assemble to view, meditate, and celebrate the fall of the dictator. Of course, numerous other structures, monuments, and symbols have been desacralized, desecrated, or recommemorated. The clock tower in downtown Tunis that once celebrated Ben Ali's 1987 coup has been renamed after Muhammad Bouazizi.

To truly grasp the role of the Mediterranean villa in coalescing collective militant action, we need to consider secret U.S. Embassy cables sent in the summer of 2009 back to Washington, DC, that were recently revealed by WikiLeaks. On July 17 of that year, the U.S. ambassador dined in what was characterized as a "lavish dinner" at the Hammamet palace of Ben Ali's son-in-law Mohammad Sakher al-Materi, who "was living, however, in the midst of great wealth and excess."[33] The cable described his home as "spacious and directly above and along the Hammamet public beach . . . with a view of the fort." Recently remodeled, it boasted an infinity pool and an immense terrace. In addition, there were "ancient artifacts everywhere: Roman columns, frescoes and even a lion's head from which water pours into a pool." In conversation with the ambassador, al-Materi averred that the Roman antiquities were "real" and mentioned that the family intended to move into its "new (and palatial) house in Sidi Bou Said in eight to ten months."[34] What kinds of culinary delights were served to the guests? "The dinner included perhaps a dozen dishes, including fish, steak, turkey, octopus, and fish couscous. The quantity was sufficient for a very large number of guests. Before dinner, a wide array of small dishes was served, along with three different juices (including kiwi juice, not normally available). The main meal over, the guests were "served ice cream and frozen yoghurt . . . brought in by plane from Saint Tropez," probably in al-Materi's private jet, piloted by an American.[35]

In conclusion, the ambassador observed, "As for the dinner itself, it was similar to what one might experience in a Gulf country, and out of the ordinary for Tunisians." The cable concluded with this prescient remark: "The opulence with which El Materi and Nesrine [his wife] live and their behavior make clear why they and other members of Ben Ali's family are disliked and even hated by some Tunisians. The excesses of the Ben Ali family are growing."[36]

By the new millennium, Tunisia had earned the sobriquet the "hunger strike" capital of the world because nonviolent public resistance had most often assumed this public guise. For example, in December 2003, Radhia Nasraoui, a human rights defender, lawyer, and prestigious member of the bar, ended a fifty-six-day hunger strike protesting the government's assault on her and an illegal search and seizure of her office.[37] Did the fact that Bouazizi was a food vendor resonate with the mobilized protesters? Tunisians had long enjoyed the relatively most secure access to food in most of Africa or the Middle East. At least in coastal cities, towns, and villages, meat, poultry, eggs, and milk products were almost always available. Indeed, Algerian families residing near the borders regularly did their food shopping in Tunisia due to shortages in their own country. But by 2009, a small can of Tunisian tuna, fished from the waters off the Cap Bon, had become really pricey, even by American standards, because the country's tuna was exported to Japan.

WOMEN, THE STATE, AND PARITY

For twenty-three years, the regime had played up Tunisia's unique Mediterranean identity for European audiences as a way of not talking about Islam and Muslims on Europe's southern frontiers. In parallel fashion, both Bourguiba and Ben Ali raised the specter of political Islam when denying the country's citizens a voice and a vote. Indeed, the Algerian Islamic Salvation Front (Front

Islamique du Salut, or FIS) and Algeria's "dark years" of civil war during the 1990s (which were sparked by contested elections) were constantly deployed by Tunisian ruling elites to quell legitimate opposition. Yet the Ben Ali regime not only manipulated religion but also stage-managed women's rights as a sort of political hedge fund against national and, above all, international accusations of human rights' abuse.[38]

However, Tunisian women had been subjected to a form of state feminism long before 1987 with the calculated incorporation of women's organizations into the party in accordance with Bourguiba's form of modern patriarchalism. As Lilia Labidi and Sophie Bessis have already pointed out, Tunisian regimes were masters in disseminating propaganda whose message about modernity drew upon the relatively (and undeniably) better status of the country's women: "Every foreign guest, each diplomatic delegation or international meeting in Tunisia was provided with ample documentation regarding female rights and progress."[39] Indeed, August 13, the date of the passage of the Personal Status Code of 1956, is a national holiday. Nevertheless, women's sociolegal status had been machinated much earlier under the French Protectorate, which after 1900 sought to promote a positive image of colonialism through its support for the newly created School for Muslim Girls in Tunis.[40]

In May 2011, Tunisia passed a parity law based upon similar legislation in France that required all political parties—over 100 parties presented themselves for the 2011 Tunisian elections—to ensure that at least half of each party's candidates were female. Some 5,000 women stood as candidates for the National Constituent Assembly, whose mandate is to govern the country while it drafts a new constitution. As a long-repressed party, Ennahda marshaled better organizational and mobilizing skills and had strongly supported the parity law; thus it ran the largest number of female candidates. As the big winner in the October 23, 2011, elections, Ennahda sent the largest single bloc of female lawmakers to the 217-member constituent assembly, although only 53 percent of the eligible electorate had exercised its right to vote. The question now is how Ennahda women will govern. Soumaya Ghannoushi, a British newspaper columnist and a scholar at the School of Oriental and African Studies in London, maintains that Ennahda is the most progressive Islamic party in North Africa or the Arab world. The daughter of Ennahda's leader, Rashid Ghannoushi, Soumaya acts as a party spokeswoman.[41] But we might wonder how well someone who was raised in England can understand the stakes and complexities of

the "woman question," which currently constitutes the single most important issue facing Tunisian state and society.

Once again, the disjuncture between the cities and the coast, on the one
hand, and the interior, on the other, became manifest during those elections.
On Sunday, October 23, 2011, in Kasserine the international media captured
an image and a message from a group of women most of whom wore head
scarves. "We are from the south and we want to vote," they declared.[42] But
no one had informed the women that they had to first register in order to cast
a ballot; they were turned away from the polling station housed in a local
school, denied a vote. Directly related, feminist historian Joan W. Scott has
raised serious questions about the very ideology of *parité* itself—equal representation of men and women in public office—because it is loaded with
inherently contradictory messages as well as ambiguous meanings, objectives,
and practices.[43]

SOCIAL PACTS: SCHOOLING AND EDUCATION

By the 1990s, the World Bank estimated that a good majority of the Tunisian
population regarded themselves as part of the middle classes. As collective
hopes for democracy were dashed by increasing authoritarianism, Tunisian
society concluded an implicit Faustian pact with Bourguiba, a social bargain
seen elsewhere in the world. In exchange for middle-class existence, achieved
mainly through education, and access to consumer culture, open political dissent was generally muted on a daily basis. In return, the Bourguiba regime
refrained from interference in the national baccalaureate examinations that
take place in early summer every year. These exams, which are critical for entry
to the university system, were the Tunisian version of an educational Ramadan.
For weeks, all eyes were glued to the "bac" process, which was fair and honest
for the most part, although social class played a considerable role, as everywhere, in outcome. After the results were published with great fanfare in Arabic and French newspapers, often with photos of the successful students, girls
and boys, family parties were organized for the winners. The losers got another
crack at the bac the following year.

But the Ben Ali regime gradually began corrupting the exam, creating an
enormous sense of grievance—and outrage—among Tunisians, which is rarely,
if at all, mentioned in analyses of the origins of the protests. In effect, families
were blackmailed, obliged to collaborate in order to assure their children's

educational future.[44] An arresting photo appeared in 2011 of an unemployed teacher in Kasserine sitting dejectedly by abandoned rail lines on a flat dusty plain. He did have a university degree, but he was one of an estimated 3,000 certified teachers without schools and classrooms. Yet there is nothing inherently Tunisian, North African, Arab, or Muslim about this image. The jobless teacher might well be from West Texas, southern Arizona, or rural Mississippi, anywhere in the United States—or the globe—beset by growing structural social inequities.

GLOBAL REPERCUSSIONS AND COMPARISONS

Kalle Lasn, "leader" of the leaderless Occupy Wall Street movement, stated during an interview, "Back in the summer of 2011 we were all talking about what we were going to do . . . and we were all inspired by what happened in Tunisia and thought that America was ripe for this type of rage."[45] Conceived of in Vancouver, the original Occupy Movement was the brainchild of a transnational activist, Kalle Lasn, who was born in Estonia, resided in Australia, and is now a Canadian citizen. After the initial launch, spin-off Occupy movements burst out in American cities and towns and subsequently were imitated across the globe. These, however, were the progeny of earlier mass action that had taken the world by surprise in the 1995—the antiglobalization protests in Seattle during the annual meeting of the World Trade Organization. In any case, huge platters of couscous, North Africa's dish par excellence, were served in Zuccotti Park in New York City by political design not by culinary accident, and that same year, 2011, Chinese prodemocracy organizers embraced the notion of a "Jasmine revolution," one of the monikers for the Tunisian Revolution, making it their own.

The "tsunami" of scholarly reflections appearing in endless profusion and diverse media since the revolutions began tends to slip in and out of comparative frames that include national and/or global frames, on the one hand, and regional and cultural—Arab or North African—frames on the other. This leads to a question: What is specifically Arab about the Arab Spring? In contrast to Algeria, which has a concentrated ethnic minority, the Kabyle, who have since 1962 increasingly demanded political and cultural autonomy, Tunisia does not have a "minority" problem, either ethnic (as in Morocco and Algeria) or religious (for example, the Copts of Egypt).[46] However, the interior functions as an internal or domestic "other."

Moreover, transnational North African communities residing permanently outside the Maghrib are historically quite old and predate independence from France. Indeed, many North Africans living in diaspora across the world are French (or Canadian or American, etc.) citizens. These communities have maintained fundamental connectivities with family members and fellow citizens suffering under repressive regimes in North Africa, furnishing access to forbidden news, information, and knowledge. Functioning as some kind of "politically active offshore" communities, the expatriates as makers of revolution have not yet gained the scholarly attention they deserve. Many questions remain. Where and how do the local, regional, transnational, and global converge? What are the most salient methodologies for comparative analysis?

If the most common comparative approach tends to be "Arab," might not a richer vein of historical comparisons open if we widen our gaze, for example, to compare Tunisia to the last years of Franco's Spain or to similar movements for democratic rights in Latin America? If fortune smiles, as it did on Francisco Franco in 1975, the dictator expires in his own bed, shriveled and incoherent. Or he flees on a private Leer jet or seeks refuge in some primitive redoubt in mountain or desert. Or he is dragged through the streets. In probing the 2011 fall of the dictator, we must extend our historical vision not only to 1987 but also, in the very least, to the transition from protectorate to nation-state, to Bourguiba himself as dictator during the latter years of his tenure in office, or, perhaps to the previous century.[47]

CONCLUSIONS: THE END OF THE AFFAIR?

This chapter's intent has been less to search for the probable or possible triggers and causalities of mass collective protest than to troll the past for long-term, tectonic transformations as well as manifest and semiconcealed continuities. Historians do not normally engage in futuristic soothsaying or oracular pronouncements. Yet the consequences that these movements hold for dominant nationalist interpretations of Tunisia's past—both recent and distant—are enormous. In the nationalist version, history merely served as both legitimizer and antechamber to the nation collapsed into the single party. In the future, historians must closely examine processes not merely by looking at places like Sidi Bou Zid but also by witnessing change through the eyes of these places and their people. The challenges are enormous. Accounts and analyses of what is transpiring, what has just transpired, occur with breathless speed; the circulation of information is so rapid that it has become uncoupled from, unbounded by, facts and attempts at verisimilitude. Social media bewitch and bedazzle by means of vertiginous flows of information and their undeniable consequences. Whatever their velocity or temporalities, moments of rupture, if conceptualized properly, offer rare glimpses into what was, as well as what might have been, and thus provide glimpses of what lies ahead. One recurrent slogan of the protesters aimed at those who once claimed absolute power in both Egypt and Tunisia—and elsewhere—has been "*Irhal*": Get lost; disengage. It is hoped that the convergence of movements that precipitated the fall of the dictator will not turn against itself—to disengagement and disenchantment.[48]

The biggest question of all pertains to the historical relationship between the fall of empire and decolonization, processes that were interconnected but that should not be conflated. One of Tunisia's best known authors, Albert Memmi (born in Tunis in 1920), in an essay devoted to the "new citizen" recently posed this poignant question: "Why, if the colonial tree produced bitter fruit, has the tree of national independence provided us only with stunted and shriveled crops?"[49]

The author expresses her profound appreciation to the Woodrow Wilson International Center for Scholars and to her Middle East Program colleagues for intellectual inspiration in writing this chapter.

NOTES

1. Formerly known as the New Constitution Party, which had led the country to independence from France beginning in the 1930s, it became after 1964 the PSD. The New Constitution arose from a rupture within the ranks of the older nationalist movement whose roots predated World War I but which was formally founded in 1920. The party's name harkened back to the 1861 Tunisian constitution.

2. Kenneth J. Perkins, *A History of Modern Tunisia* (Cambridge: Cambridge University Press, 2004), 157–176; and Christopher Alexander, *Tunisia: Stability and Reform in the Modern Maghreb* (Oxon, UK: Routledge, 2010).

3. Perkins, *A History*, 170.

4. The most comprehensive analysis of state repression under the Ben Ali regime is Béatrice Hibou, *The Force of Obedience: The Political Economy of Repression in Tunisia* (Cambridge: Cambridge University Press, 2011), an expanded and

updated version of the French edition, *La force d'obéissance: Economie politique de la repression en Tunisie* (Paris: La Découverte, 2006).

5. Rikke Hostrup Haugbølle and Francesco Cavatorta, "Beyond Ghannouchi: Islamism and Social Change in Tunisia," *Middle East Report* 260 (Spring 2012): 20–25.

6. Mounira M. Charrad, *States and Women's Rights: The Making of Postcolonial Tunisia, Algeria, and Morocco* (Berkeley and Los Angeles: University of California Press, 2001); Jane Tchaïcha and Khedija Arfaoui, "Tunisian Women in the Twenty-First Century: Past Achievements and Present Uncertainties in the Wake of the Jasmine Revolution," *Journal of North African Studies* 17, 2 (March 2012): 215–238; and the *International Journal of Middle East Studies* 43, 3 (August 2011), special section on women and the Arab uprising. See also Lilia Labidi's important research on women and oral history: *Joudhour al-harakat al-nisa'iyya: Riwayat li-shakhsiyyat tarikhiyya* (Origins of Feminist Movements in Tunisia: Personal History Narratives) (Tunis: Imprimerie Tunis-Carthage, 2009); and *Qamus as-siyar li-lmunadhilat at-tunisiyyat, 1881–1956* (Biographical Dictionary of Tunisian Women Militants) (Tunis: Imprimerie Tunis Carthage, 2009).

7. Perkins, *A History*, 135–139; and Charrad, *States and Women's Rights*, 219–231.

8. Nouradin Dougi, *Histoire d'une grande entreprise coloniale: La Compagnie des Phosphates et du chemin de fer de Gafsa, 1897–1930* (Tunis: Publications de la Faculté de la Manouba, 1995); and Silvia Finzi, ed., *Mestieri e professioni degli Italiani di Tunisia* (Tunis: Éditions Finzi, 2003).

9. Perkins, *A History*, 84, 99, 145–115.

10. Ibid., 138–141.

11. Mehdi Mabrouk, "A Revolution for Dignity and Freedom: Preliminary Observations on the Social and Cultural Background to the Tunisian Revolution," *Journal of North African Studies* 16, 4 (2011): 625–635; on the "culture of suicide," see 629. See also Amy Aisen Kallander, "Tunisia's Post–Ben Ali Challenge: A Primer," in *MERIP Middle East Report Online*, January 26, 2011, www.merip.org; and David Ottaway, "Tunisia's Islamists Struggle to Rule," Woodrow Wilson International Center for Scholars Occasional Papers (April 2012).

12. It is a pity that political science research, such as Natasha Ezrow and Erica Frantz's *Dictators and Dictatorships: Understanding Authoritarian Regimes and Their Leaders* (New York: Continuum, 2011), 61–62, went to press before the Tunisian Revolutions; the authors tend to undervalue the potential of mass civic action in the unmaking of dictatorial systems of rule.

13. Naming the movement produced an increasingly heated debate over the moniker, "Jasmine Revolution," a label that has been around since Ben Ali seized power in 1987 when that event was curiously labeled the "Jasmine Revolution." Some scholars maintain that the CIA coined the term at the time as a marketing device. For the uprisings since 2010, Tunisians have generally employed *Thawrat al-Karamah* (The Dignity Revolution) or *Thawra Sidi Bou Zid* (The Revolution of Sidi Bou Zid), although currently, *al-Thawra al-Tunisiyya* (The Tunisian Revolution) seems to prevail.

14. Richard Reid, "Past and Presentism: The 'Precolonial' and the Foreshortening of African History," *Journal of African History* 52, 2 (2011): 135–155.

15. Italics are mine. For example, Angelique Chrisafis rejoiced in "the Arab world's first modern popular revolution" in *The Guardian*, February 9, 2011, an assertion that is historically inaccurate. Other journalists claimed that Tunisia had experienced less violence than Egypt during the Arab Spring because it had been so thoroughly colonized by Rome and that the French or, as improbably, the British had "liberated" North Africa from Ottoman imperial rule.

16. Stuart Schaar, "Arab Dictatorships Under Fire in the New Information Age," *Economic and Political Weekly* 46, 6 (February 5, 2011): 12–15.

17. Environmental forces and youth did not receive the scholarly attention they merited in the field of Middle East and North African studies until recently; the Tunisian and other Arab revolutions have brought these fundamental problems to the fore.

18. James L. Gelvin, *The Arab Uprisings: What Everyone Needs to Know* (New York: Oxford University Press, 2012).

19. Julia Clancy-Smith, "Ruptures? Governance in Colonial-Husaynid Tunisia, 1870–1914," in *Colonial and Post-Colonial Governance of Islam: Continuities and Ruptures*, ed. Veit Bader, Annelies Moors, and Marcel Maussen (Amsterdam: University of Amsterdam Press, 2011), 65–87.

20. An arresting photo of a protester brandishing a baguette in Tunis on January 18, 2011, appears in Nadia Marzouki, "From People to Citizens in Tunisia," *Middle East Report* 259 (Summer 2011): 16–19. See also Hibou, *The Force of Obedience*; Mabrouk, "A Revolution"; and "Food and the Arab Spring," *The Economist*, March 17, 2012, 59.

21. Perkins, *A History*, 157–165; and Stephen J. King, "Economic Reform and Tunisia's Hegemonic Party," in *Beyond Colonialism and Nationalism in the Maghrib: History, Culture, and Politics*, ed. Ali Abdullatif Ahmida (New York: Palgrave, 2000), 165–193.

22. Julia Clancy-Smith, *Mediterraneans: North Africa and Europe in an Age of Migration, c. 1800–1900* (Berkeley and Los Angeles: University of California Press, 2011).

23. Maude Barlow and Tony Clarke, *Blue Gold: The Fight to Stop the Corporate Theft of the World's Water* (New York: The New Press, 2005); and Stewart M. Patrick, "Not a Drop to Drink: The Global Water Crisis," Council on Foreign Relations, May 8, 2012.

24. My thanks to Jemel Derbali of Pomona College for sharing this information with me.

25. Jacques Berque, *Le Maghreb entre deux guerres* (Paris: Seuil, 1979).

26. John R. McNeill, *Mountains of the Mediterranean: An Environmental History* (Cambridge: Cambridge University Press, 1992); Faruk Tabak, *The Waning of the Mediterranean, 1550–1870: A Geohistorical Approach* (Baltimore, MD: Johns Hopkins University Press, 2008); Edmund Burke III and Kenneth Pomeranz, eds., *The Environment and World History, 1500–2000* (Berkeley and Los Angeles: University of California Press, 2009); and Julia Clancy-Smith, "Mediterranean Historical Migrations: An Overview," in *Encyclopedia of Global Human Migration*, ed. Dirk Hoerder and Donna Gabaccia (London: Wiley Blackwell, 2012).

27. The best study of the 1864 revolt is Silvia Marsans-Sakly, "The Revolt of 1864 in Tunisia: History, Power, and Memory" (PhD diss., New York University, 2010). See also Ilham Khuri-Makdisi, *The Eastern Mediterranean and the Making of Global Radicalism, 1860–1914* (Berkeley and Los Angeles: University of California Press, 2010).

28. Perkins, *A History*, 126–129.

29. See Hibou, *The Force of Obedience*, 31, on the abuses of the internationally financed tourist industry.

30. As is true of all social movements, the December 2010 events produced a tangle of contradictory stories: Laila Lalami, "Tunisia Rising," *The Nation*, February 7, 2011, 7, stated that Bouazizi had a university degree, which was patently untrue: "The Tunisian uprising began when Mohammed Bouazizi—a college graduate eking out a living selling vegetables whose unlicensed cart was confiscated by the police. . . ."

31. Isabelle Mandraud, "Un portfolio sonore sur Sidi Bouzid," *Le Monde*, December 17, 2011.

32. Clancy-Smith, *Mediterraneans*, 313–314.

33. On November 28, 2010, WikiLeaks and five international newspapers including *The Guardian* agreed to simultaneously publish a number of leaked diplomatic cables from U.S. embassies around the world, covering the period from 1966 until early 2010. The report on Ben Ali's son-in-law was reported by *The Guardian*, December 7, 2010, www.guardian.co.uk/world/us-embassy -cables-documents/218324.

34. Ibid. Later in the same cable, the ambassador remarked apropos of the new Sidi Bou Said house, "Even more extravagant is their home still under construction in Sidi Bou Said. That residence, from its outward appearance, will be closer to a palace. It dominates the Sidi Bou Said skyline from some vantage points and has been the occasion of many private, critical remarks."

35. Ibid.

36. Ibid.

37. "Radhia Nasraoui on Hunger Strike in Tunisia, December 2003," www .frontlinedefenders.org/taxonomy/term/779, accessed May 11, 2012.

38. On associations, especially human rights organizations, in Tunisia, see Hibou, *The Force of Obedience*, 95–105.

39. Lilia Labidi, "Islamic Law, Feminism, and Family: The Reformulation of *Hudud* in Egypt and Tunisia," in *From Patriarchy to Empowerment: Women's Participation, Movements, and Rights in the Middle East, North Africa, and South* Asia, ed. Valentine M. Moghadam (Syracuse, NY: Syracuse University Press, 2007); and Sophie Bessis "Le féminisme institutionnel en Tunisie," *CLIO: Histoire, femmes et sociétés* 9 (1999), accessed May 10, 2012, http://clio.revues.org/286, doi: 10.4000/clio.286.

40. Julia Clancy-Smith, "Envisioning Knowledge: Educating the Muslim Woman in Colonial North Africa, 1850–1918," in *Iran and Beyond: Essays in Middle Eastern History in Honor of Nikki R. Keddie*, ed. Beth Baron and Rudi Matthee (Los Angeles: Mazda Press, 2000), 99–118.

41. See, for example, Soumaya Ghannoushi, "Perceptions of Arab Women Have Been Revolutionised," *The Guardian*, March 11, 2011.

42. Euroenews, October 23, 2011.

43. Joan W. Scott, *The Politics of the Veil* (Princeton, NJ: Princeton University Press, 2007).

44. I gathered evidence for this during years of interviews and conversations in Tunis with high school teachers who drew up, oversaw, and corrected the annual examination, as well as with the families of students presenting themselves for the bac.

See also Julia Clancy-Smith, *From Household to School Room: Education and Schooling in North Africa, c. 1830–2000* (Cambridge University Press, forthcoming).

45. "The Brains Behind 'Occupy Wall Street': Kalle Lasn Talks to Kenneth Rapoza," *Forbes*, October 14, 2011, http://www.forbes.com/sites/kenrapoza /2011/10/14/the-brains-behind-occupy-wall-street-and-where-its-heading.

46. The Berber Spring of 1980 has been largely neglected in recent analyses. In 1980 when a lecture on Kabyle poetry to be given by popular Berber writer Mouloud Mammeri was announced at the University of Tizi-Ouzou and subsequently forbidden by the Algerian government, protests exploded in the Kabylia calling for official recognition of Berber as a national language and its use in national curricula. These cultural demands translated larger political and social struggles for democratic forms of governance and more open society. Although rapidly suppressed by the state, the Berber Spring nurtured regional and national identity and a continuing Berber movement in Algeria and France. Widely divergent explanations for the long-term origins, short-term triggers, and social meanings of the Berber Spring persist to this day. See Judith Scheele, *Village Matters: Knowledge, Politics, and Community in Kabylia, Algeria* (Suffolk, UK: James Currey, 2009).

47. However, as many Tunisians and scholars have pointed out, Bourguiba died in rather modest social circumstances, owning few possessions; a simple visit to the museum in his memory in Bourguiba's hometown of Munastir demonstrates that, much in contrast to Ben Ali, the first president did not regard Tunisia's wealth and resources as his personal property or fief. This fact should introduce more nuanced theoretical distinctions into discussions of the nature of dictatorship or authoritarian rule. See Pierre-Albin Martel, *Habib Bourguiba: Un home, un siècle* (Paris: Jaguar, 1999).

48. Clearly, the recent parliamentary elections in Algeria, held on May 10, 2012, demonstrate disenchantment on the part of Algerian voters, who showed up at the polls in small numbers and who also cast a very high percentage (17 percent) of blank ballots to protest the process. See David Ottaway, "Algeria's Islamists Crushed in First Arab Spring Elections," Woodrow Wilson Center for Scholars Occasional Papers (May 2012).

49. Albert Memmi, *Decolonization and the Decolonized*, trans. Robert Bononno (Minneapolis: University of Minnesota Press, 2006), 21.

2

Egypt: The Origins and Consequences of the January 25 Uprising

BRUCE K. RUTHERFORD

FOR MANY OBSERVERS, the uprising that removed Husni Mubarak on February 11, 2011, was a surprise.[1] Mubarak's regime had been the model of authoritarian stability. Scholars had written careful studies of how Mubarak, the ruling National Democratic Party (NDP), and the intelligence services created a uniquely durable and adaptive form of authoritarianism. They used cooptation and coercion with equal skill to build a wide circle of supporters and to keep opponents at bay.[2]

In reality, the foundations of the Mubarak regime had been eroding for decades. Its origins lay in the revolution begun by Gamal Abd al-Nasser in 1952, which created a political order based on an informal social contract: citizens would cede the political arena to Nasser and the ruling party; in exchange, the regime would provide material prosperity and security. The regime's side of this contract entailed building a massive public sector that, at its peak in the early 1980s, produced 50 percent of GDP and consumed 75 percent of gross domestic fixed investment.[3] It also created an extensive network of subsidies that provided food, electricity, gasoline, public transportation, education, medical care, and a host of other services either free or at heavily subsidized prices.

This system was doomed by two developments. As medical care and nutrition improved (partly due to Nasser's policies), Egypt's population grew at unprecedented rates in the 1970s, 1980s, and 1990s. By the mid-1990s, 1.3 million new Egyptians were born every year. Each of these new citizens expected the full panoply of state subsidies promised by Nasser as well as a decent job for life. But the state-centered economy that Nasser had built simply could not meet these demands. The public sector produced shoddy goods at relatively high prices and, because of its poor performance, was unable to provide the generous salaries and benefits that Nasser and his successors promised. It became an enormous drain on the state budget, which, in turn, made the subsidies that were essential to the Nasserist social contract unaffordable. The government attempted to deal with this problem through borrowing, getting itself into a deep financial hole. By the late 1980s, Egypt had one of the largest debt burdens in the world—184 percent of GDP, if calculated at the free-market exchange rate.[4]

In the early 1990s, the United States and Europe agreed to help Egypt out of this hole through a combination of bilateral and multilateral assistance. This assistance, however, came at a price: Egypt must mend its ways and create a more market-driven, export-oriented economy that was fully integrated into the global economy. Mubarak had little choice but to comply, and Egypt embarked on a neoliberal reform plan in 1991 that was crafted in consultation with the International Monetary Fund. At the heart of this plan lay the dismantling of the social contract that was the foundation of the regime's legitimacy. The public sector would be largely sold off, the subsidy system cut, and the state's role in the economy reduced.

The architects of this reform plan were sensitive to the political repercussions of dismantling this safety net and attempted to design their plan to minimize its pain. Public sector firms would be privatized, but at a market price and only to buyers who agreed not to dismiss workers for several years. Any workers who were made redundant would receive training that enabled them to find new jobs, and they would retain access to subsidized housing and other benefits while they were looking. The implementation of the plan, though, fell far short of these goals. Public sector firms were sold at bargain-basement prices, often to businessmen with close political connections to Mubarak and his family. Promises to keep workers on the payroll were evaded or ignored, leading to widespread dismissals. Assurances of additional training and benefits went unfulfilled. At the same time, state subsidies were cut and state investment in the public sector was sharply curtailed.

The regime and its advisers hoped that the private sector would pick up the slack and establish new, dynamic enterprises that would create thousands of new jobs. Indeed, a new private sector emerged. Some parts of the Egyptian economy grew—particularly, technology services (Egypt became a major provider of call center services) and exports of agricultural products. Overall, the economy reached very respectable growth rates of 6–7 percent in the mid-2000s. Egyptians with the specialized skills and the connections needed to perform these new jobs did well. But Egyptians without these skills and connections saw their quality of life deteriorate steadily. Public sector workers, civil servants, and pensioners saw their incomes remain largely stagnant while inflation rose at double-digit rates for much of the 2000s. Families who thought of themselves as solidly middle class saw their standard of living steadily decline until they were poor. Those who were on the edge of poverty slipped into it. At the time of the January 2011 uprising, more than 40 percent of the population fell below the poverty line.[5] In 2008, unemployment among university graduates reached 25 percent.[6]

As many Egyptians watched the purchasing power of their salaries fall, corruption became much more common. Civil servants routinely asked for a "tip" for the services they provided, largely because it was the only way to acquire the income needed to survive. Teachers in public schools began to charge for "extra lessons" after school, which in reality were essential for the student to pass exams for admission to university. This small-scale corruption led the large and unwieldy apparatus of the Egyptian state to become almost thoroughly dysfunctional. It was unable to meet even the smallest expectations of the public for the services that had been promised by the glowing rhetoric of the Nasser era.

By the mid-2000s, the social contract of the Nasser era was long dead and, with it, the basis for the regime's legitimacy. In its place had emerged a corrupt and ineffective state that served the interests of a small elite consisting of the ruling party, businessmen with close ties to the regime, and Mubarak's family and close confidants. Their power was backed by the military, whose officers also benefited from this order. This system was propped up by an increasingly brutal and arbitrary security service. Egypt under Nasser and his successor, Anwar Sadat, had always had a strong security apparatus. However, its power and breadth of jurisdiction were widened dramatically under Mubarak in the early 1990s after the regime faced a surge of attacks by violent Islamic groups. It responded to these attacks by granting the security services extensive authority, with few legal constraints, to arrest and detain citizens. Once police officers began using these new powers, it did not take long for abuse to set in.

It became routine for anyone suspected of a crime to face beatings at the local police station, and for persons suspected of political subversion to face long detention without trial. In addition, individual police officers often abused their power for personal gain. By 2010, the police and the security services were deeply feared and loathed by much of the population.

As the legitimacy of the regime steadily declined and the economic situation for many citizens continued to deteriorate, Egyptians had few peaceful ways to express their anger. Opposition parties had been permitted since the mid-1970s, but they had long been rendered mute and politically irrelevant. Mubarak's men sometimes allowed them to win a few seats in parliament, but they did not play a role in the formulation of policy and were prevented from building a national organization that might lead to real political power. The Muslim Brotherhood was a tenacious and durable opponent that the regime managed with a variety of tactics, including brutal repression under Nasser; a brief opening under Sadat, followed by another round of repression; and limited freedom in the early years of Mubarak's rule, but then waves of repression in the 1990s and 2000s as Mubarak came to believe that the Brotherhood was an irredeemable threat to him and his regime. A wide array of civil society groups existed—from professional associations to charitable groups to labor unions—but all were carefully monitored and regulated by the state.

Beyond this carefully managed political arena, some pockets of opposition began to emerge. Most notably, the independent labor movement organized more than 1,900 labor actions of various sizes from 2004 to 2008 that protested poor wages, inadequate benefits, and declining working conditions.[7] On a few occasions, these labor actions managed to achieve some concessions from employers. Some independent political groups also arose. The best known was the *Kefaya* (Enough) movement, which organized demonstrations in 2005 calling for Mubarak to leave office. In 2008, the April 6 movement was formed. It was initially established to support striking workers in Egypt's delta region, but soon expanded to call for broad political and economic reform. In addition, online communities provided an important arena for Egyptians to share their anger and their hopes for change. A website established to commemorate a businessman beaten to death by police in 2010—We are all Khalid Said[8]—attracted 400,000 members in the months preceding the uprising. The April 6 website had 70,000 members on the eve of the uprising.[9] These groups and organizations gave some voice to the growing public anger with the status quo. To some degree, they also helped to erode the public's fear of the regime. The fact that independent labor unions, in particular, could demonstrate and achieve concessions without severe retaliation from the regime was an important source of encouragement for some activists.

In 2010, several developments helped to intensify the economic and political pressures that led to the uprising. As noted earlier, inflation had been a constant bane to the lives of many Egyptians, averaging more than 10 percent for much of the decade preceding the uprising, with few salary increases to preserve peoples' purchasing power. This problem worsened sharply, with food prices rising 37 percent in the two years prior to the uprising.[10] As many citizens' economic situation deteriorated, the political institutions that ostensibly represented them became even less responsive. This was particularly true during the parliamentary election in November 2010. In the previous election in 2005, opposition parties managed to win 22 percent of the seats with most of these held by the Muslim Brotherhood (88 seats)—not enough to pose a meaningful challenge to the ruling party's control of the chamber, but enough to lend some credibility to the parliament and provide a forum for venting some public anger at the status quo. In November 2010, Mubarak and his advisers lost all sense of proportion and managed the elections to produce a lopsided victory for the ruling party. The NDP won 93 percent of the seats. The Brotherhood won only 1 seat. The regime also embarked on a new round of steps to rein in the opposition press and limit the capacity of private satellite stations to criticize the government. In addition, it took steps to silence the reformist wing of the judiciary, which had been an important voice for electoral honesty in the 2005 elections. Thus, as the public was pushed even closer to economic desperation, the peaceful avenues for venting its anger—whether through parliament, the press, or the judiciary—were closed off.

On top of these deteriorating economic and political conditions, there were growing rumors about Mubarak's health. The president was eighty-three years old in 2011 and had spent several months abroad for medical treatment in 2010. For some of the demonstrators who would flow to Tahrir, there was a sense that Egypt was at a pivotal moment of succession, and they wanted to have some input into how it would unfold.

The key to the success of Egypt's uprising was the extraordinary size of the crowds. By some estimates, they exceeded 1 million people on several occasions.[11] The sheer number of demonstrators provided irrefutable evidence of the public's anger with the status quo and its determination to achieve change.

They led the key supporters of Mubarak in the military and in the United States to conclude that it was time for a new leader.

It is useful to remember that the Internet activists who spearheaded the demonstrations on January 25 had called for similar demonstrations on several occasions in the past. The results on these previous occasions had been disappointing. They produced small turnouts of a few hundred die-hard activists who were easily dispersed by the security services. This had been a long-standing feature of Egyptian politics. In essence, average Egyptians concluded that the continued survival of the regime was inevitable. They might not like it, but they were powerless to change it. Demonstrations were a waste of time. And they were very risky. A participant could be arrested, tortured, and possibly killed.

For the January 25 demonstrations to succeed, many average Egyptians had to reach two conclusions that were new: they had to be willing to take on risks that they were unwilling to endure previously, and they had to believe that the regime's survival was no longer inevitable (and thus the risk was worth taking).

What conditions led to this change of calculation by the average Egyptian? At least four factors were involved.

1. *Online communities:* Facebook, blogs, and other social media played an important role in building a shared identity and purpose among critics of the regime. Dissidents often feel alone and powerless. Social media helped to overcome these feelings of isolation and provided many thousands of Egyptians with a sense of connection to the noble cause of transforming their country. This connection was so strong that it pushed many first-time demonstrators on to the street. Many more came out as the demonstrations unfolded once they saw their online friends (or people like them) being beaten by security police on satellite TV. These were no longer "other people" who were being attacked. They were people that members of these communities saw as their friends and comrades. Social media helped to create strong emotional bonds that led some young people to risk their lives.

2. *Tunisia:* The Arab Spring began with the departure of Tunisia's dictator, Zine al-Abidine Ben Ali, on January 14, 2011, after thirty days of protests. Prior to Ben Ali's departure, most Egyptians reasoned that there was little point in demonstrating. They would achieve nothing and would be beaten up by the security police. After Ben Ali's exit, many thousands of Egyptians concluded that meaningful political change could be accomplished by going to the street. The events in Tunisia altered the cost-benefit assessment of participat-

ing in demonstrations. They also had an inspirational effect. After watching the demonstrations in Tunis, many people decided that the time had come to change a system that had produced sweeping indignity and poverty.

3. *Satellite television:* Satellite receivers are widely available in Egypt, and most of the population was able to watch events unfold on Tahrir Square in real time. Satellite news programs (particularly Al-Jazeera) enabled a broad audience of Egyptians to see both the size of the demonstrations and the brutality of the regime that tried to suppress them. The size of the crowds, combined with the recent memory of events in Tunisia, reinforced the impression that the regime was vulnerable and, thus, participation in demonstrations could accomplish meaningful change. The brutal tactics employed on February 2 and 3 to disperse the demonstrators were broadcast for all to see and added moral urgency and legitimacy to the cause of confronting the regime.

4. *The organizational skill of the youth movement:* Youth activists such as the April 6 movement were essential to the success of the demonstrations.[12] Partly by following the examples of other protests movements (particularly in Serbia) and partly through their own creativity, these activists developed novel ways to outmaneuver Egypt's vast and plodding security apparatus. They tricked the security police into sending troops to the wrong sites, mobilized unexpected groups (particularly from the poor neighborhoods near Tahrir Square) for the first big march on the square on January 25, and made skillful use of the international media.[13] They managed to get much larger crowds to Tahrir on January 25 than anyone expected. The presence of these crowds and the regime's brutal response were immediately broadcast on satellite TV, and then the cascade effect began. The TV images led more people to conclude that the regime was vulnerable and that demonstrations were worth the risk; more people turned out; as the demonstrations became ever larger, the vulnerability of the regime became even more apparent and the marginal risk to each new participant became lower, so the crowds grew at an even faster pace.

Of course, all of these efforts would have been for naught if the military had intervened to disperse the demonstrators. The military leadership's decision not to fire on the protesters was pivotal and was a surprise to many. The senior officer corps were all Mubarak's men. They were appointed by him and rewarded with relatively high salaries and an array of privileges. They owed their careers, status, and prosperity to him. Furthermore, they saw themselves as an integral part of the ruling elite. Yet at the critical moment, they showed

Mubarak the door. We still do not know the complete story of why the generals made this decision. It may have been a purely pragmatic calculation. Senior officers may have concluded that Mubarak had lost the support of the public and key international actors, particularly the United States. The writing was on the wall: Mubarak's days were numbered, so the generals simply facilitated his departure as quickly as possible. The structure of Egypt's military may have also been a factor. Egypt has a conscript army drawn from every corner of the country. The demands made at Tahrir Square—for more jobs, less corruption, and better protection of rights—resonated at all levels of Egyptian society and led parts of the rank and file to support the protesters. As a result of these sympathies, the generals may have feared that an order to fire on the protesters would have been ignored by some soldiers, leading to a paralyzing split in the military. In addition, there was growing disenchantment with the regime. As rumors of high-level corruption became commonplace over the previous decade, some military men concluded that Mubarak was acting against the best interest of the country. There was particular criticism of the privatization process, which many believed was rigged to provide sweetheart deals to the president's family and friends. The secretive military rarely expressed these criticisms publicly, but they occasionally leaked out through statements and letters by retired officers. The cancer of corruption eroded the military's loyalty to the regime, even while some officers benefited from it.[14]

Finally, there was concern among the generals over who would succeed Mubarak as president. Ever since the 1952 coup, Egypt has been led by presidents drawn from the military—Muhammad Naguib, Nasser, Sadat, and Mubarak. With one of their own at the top of the political hierarchy, the military was assured that its status, budget, and privileges would be protected. However, Mubarak appeared to be steering the succession toward his son Gamal Mubarak, a Western-trained banker with longstanding connections to the corrupt businessmen who had benefited from the privatization process. He was largely an unknown figure to the generals. Furthermore, his close ties to supporters of market reform raised the possibility that he might try to restructure or even privatize the vast web of commercial enterprises controlled by the military. These enterprises produce a wide range of products sold into the civilian economy and are a key source of revenue for sustaining the relatively high salaries and standard of living enjoyed by the officer corps. The generals' decision to end Mubarak's rule may have been the product of a clear-eyed calculation of how to protect their interests in post-Mubarak

Egypt. Rather than trust Gamal's promises that he would continue his father's policies, the generals decided to take matters into their own hands and manage the succession themselves.

Regardless of the generals' motives, we know that their position evolved quickly. When the demonstrations began on January 25, the generals were studiously neutral, watching to see if Mubarak and his central security forces could manage the situation. Mubarak's political judgment failed him. He underestimated the popular appeal of the demonstrators and missed several opportunities to offer concessions that might have slowed their momentum.[15] Instead, he remained dismissive of the "children" on the square and sent in thugs from the security forces to subdue them.

It is unclear whether Mubarak ordered the military to fire on the demonstrators. Defense Minister Field Marshall Hussein Tantawi testified in court that he had received no such order. In any event, by the time Mubarak would have given such an order, the die had been cast. The military had decided to jettison its patron of thirty years and take the reins of power itself in the form of the Supreme Council of the Armed Forces (SCAF). This committee of twenty senior generals assumed all executive and legislative power on February 11, 2011. It immediately suspended the constitution and disbanded the parliament. It announced plans to supervise elections for a new parliament and president, as well as preside over the drafting of a new constitution. In the interim, the SCAF released a "Constitutional Declaration" that functioned as a de facto constitution. This declaration was based largely on the amended 1971 constitution of the Mubarak period, with a few modifications that allowed for competitive elections for parliament and the presidency.

Elections for both the lower and upper houses of parliament were held in late 2011–early 2012. The Muslim Brotherhood was the only competitor with a strong national organization, which paid off. The Brotherhood won 45 percent of the seats in the lower house (the People's Assembly) and 58 percent of the contested seats in the upper house (the Shura Council). The Salafi movement's main representative, the al-Nur (Light) Party, won 25 percent in the lower house and 25 percent in the upper house. This came as a surprise to many observers. The Salafis were a highly conservative Islamic movement that had been uninvolved in Egyptian politics prior to 2011 Their leaders had openly opposed the January 25 uprising on the grounds that it was better to accept Mubarak's authority than to risk the disorder that might flow from a change of regime. The liberal parties came in a distant third. The largest liberal party, the Wafd (Delegation) Party, won only 7.5 percent of the seats in the lower house and 8 percent in the upper house. An alliance of other liberal parties, the Egyptian Bloc, won 6.7 percent of the seats in the lower house and 4.5 percent in the upper house.

The first round of presidential elections occurred on May 23–24, 2012. Thirteen candidates entered the contest and received the necessary approvals from the Presidential Election Commission to compete.[16] In the run-up to the balloting, five candidates led the race: Muhammad Mursi, a senior Muslim Brotherhood leader and president of the Brotherhood's Freedom and Justice Party (FJP); Abd al-Monam Abu al-Fatuh, a prominent former leader of the Brotherhood who had led efforts in the 1990s and 2000s to revise Brotherhood doctrine to support a more open and democratic political system;[17] Hamdin Sabahi, a Nasserist and poet who emphasized the importance of economic reforms that would broaden workers' rights and expand social services; Amr Moussa, who had been foreign minister under Mubarak from 1991 to 2001 and secretary general of the Arab League from 2001 to 2011; and Ahmad Shafiq, a former military officer who had led the Egyptian air force from 1996 to 2002, had been minister of civil aviation from 2002 to 2011, and had briefly served as prime minister at the end of Mubarak's reign.

Mursi received the largest share of the vote, with 24.8 percent, and Shafiq was runner-up with 23.7 percent, setting the stage for a runoff on June 16–17 to determine who would be Egypt's first elected president. Many supporters of Egypt's revolution were disappointed with this range of choices. Mursi was seen as a machine politician who lacked the charisma and political skill needed to unify the country. Shafiq's commitment to the goals of the revolution was in serious doubt. Of all the candidates in the race, he was the figure most associated with Mubarak's regime. Indeed, he described Mubarak as his role model and criticized the January 25 demonstrators as disrespectful children who had slapped their father.[18] Shafiq promised during the campaign that he would restore order, revive the economy, and counterbalance the influence of the Islamists who controlled parliament.

Two days before the runoff election began on June 16, the Supreme Constitutional Court (SCC) issued a dramatic ruling that declared the law governing the election of the lower house of parliament (the People's Assembly) unconstitutional.[19] Based on this ruling, the SCAF dissolved the People's Assembly. As noted earlier, the Muslim Brotherhood's Freedom and Justice Party held a large plurality of seats in this chamber (45 percent). The Brotherhood and some observers asserted that the SCC ruling and the SCAF decision to dissolve the People's Assembly were politically motivated efforts to deny the Brotherhood the political power that it had earned at the ballot box. The Brotherhood's presidential candidate, Muhammad Mursi, portrayed the dissolution of the People's Assembly as an attack on both the Brotherhood and the democratic principles of the January 25 uprising. He campaigned as the "candidate of the revolution" who would fight against the counterrevolutionary forces in the military, the judiciary, and the security services.

Mursi's efforts were successful. He won 52 percent of the vote to Shafiq's 48 percent. The military accepted the defeat of Shafiq and allowed Mursi to assume office. For the first time in Egypt's 5,000-year history, the country had an elected national leader. In his inaugural address, Mursi promised to be the president of all Egyptians and to build a new Egypt that is "civil, national, constitutional, and modern."[20] He also announced plans to create a national unity government that would include all of Egypt's political currents.

However, the struggle between the Brotherhood and the military was not yet over. Within hours of the polls closing on June 17, the SCAF decreed several amendments to the de facto constitution that significantly altered the political landscape. The amendments expanded the SCAF's powers by granting it the legislative authority previously held by the parliament, complete control over all matters related to the military, immunity from civilian oversight, and the capacity to block virtually any policy initiative that the new president might pursue. The amendments also gave the SCAF an important role in the drafting of the new constitution. Prior to these amendments, the constitution was to be written by a constituent assembly selected by the parliament and then submitted to the public for approval. After issuing the new amendments, the SCAF assumed the power to appoint a new constituent assembly if the existing assembly failed to complete its work. The SCAF also granted itself a formal mechanism to object to specific clauses of the proposed constitution.[21]

These amendments marked a striking change in the SCAF's political role. Prior to June 17, the SCAF had stated repeatedly that it planned to turn over all political power to civilian officials on June 30 and withdrawal to the barracks. By issuing these amendments, the SCAF made clear that it planned to play a central role in the development of the political and legal system at least until a new constitution was adopted and a new lower house of parliament was elected.

As Egypt's politics have become more open since the January 25 uprising, five actors have emerged as particularly important for influencing the country's future: liberals, the Muslim Brotherhood, the Salafis, the military, and remnants of the old regime.

LIBERALS

Many of the young people who organized the demonstrations on January 25, 2011, described themselves as supporters of liberal democracy or expressed views that placed them in this camp. They joined a long tradition of liberal thought that extends back to the late nineteenth century and reached its heyday in the early years of Egypt's independence in the 1920s. They hold a view of constitutional order that contains many features of classical liberalism, including a civil state in which military and religious institutions play no role in politics; sovereignty residing with the people; laws originating in an elected parliament that is accountable to the people; state power divided into three branches, with checks and balances among these branches; an independent and well-trained judiciary; equality of all citizens regardless of religion or gender; protection of basic civil and political rights, including freedom of speech, inquiry, and assembly; and a market-based economy that is regulated in a manner that improves social justice.

There are some elements of this view that are at odds with classical liberalism. Most notably, many proponents of liberalism have indicated their willingness to accept Article 2 of the 1971 constitution, which declares that Islam is the religion of the state and sharia is the primary source of law. This formulation gives religion a role in public life that differs from classical liberalism. Thus, Egyptian liberalism has a distinctive character, but the large majority of its positions fall squarely within the scope of classical liberal thought.

In the aftermath of Mubarak's ouster, liberals organized into several parties. The largest were the Wafd, the Justice Party, the Free Egyptians, the Democratic Front Party, the Social Democratic Party, and the Free Egypt Party. Each party competed in the parliamentary elections. However, the liberals were unable to translate their remarkable skills at political mobilization (manifest so clearly during the uprising) into effective campaigning. As noted earlier, the largest liberal party—the Wafd—won only 7.5 percent of the seats in the lower house and 8 percent in the upper house. The liberal parties simply failed to connect with the masses of the Egyptian public. They were widely seen as urban, elitist, and out of touch with the challenges facing the average Egyptian. Despite their poor electoral performance, advocates of liberalism play a prominent role in public debates over politics and the constitution. They are well represented in the media (both newspapers and TV) as well as in the legal community, which is likely to have an important role in the drafting of the constitution.

The Muslim Brotherhood

The Muslim Brotherhood has been vague about its political goals for much of its eighty-four-year history. While it often intoned that "Islam is the solution," it studiously avoided spelling out what this meant. This began to change in the mid-1990s, when the Brotherhood started to issue political documents that drew on the ideas of several reformist Islamic thinkers—particularly Yusuf al-Qaradawi, Tariq al-Bishri, Kamal Abu al-Magd, and Muhammad Salim al-Awwa. This reformist trend in the Brotherhood's thinking became especially pronounced in its platform and other campaign materials for the 2005 parliamentary elections and its draft party platform in 2007. These documents began to define an Islamic conception of constitutionalism (IC) that became increasingly influential in Egyptian political debates. It drew on Islamic tradition and doctrine to advocate positions that many liberals would find appealing, including legal and institutional constraints on state power, protection of many civil and political rights, the rule of law, and the principle that laws are written by elected representatives who are accountable to the people.

However, the form of IC that emerged in 2005–2007 differed from liberal constitutionalism in several important respects. These differences were clearest in the draft party platform that the Brotherhood issued in 2007,[22] which articulated three controversial positions:

1. It proposed that a body of religious scholars be empowered to review draft legislation to determine whether it conformed to sharia. In the text of the draft platform, it was unclear whether this body's opinions would be binding on legislators or simply advisory.
2. It opposed allowing women to hold the presidency on the grounds that they lacked the temperament to perform the job effectively. Brotherhood leaders later explained that they would not call for a law that prohibited women from holding the presidency. Rather, they would simply oppose a female candidate for the office.

3.   It opposed allowing a Copt to hold the post of either president or prime
     minister (Copts are the largest Christian group in Egypt, accounting
     for an estimated 10 percent of Egypt's population). The platform ar-
     gued that the state plays a fundamental role in enforcing sharia and in
     building the Islamic character of individuals and society. For this rea-
     son, a non-Muslim could not hold either of the most senior political
     posts. As with the issue of women in senior positions of power, the
     Brotherhood did not call for a law that prohibited Copts from holding
     these senior posts. Rather, it declared that it would oppose a Coptic
     candidate for them, regardless of his qualifications.

Since the January 25 revolution, these illiberal features have been largely
discarded in the Brotherhood's official documents and statements. The clearest
evidence of this change lies in the platform of the Muslim Brotherhood's political party, the Freedom and Justice Party.[23] This platform makes no reference to a body of religious scholars that would vet legislation. It also makes no
mention of opposing Copts or women holding the country's most senior political posts. The leaders of the FJP have indicated that they would accept a
women or a Copt holding senior political posts if she or he were chosen
through free and fair elections. In addition, the FJP platform does not contain
a controversial passage from the 2007 draft platform declaring that the state
plays an important religious role in society. This passage was interpreted at
the time to mean that a non-Muslim could not be head of state and that the
state would play a prominent role in regulating public morality. However, the
FJP platform still contains a passage asserting that the party seeks to "enhance
Islamic morals, values, and concepts in individuals' lives and society."[24] It is
unclear whether the state would play this role or whether private actors would.

In addition, al-Azhar University—the most prominent center of Sunni
thought in Egypt—has adopted a view of political order that aligns with Islamic constitutionalism. The sheikh of al-Azhar issued a statement in June
2011 reinforcing the view espoused by the FJP.[25] Drawing on Islamic principles
and doctrine, it expressed support for a democratic state based on a constitution approved by the citizenry. It called for a separation of powers, protection
of civil and political rights, equality for women and Copts, and a freely elected
parliament with unrestricted authority to draft and adopt laws.

These changes in Islamic constitutionalism constitute one of the most important developments in constitutional thinking since the January 25 uprising.

In essence, the boundary between liberal thought and IC has largely disappeared. In official documents and statements, liberal thinkers and moderate Islamic thinkers have converged around a conception of constitutionalism that is supportive of democratic transition and consolidation.

This convergence was largely the product of the FJP and al-Azhar moving toward the center of the political spectrum in order to find common ground with liberal and secular actors. This effort continued through the parliamentary elections in late 2011–early 2012. In March 2012, the Brotherhood decided to enter the race for the presidency. It initially nominated its most prominent financier and strategist, Khairat al-Shater. However, he was disqualified by the Presidential Election Commission on the grounds that he had been convicted of fraud during the Mubarak era and thus was ineligible to enter the race. He was quickly replaced by Muhammad Mursi, the FJP's president. Mursi's presidential campaign in April and May 2012 emphasized several conservative themes. For example, he called for implementation of sharia, rather than simply drafting of legislation within the framework of sharia. While Mursi emphasized that legislation should be written and adopted by elected representatives of the people in parliament (not by religious scholars), this shift in language reflected the more conservative strand of thought within the Brotherhood. Mursi also asserted that the Quran should serve as the foundation for the new constitution and expressed his personal opposition to women or Copts running for the presidency.

Mursi did not renounce the moderate positions advocated by the FJP during the parliamentary race, but his presidential campaign placed greater emphasis on views that would appeal to the Brotherhood's more conservative supporters. The campaign also used conservative Salafi clerics, such as Safwat Hegazy, to speak at rallies and mobilize the conservative base. This decision by Mursi and his advisers to invoke conservative themes during the campaign appears to have been driven by several considerations: Mursi wanted to consolidate his support among the more conservative elements of the Brotherhood; the conservative Salafi parties (particularly al-Nur) performed surprisingly well in the parliamentary election, and Mursi hoped to gain their backing; and Mursi's primary Islamist challenger in the presidential race was Abd al-Monam Abu al-Fatuh, a former Muslim Brother who was a long-standing supporter of a moderate view of Islam and Islamic governance. Mursi wanted to distinguish himself from Abu al-Fatuh by advocating a more conservative view of the faith. In the first round of the presidential election on May 23 and 24, Mursi emerged as the highest vote getter, with 24.8 percent of the vote. Abu al-Fatuh came in fourth, with 17.5 percent. Mursi then proceeded to a runoff on June 16–17 against Ahmad Shafiq, a former prime minister and protégé of Husni Mubarak. During the campaign for the runoff, Mursi reemphasized the moderate themes of the FJP platform in an effort to gain support from Abu al-Fatuh and his followers. Mursi's adoption of a more conservative posture during the first round of the presidential race made sense politically, but it raised concerns that he lacks a sincere commitment to the moderate language expressed in the FJP platform and the al-Azhar document. Others assert that this maneuvering shows that Mursi and the Brotherhood's leadership are pragmatic. They adjust their ideology in order to gain support, form alliances, and achieve their political goals.

Regardless of his motives, Mursi's shift to the right during the first round of the presidential election raised fears that the Brotherhood's commitment to moderation is skin deep. Advocates of women's rights are particularly worried. As noted earlier, the FJP platform made no reference to opposing a woman's candidacy for president. However, Mursi stated his personal opposition to the idea during the campaign. In addition, the FJP platform calls for repealing laws from the Mubarak era that broadened women's rights (particularly their right to divorce) on the grounds that these laws were imposed under foreign pressure. The FJP and Mursi have not proposed alternative laws that would strengthen women's rights. Furthermore, the Brotherhood ran very few women on the FJP's parliamentary list, and as a consequence there were only 7 women in the FJP's parliamentary delegation of 213. The FJP also placed only 6 women on the short-lived committee of 100 persons tasked in March 2012 with drafting the new constitution.[26] Finally, no women hold positions of leadership within the Brotherhood, despite the organization's claim that it supports women holding leadership posts throughout society.

Thus, a gap has emerged between the Muslim Brotherhood's rhetorical support for civil and political rights and some of its positions regarding women's rights. Critics argue that this gap reveals the Brotherhood's deep-rooted opposition to full legal and political equality for women. Others assert that we are watching the early stages of an ideologically based social movement becoming a political party. This process includes wide-ranging policy debates within the movement that have not yet been resolved. A key question remains: Are these less tolerant positions a reflection of the deep-seated political values of the organization, in which case they are unlikely to change? Or are they the result of political jockeying among the Brotherhood's leaders as they court supporters and build alliances among themselves and other movements? If this is the case, the Brotherhood's positions may change as the political arena continues to broaden and new constituencies (particularly women) become more politically important.

The Brotherhood's documents and leaders support many aspects of democracy, including free elections, an elected parliament that is fully empowered to draft legislation, an independent judiciary, and legal and institutional constraints on state power. However, the Brotherhood is an imperfect advocate of democracy. On the issue of women's rights, in particular, it has fallen short of the democratic ideal.

THE SALAFIS

As the Brotherhood put forward a moderate platform in the spring and summer of 2011, the more conservative elements of the Brotherhood and of al-Azhar developed a third view of constitutional order: Salafi constitutionalism. The Salafi end of the political spectrum is very fragmented along ideological, personality, and geographic lines. In addition, it has undergone considerable evolution since it first arose in the spring of 2011. Indeed, there have been two waves of Salafist constitutional thinking since the January 25 uprising. The first occurred in the spring and summer of 2011 and was led by two voices: the Legitimate Body for Rights and Reform (al-Hayt al-Sharaiyya li al-Huquq wa al-Islah), a group of mostly al-Azhar scholars, and Abd al-Monam al-Shahat, a prominent intellectual and commentator who defined himself as Salafi and assumed a high public profile in the spring and summer of 2011. The second wave arose in the summer and fall of 2011 and was led by the al-Nur Party, which emerged as the primary political voice of the Salafis.

Prior to the January 25 uprising, Salafis played very little role in Egyptian political and legal debates. Their leaders opposed participation in political life on the grounds that it was corrupting and distracted devout Muslims from their spiritual obligations.

After the uprising, some thinkers and leaders who described themselves as Salafi began to give interviews, present speeches, and release documents regarding their view of the legal order that best suited Egypt's Islamic character. They justified this increased participation in political and legal discussions by emphasizing the importance of expanding the role of Islam in Egyptian society.

They also wanted to counteract what they regarded as the excessive influence of liberal ideas over constitutional debates.

This first wave of Salafi constitutional thinking differed from liberalism and Islamic constitutionalism in several important ways.[27] It called for an Islamic state rather than the civil state supported by liberals and the Muslim Brotherhood; a limit on the authority of an elected parliament to issue legislation and an expansion of the role of religious scholars in this process; the exclusion of Copts from any political post on the grounds that a non-Muslim should not hold power over a Muslim; and opposition to women holding positions of leadership in society on the grounds that their involvement in public affairs would distract them from their familial duties, which in turn would weaken the family and thus the foundation of society. Involvement in public life would also compromise a woman's honor.

Some prominent Salafists—particularly Emad al-Din Abd al-Ghafur, Nadir al-Bakaar, and Yusri Hamaad—claimed that these views were not representative of Salafi thought. Their subsequent writings and speeches delineated the second wave of Salafi thinking on political reform, which coalesced around the al-Nur Party. As the fall 2011 parliamentary elections approached, al-Nur developed a platform that spelled out in considerable detail its view of Egypt's political future. This platform was reiterated and developed in statements and interviews by the leaders of al-Nur.[28] These documents, statements, and interviews articulated a conception of constitutionalism much closer to the Islamic constitutionalism discussed earlier. The al-Nur Party made considerable effort to distance itself from the first wave of Salafi constitutional thinking. For example, it declared that Abd al-Monam al-Shahat—one of the most prominent voices in the first wave of Salafi constitutionalism—did not speak for it and called on him to stop making public statements. This was easier to do after al-Shahat lost his race for a parliamentary seat in Alexandria.

This second wave of Salafi thinking retained some of the underpinnings of the earlier wave. Advocates of this view seek an Islamic state, consider sharia the primary source of law, and want to prevent liberal thinkers from dominating the political debate. However, beyond these general principles, the second wave adopted specific stances similar to the Islamic constitutionalism found in the FJP's platform. The al-Nur Party's platform states that its goal is "democracy within the framework of *Shari'a*." Its key points include acceptance of a wide range of civil and political rights, including freedom of assembly, speech, inquiry, and property ownership; "equal dignity" for men and women, with women permitted to undertake higher education, pursue careers outside the home, and vote; full legal equality for Copts, who would be permitted to run for all political offices and utilize their religious laws in matters of personal status; and a parliament chosen through free elections and possessing unrestricted power to draft legislation. There is no mention of a body of religious scholars that vets legislation. This platform received a surprisingly strong endorsement in the 2011–2012 elections to the parliament when al-Nur won 25 percent of the seats in both houses.

It would be an overstatement to suggest that the boundary between the al-Nur Party and the FJP has disappeared. Individual al-Nur politicians have expressed views that are much less tolerant than those in the al-Nur platform. Al-Nur political figures tend to emphasize a conservative social agenda that includes banning alcohol, limiting the mixing of genders outside the home, and regulating media and books to ensure that they uphold Islamic moral standards.[29] In general, they are more critical of Western culture and ties to the West than FJP politicians are. In addition, FJP leaders remain wary of the more extreme voices in the Salafi movement and have said repeatedly that they would not form a governing coalition that drew solely on the al-Nur Party. Instead, they have announced plans to work with liberal parties, despite their relatively poor showing in the parliamentary elections.

However, on matters of political reform, there is considerable overlap between the positions of the FJP and al-Nur. Fundamentally, they agree on empowering elected representatives of the people to draft laws, on protecting many civil and political rights, and on placing legal and institutional constraints on state power. Thus, contrary to the assumptions of some analysts, the rise of political Islam in Egyptian politics may strengthen efforts to build a more democratic political order. Furthermore, these positions are also found among the liberal parties. In other words, the three major schools of political thought that have emerged after the January 25 uprising—liberal constitutionalism, Islamic constitutionalism, and Salafi constitutionalism—agree on many political principles that support democratic transition and consolidation.

These different schools of thought also share several themes in their approaches to foreign policy. Each of their parties' platforms speaks of Egypt's historic greatness as a major power in the region and underscores that this greatness waned under Mubarak. For most of the parties, this decline in power and status stems in part from Egypt's close ties to the United States. In this

view, Egypt under Mubarak became an appendage of American policy in the
region and failed to defend the country's distinct national interests. The Camp
David Accords, in particular, are viewed with mixed feelings. On the one hand,
there is widespread awareness that another war with Israel would be a disaster
for Egypt—the country would be unlikely to win such a conflict, and most of
its international aid would be cut off. A cut in aid would have a particularly
negative effect on the country's military readiness, as U.S. military assistance
accounts for roughly one-third of Egypt's official defense budget. However,
there is a widespread belief that the Camp David Accords included a commitment by all parties to address the Palestinian issue, which has not yet occurred.
In addition, the Camp David Accords place restrictions on the deployment of
Egyptian troops in Sinai that most Egyptian political parties regard as an
unacceptable infringement on the country's sovereignty. Most parties call for
renegotiating these aspects of the agreement.

The liberal parties further emphasize the need to strengthen the Palestinian
Authority and to lean on the United States to play a more active role in per-
suading Israel to address Palestinian grievances. The Muslim Brotherhood
and the Salafi al-Nur Party state that they will abide by all of Egypt's existing
international treaties, including Camp David. However, both groups also speak
of Egypt's obligation to help "liberate Palestine." Their leaders have indicated
that this obligation includes support for groups that confront Israel militarily
such as Hamas, but have not specified whether this support would be economic, humanitarian, or military.

In addition, each of the parties' platforms speaks of the need to broaden
Egypt's foreign alliances and reduce its degree of dependence on the United
States. For al-Nur, this includes ending Egypt's acceptance of conditional aid
from the United States. Each party emphasizes the importance of expanding
Egypt's ties to Africa, Turkey, the Islamic world, and Asia. In addition, they
support increased integration among Arab countries through greater inter-
Arab trade and strengthening of the Arab League.

THE MILITARY

The SCAF's foreign policy calls for continued Egyptian support for Camp
David, strong relations with the Arab countries of the Persian Gulf, and close
ties with the United States. However, the SCAF is less committed to democracy than the civilian actors discussed above. Its legal adviser called in May

2011 for a clause in the constitution that protects the military from civilian scrutiny in every dimension of its operations.[30] In his view, military matters should not even be discussed in parliament and the president should play no role in formulating security policy. The SCAF made its political goals even clearer on November 1, 2011, when the SCAF-appointed Cabinet released a "proposal of basic principles for the new constitution" (sometimes called the "supra-constitutional" principles).[31] Article 9 of this document rejected any form of civilian scrutiny over the military and identified the armed forces as the "protector of constitutional legitimacy." If this language were adopted, it would create a constitutional basis for the military to intervene in domestic politics and, possibly, to remove an elected government.

It is not difficult to understand why the military is deeply worried by democratic change. As Tarek Masoud argues, it has several reasons to fear democracy:[32]

- *Political:* The military currently enjoys complete autonomy from civilian officials and other state institutions. It has unrestricted power to formulate policy, decide on promotions, administer its budget, and handle internal discipline. This degree of autonomy and privilege would almost certainly decline in a democratic system.
- *Economic:* The military has wide-ranging economic interests. It owns at least thirty-five companies that produce everything from automobiles to foodstuffs to washing machines.[33] By some estimates, this economic activity accounts for 12–18 percent of GDP.[34] The budgets of these companies are not subject to review or audit by any other state institution. This degree of economic independence and lack of transparency would almost certainly be reduced in a democratic order.
- *Geopolitical:* The military relies on the United States for military assistance ($1.3 billion in 2011) and also utilizes American cooperation and support to enhance its regional power and influence. The cornerstone of this relationship is the Camp David Accords. If democracy were to grow, voices in Egyptian society that are critical of the peace with Israel might gain strength and might even succeed in modifying parts of the agreement. Such a step might weaken the relationship between Egypt and the United States and, as a result, damage an essential source of military aid and regional influence for Egypt's generals.

The military's actions during its first year in power confirmed fears about its commitment to democracy. More than 12,000 civilian demonstrators were tried in military courts without any compelling legal reason beyond the assertion of the need to obtain quick convictions—a sentiment hardly consistent with strengthening the rule of law.[35] The SCAF also insisted on utilizing the Emergency Law, which empowered it to arrest and detain civilians without judicial oversight. When the Emergency Law expired on May 31, 2012, the SCAF effectively continued its key provisions by asserting that military personnel still had the authority to arrest civilians and try them before military courts.[36] When soldiers have been accused of human rights abuses, the military has taken little action to investigate the claims or to discipline those responsible. Civil society groups have been tightly monitored and, in some cases, face a degree of repression comparable to what they endured during Mubarak's rule.[37] There have also been reports of the military interfering with the media and, effectively, enforcing de facto censorship over coverage of numerous issues related to the country's future.[38]

The military took several additional steps in June 2012 to slow the process of democratic change. In response to a ruling by the Supreme Constitutional Court, the SCAF dissolved the elected lower house of parliament. It then issued several constitutional amendments on June 17, 2012. As noted earlier, these amendments transferred legislative power to the SCAF, limited the powers of the elected president, granted the SCAF full authority over all matters related to the military, and gave it an important role in the drafting of a new constitution. The amendments sparked intense debate among Egyptians. Some called them a de facto coup that aimed to frustrate the will of the people and prevent a transition to democracy. For these critics, the SCAF was holding progress toward democracy hostage until the Brotherhood and other groups agreed to protect its interests and privileges. Others believed the SCAF was playing a constructive role by preventing Islamists from dominating the legislature and the drafting of the new constitution, thereby ensuring that all segments of Egyptian society would be included at this formative stage of Egyptian democracy. In this view, the military was the only institution capable of balancing the power of Islamists. It was the defender of a civil state at a time when some populist figures in the Brotherhood and the Salafi movement were calling for a state with a strong Islamic character. Still others saw the military's intervention as a healthy (albeit undemocratic) step toward a more stable political order. In this view, a new constitution must reflect and embody the realities of power within Egyptian society. The military is a powerful actor, and thus its interests and concerns must be addressed in order for the new constitution to endure.

At the very least, the amendments showed the military's lack of confidence in democracy. The SCAF justified its intervention in political life on the grounds that it was stabilizing Egyptian politics at a critical moment and preventing the Muslim Brotherhood from dominating the formation of Egypt's new political order. The SCAF's stance appeared to enjoy some popular support, particularly among Coptic Christians and some mainstream Muslims who feared that the Brotherhood held a hidden political agenda that would infringe on their rights. At the time of this writing, it is difficult to gauge the breadth of this support.[39]

REMNANTS OF THE OLD REGIME

The regime that was challenged by the demonstrators on January 25 has very deep roots. In the sixty years since its founding, its influence has spread to every corner of Egyptian society. As noted above, the military is at the heart of the regime and still retains a great deal of power. The domestic security services—housed in the Ministry of Interior (MOI)—are also pillars of the old order. With more than 400,000 men and a vast amount of resources, this security apparatus remains an influential force.[40] To date, the leaders of the MOI have largely resisted efforts to reform their ministry or allow greater civilian scrutiny of its conduct. The SCAF and its civilian cabinet have chosen not to confront the MOI, perhaps for fear of provoking a backlash. One of the more notable features of this deference to the MOI's power is the decision not to prosecute any security officials for alleged abuses committed during the Mubarak era. This decision is especially striking given that abuses by the security services were one of the primary reasons that so many Egyptians flocked to Tahrir.[41] To the extent that security officials have been prosecuted, it is only for alleged crimes committed against the January 25 demonstrators. Other appendages of the old regime are also still in place or can be easily reconstituted, including the local networks that were the foundation of the NDP's power and the gangs of professional thugs who were an important tool of intimidation under the old regime.

CONCLUSION

In the months since the January 25 uprising, a surprising degree of consensus has emerged among civilian actors regarding the broad outlines of Egypt's political future. This consensus supports a constitution that would facilitate democratic transition and consolidation by protecting many civil and political rights, ensuring that senior political posts are chosen through free elections, and creating legal and institutional constraints on state power. However, the military and the remnants of the old regime have substantial interests that would be threatened by democratic change.

The military may well succeed in creating an enclave that insulates it from civilian accountability. The only question is how extensive this enclave will be. Will it encompass all aspects of the military's operations or only some? It is conceivable, for example, that the military might accede to some restructuring of its economic enterprises or very limited and general civilian review of its budget by a small committee of parliament. But on the core issues—such as its role in security decisionmaking, immunity of officers from civilian judicial proceedings, appointment and promotion of officers, and preservation of its privileges and perks—it is likely to hold fast and to get what it wants. The result will be, at best, an imperfect democratic transition. The key remaining questions are whether the military's reserve domains can be gradually eroded over time and how this might occur.

In addition, Mubarak appointees remain throughout the state apparatus. They are in every ministry, the tax authority, the education system, and beyond. In general terms, any movement that aims for change must make a fundamental tactical decision: whether to purge the state apparatus of old regime apparatchiks, which "cleans house" but also paralyzes the state by removing most of its leadership; or to leave the old appointees in their posts, which slows the pace of change but may allow for gradual reform without severe disruptions to the state, the economy, and society. So far, Egypt has opted for the second path. Most of the structures and personnel of the old regime are still in place.

There is little evidence of any coordinated effort by these old regime elements to resist reform. Rather, their resistance is decentralized and appears more a result of self-interest and self-preservation than of philosophical opposition to the uprising. Nonetheless, their presence puts a brake on the pace of change and effectively rules out the sweeping social and economic transformations normally associated with a revolution. Change in Egypt is likely to be a slow and halting process that will prove frustrating to the idealistic young people who initiated the uprising. We may see continued demonstrations in the comings years, as the supporters of the uprising try to push a large and well-entrenched state to fulfill their dream of a more democratic, just, and accountable society. The Egyptian revolution will be a long and difficult struggle, and it has only just begun.

NOTES

1. Portions of this chapter utilize material from the introduction to the paperback edition of my book *Egypt After Mubarak: Liberalism, Islam, and Democracy in the Arab World*. (Princeton, NJ: Princeton University Press, 2012). Also, I am grateful for excellent research assistance from Thomas Ellison and Mark Robson.

2. Lisa Blaydes, *Elections and Distributive Politics in Mubarak's Egypt*. (New York: Cambridge University Press, 2011); Jason Brownlee, *Authoritarianism in an Age of Democratization* (New York: Cambridge University Press, 2007).

3. Khalid Ikram, *The Egyptian Economy, 1952–2000: Performance, Policies, and Issues* (New York: Routledge, 2006), 92.

4. Ibid., 56.

5. At the time of the uprising, 44 percent of Egyptians were "extremely poor" (unable to meet minimum food needs), "poor" (unable to meet basic food needs), or "near-poor" (able to meet basic food needs, but not much more). Joel Beinin, "The Working Class and the Popular Movement," in *The Journey to Tahrir*, ed. Jeannie Sowers and Chris Toensing (New York: Verso, 2012), 105.

6. *Egypt Human Development Report, 2008* (New York: United Nations Development Programme, 2008), 296.

7. Joel Beinin, *The Struggle for Worker Rights in Egypt* (Washington, DC: The Solidarity Center, 2010), 14.

8. http://www.facebook.com/ElShaheeed.

9. http://6april.org/.

10. "Food and the Arab Spring: Let Them Eat Baklava," *The Economist*, March 17, 2012, 59. The world price for wheat more than doubled between July 2010 and January 2011, due to drought and brushfires in Russia, Ukraine, and Kazakhstan. Egypt is the world's largest importer of wheat. Sarah Johnstone

and Jeffrey Mazo, "Global Warming and the Arab Spring," *Survival* 53, 2 (April-May 2011): 12.

11. Adel Iskandar, "Egypt Defies All," Huffington Post, February 14, 2011, http://www.huffingtonpost.com/adel-iskandar/egypt-defies-all_b_822336.html.

12. Other youth movements included We Are All Khalid Said, youth of the Muslim Brotherhood, youth of *Kefaya*, and youth of the Democratic Front Party.

13. See Wael Ghonim, *Revolution 2.0: The Power of the People Is Greater Than the People in Power: A Memoir* (New York: Houghton Mifflin Harcourt, 2012); Ashraf Khalil, *Liberation Square: Inside the Egyptian Revolution and the Rebirth of a Nation* (New York: St. Martin's Press, 2012). See also Charles Levinson and Margaret Coker, "The Secret Rally That Sparked an Uprising," *Wall Street Journal*, February 10, 2011.

14. This paragraph utilizes material from my essay "Egypt: Citizens and Soldiers," *Montréal Review*, March 2011, http://www.themontrealreview.com/2009/Egypt-Citizens-and-Soldiers.php.

15. See Emad Shahin, "Mubarak's 5 Fatal Mistakes," *The Atlantic*, February 24, 2011, http://www.theatlantic.com/international/archive/2011/02/mubaraks-5-fatal-mistakes/71661/.

16. Several prominent candidates were disqualified by the commission for failing to meet the legal requirements for entering the race. Omar Suleiman, a former head of Egyptian intelligence and a close adviser to Husni Mubarak, was disqualified for not having enough signatures on his petitions for candidacy. Khairat al-Shater, the Muslim Brotherhood's leading strategist and financier, was prevented from running because of a conviction for fraud during the Mubarak era. Hazem Abu Ismail, a charismatic Salafist preacher, was disqualified because his mother held dual citizenship (the presidential election law specified that both of a candidate's parents must hold only Egyptian citizenship).

17. Abu al-Fatuh was expelled from the Brotherhood in June 2011. At the time, the Brotherhood leadership decided that the organization would not run a candidate for president and that no member of the organization should run for the post. Abu al-Fatuh disregarded this order and announced his candidacy. He was promptly expelled for defying the organization's leadership.

18. David D. Kirkpatrick and Kareen Fahim, "In Egypt's Likely Runoff, Islam Vies with the Past," *New York Times*, May 25, 2012.

19. The law stated that two-thirds of the seats in the People's Assembly would be chosen through competition among party lists and one-third would be selected

by competition among individual candidates. The law allowed members of parties to run both as members of a party list and as individual candidates. The Supreme Constitutional Court ruled that this structure gave candidates with party affiliations an unfair advantage over independent candidates, as they effectively had two opportunities to win a seat in the chamber. On the same day, the SCC issued another important decision regarding the political isolation law, which banned senior Mubarak-era officials from participation in political life on the grounds that they were responsible for widespread corruption and abuse of power. If implemented, the law would have prevented Ahmad Shafiq from running for president. However, the SCC ruled the law unconstitutional and cleared the way for Shafiq to run.

20. "President Mursi's Remarks upon Taking the Oath of Office," June 30, 2012, http://www.ikhwanonline.com/new/president3/Article.aspx?ArtID=112981&SecID=470.

21. If the head of the SCAF disagreed with a proposed clause of the constitution, he could call on the constituent assembly to reconsider it. If the assembly did not do so, the matter would be referred to the Supreme Constitutional Court, which would make the final decision on whether the clause would be modified to accommodate the SCAF's concerns. Three other individuals were also granted the same power to challenge clauses of the draft constitution: the president, the prime minister, and the head of the Supreme Council of Judicial Bodies. In addition, the same power could be exercised by one-fifth of the constituent assembly if they objected to a clause in the proposed constitution.

22. *"Birnamij Hizb al-Ikhwan al-Muslimin: Al-Isdar al-Awal,"* August 25, 2007.

23. *"Birnamij Hizb al-Huriyya wa al-Adala,"* n.d.

24. Ibid., 5.

25. "Al-Azhar Document on the Future of Egypt," www.sis.gov.eg, accessed August 5, 2011.

26. This committee was dissolved as a result of a court order in April 2012.

27. The following discussion utilizes materials from the Legitimate Body for Rights and Reform website (www.forislah.com), as well as the following interviews and statements by Abd al-Monam al-Shahat: "The Salafi Spring," *al-Majalla,* July 17, 2011; "The Salafis," *al-Nahar,* November 14, 2011; http://www.sotelmalayin.com/products15.php?id=75; http://www.youtube.com/watch?v=iqIbLqCxbiA); (http://muslm.net/vb/showthread.php?t=444098); and http://www.bbc.co.uk/arabic/multimedia/2011/12/111210_interview_alshahat.shtml.

28. The al-Nur platform is available on the party's website: www.alnourparty
.org. As the parliamentary elections approached, the party also created a separate
website that focused on the campaign: www.nour4egypt.com. Senior party leaders
have given numerous interviews, including Emad al-Din Abd al-Ghafur:
http://www.majalla.com/arb/2011/12/article55230222, http://www.ahram.org
.eg/Investigations/News/124620.aspx, and http://www.almasryalyoum.com/node
/553141; and Yusri Hamaad: http://www.shorouknews.com/news/view.aspx
?id=1f4d77aa-175b-434d-a726-deff64079954; and http://www.alnas.tv/Pages
/Public/Videos/VideoInfo.aspx?ID=a64d3797-fda9–447a-9558–8e5f2a872ebc.
The following analysis utilizes all these sources.

29. However, the al-Nur Party endorsed the candidacy of Abd al-Monam Abu
al-Fatuh in the first round of the presidential race. Among the Islamist candidates
in the contest, he was the most moderate regarding social issues and women's rights.
Al-Nur did not support the Muslim Brotherhood's Muhammad Mursi, who held
more conservative views on these topics than Abu al-Fatuh. This step was widely
seen as an attempt by al-Nur to block the Brotherhood's efforts to control both the
presidency and the parliament. It suggests that al-Nur is willing to compromise on
important ideological points in order to achieve political goals.

30. "Mamdouh Shahin: New Constitution Must Protect Army from Whims
of Next President, No President in World Heads Military Council," *al-Youm
al-Saba*, May 26, 2011.

31. The text of the supraconstitutional principles is available at http://www
.masrawy.com/news/Egypt/Politics/2011/November/2/4559080.aspx%
2f4559080.aspx#. A translation is available at http://fjponline.com/article.php
?id=84.

32. Tarek Masoud, "The Road to (and from) Liberation Square," *Journal of
Democracy* 22, 3 (July 2011): 25–26.

33. Zeinab Abul-Magd, "The Generals' Secret: Egypt's Ambivalent Market,"
February 9, 2012, http://carnegieendowment.org/sada/2012/02/09/generals
-secret-egypt-s-ambivalent-market/9j3k. See also Robert Springborg, *Mubarak's
Egypt: Fragmentation of the Political Order* (Boulder, CO: Westview Press, 1989),
109–118; and Stephen H. Gotowicki, "The Military in Egyptian Society," in *Egypt
at the Crossroads: Domestic Stability and Regional Role*, ed. Phebe Marr (Washington, DC: National Defense University Press, 1999), 114–116.

34. Personal interview with Ahmad Ghoneim, professor of economics at Cairo
University, June 25, 2011. Professor Ghoneim was quick to note that this was

"only a guess," as there are no reliable data publicly available regarding the military's economic role.

35. This number is larger than the total number of civilians tried before military courts during the entire thirty years of Mubarak's rule. Amnesty International, *Year of Rebellion: The State of Human Rights in the Middle East and North Africa* (London: Amnesty International, 2012), 9–15.

36. This authority was granted by the SCAF-appointed minister of justice. At the time of this writing, an administrative court had suspended implementation of this order.

37. Human Rights Watch, "Egypt: National and International Human Rights Organisations Are Under Attack." December 29, 2011, www.hrw.org.

38. Human Rights Watch, "Egypt: A Year of Attacks on Free Expression," February 11, 2012, www.hrw.org.

39. This chapter was finalized on July 3, 2012.

40. Some observers claim that the forces controlled by the Ministry of Interior are substantially larger—perhaps as large as 1.4 million. See Saad Eddin Ibrahim, "Egypt's Unchecked Repression," *Washington Post*, August 21, 2007; and "Bashing the Muslim Brothers," *The Economist*, September 1, 2007, 38. For further details on Egypt's security forces, see Anthony H. Cordesman, *The Military Balance in the Middle East* (Westport, CT: Praeger, 2004), 172–186.

41. Indeed, January 25 was chosen as the first day for the demonstrations precisely because it was "Police Day"—an annual holiday to celebrate the police. Demonstrators wanted to use this holiday to draw attention to police abuses.

3

The Arab Spring:
Libya's Second Revolution

MARY-JANE DEEB

LIBYA WAS THE THIRD COUNTRY after Tunisia and Egypt to experience
the Arab Spring.* On February 15, 2011, the first protests began in Benghazi, the second most important city in Libya, when hundreds of protesters
gathered in front of a police station. They were shot at, and a number died.
Two days later, on February 17 the official date of the start of the uprising,
thousands of demonstrators began protesting peacefully throughout eastern
Libya in Benghazi, Ajdabiyah, Darnah, and Zintan. Security forces responded
with live ammunition, and about a dozen people were killed.

Rather than putting an end to the protests, the government actions created
more anger and led to a rebel takeover of Benghazi on February 20. Army
forces defected and joined the rebels, and they were able to break into the city's
well-stocked military garrison and obtain weapons, which they used against
Muammar al-Gadafi's forces.

As the takeover of Benghazi was unfolding, a group of people, including a
former minister of justice, Mustafa Abd al-Jalil, a human rights activist, Fathi
Tarbil, and a Libyan professor teaching in the United States, Abd al-Rahim
al-Keib, formed the National Transitional Council (NTC). They claimed
that they and not Gadafi represented the Libyan people. The NTC played a
critical role in getting European powers and eventually the United States to

---

*Disclaimer: the views expressed here are my own and not those of the Library of Congress.

recognize it as the legitimate interim government and in obtaining military and other forms of aid for the rebels.

Meanwhile at the United Nations, ten members of the Security Council voted on Resolution 1973 on March 17, 2011, to impose a no-fly zone on Libya (five abstained: Russia, China, Germany, India, and Brazil) to prevent Gadafi's forces from bombing civilians. The resolution authorized international military action to protect civilians. The British representative pledged that NATO partners and members of the Arab League would act upon this resolution.

Two days later, on March 19, 2011, NATO military operations against Gadafi's forces began with air strikes by French fighter jets against Libyan army tanks. They were followed by British and American forces firing Tomahawk cruise missiles and the British and French air forces bombing Libya. The British Royal Navy at the same time imposed a blockade on the ports of Libya to prevent weapons from entering the country. Qatar and the United Arab Emirates were the only two members of the Arab League that participated in the operations, providing the NATO forces with logistical support. These actions were welcomed by the Libyan rebels, who were for the most part unarmed and untrained in military warfare and faced Gadafi's overwhelming military power.

Despite NATO's airpower, the fighting in Libya lasted eight months. Libyans fought city by city and town by town, encountering resistance not only from Libyans who supported Gadafi, but also from both African mercenaries and prisoners who were released from jail and purportedly given money and ammunition to fight against the rebels. After conquering Cyrenaica, the rebels were joined by others, including Islamists who wanted to rid themselves of Gadafi, and began moving westward. Some of the fiercest and longest battles were for the towns of Misratah, in Tripolitania, not very far from the capital city of Tripoli, which the rebels took over in May 2011.

The strategy of the rebels was to surround the main holdouts of Gadafi, his family, and his supporters in Tripoli, Bani Walid, and Sirte (the birthplace of Gadafi and his tribal base). Throughout the month of August, the rebels fought in and around Tripoli, and by the end of the month, Tripoli fell into their hands. Gadafi went into hiding, and his wife, Safiyah, daughter Aisha, and two of his sons, Muhammad and Hanibal, fled to Algiers.

Finally, the rebels converged on Sirte, and after more than two months of fighting, Sirte fell on October 20, and Gadafi was captured and killed. One of his sons, Saif al-Islam, and presumptive heir, was eventually captured, while another, Mutassim, the head of a militia protecting Gadafi, was killed. The forty-two-year-old rule of Gadafi in Libya thus came to an end.

The Historical Context

To understand the Arab Spring in Libya (and in the rest of the Arab world), it is important to place the events of 2011 within a historical framework. That framework can best be represented by three evolving and overlapping paradigms of the social order in the region, namely, a socialist paradigm, an Islamist paradigm, and a secular democratic paradigm.

During the 1960s and 1970s, the dominant ideological paradigm in the region, first propounded by Gamal Abd al-Nasser of Egypt, and then adopted by Syria, Iraq, the Sudan, Libya, Algeria, southern Yemen, and, briefly, by Tunisia, was socialist and Arab nationalist. The socialist paradigm reflected not so much the Soviet Union's communist worldview, but rather that of the nonaligned nations, countries like Yugoslavia, India, and Indonesia. This socialist paradigm was based on major economic, social, and political reforms; was secular and anti-imperialist; and in the Arab world was led in almost all cases by the military.

As the socialist paradigm failed to keep its promises and people became disenchanted with this model of governance, the voices of those who had questioned and fought against it became louder. Throughout the region, Islamists became more vociferous and more active, calling for the implementation of sharia and a greater role for religion in the social and political spheres. But it was in Iran, and not in the Arab world, that the paradigm finally shifted.

In February 1979, after months of demonstrations and strikes, the shah of Iran left his country, and on April 1, 1979, Iranians voted in a referendum to become the first ever Islamic Republic, and they eventually approved a constitution in which sharia became the law of the land. The Grand Ayatollah Rouhollah Mousavi Khomeini became the supreme leader, and the governing body was constituted not by the military, as in the socialist paradigm, but by the clerics, the ayatollahs. The "Islamist paradigm" had come into being.

The Arabs witnessed the overthrow of the Iranian shah and the creation of an Islamic Republic and wondered why that should not happen in other parts of the Muslim world as well. The Islamist paradigm spread, as did its various conceptual manifestations. It was messianic in nature: it was not enough for one country to be ruled by Islamic law, but the entire Muslim world had to follow suit. From the most moderate Islamists to the most radical, all advocated their version of the Islamist paradigm, which would eventually lead to "the good society." The motto was *Islam huwa al hal*—"Islam is the solution." Islamists challenged the state in every Muslim country and became one of the major organized opposition in the region. In Tunisia, for example, it was the Nahda Party in the 1980s that opposed President Habib Bourguiba and later President Zine al-Abidine Ben Ali, and in Libya it was the Islamic Front for the Salvation of Libya that acted similarly.

The failure of the Islamic Republic of Iran to deliver the good society to its citizens, and the violence of the radical Islamists, much of which was directed against Muslims, eroded the support of many young people in the Muslim world for this ideology. In the past few years, the Islamist paradigm has been losing ground, although it is resisting strongly. The decline in the appeal of radical Islamism is best illustrated by the reaction to the news of the shooting of Osama bin Laden in Pakistan in May 2011. Basically, there was no public reaction; there was just silence in the Arab world. A few lonely voices mourned his death, such as that of Hamas in Gaza and those of some Salafists in Egypt and elsewhere in the region. Only in Pakistan and Afghanistan was there some outpouring of grief and anger, but even there the reaction was rather muted (in contrast, for example, to the reaction to the Danish cartoons depicting the Prophet Muhammad as a terrorist or the burning of the Quran by a Florida pastor in March 2011).[1]

Brian Murphy, a foreign correspondent for the Associated Press, wrote a piece after the killing of Bin Laden entitled "Islamic World Quiet as Bin Laden Age Closes."[2] He interviewed a number of people in the region and asked them why there had been no reaction. A professor of political science at United Emirates University answered him: "Bin Laden died in Egypt before he was killed in Pakistan"—meaning that the paradigm of radical and violent Islamism no longer had any appeal there. In a similar statement, Amr al-Shubaki, the head of the Arab European Unit in the Cairo Al-Ahram Center for Political and Strategic Studies, the premier think tank in Egypt, was quoted in the *Washington Post* as saying, "Al-Qaeda, through its violent operations in the Arab states and all over the world, has lost all sympathy."[3]

The point these individuals were making here is that the violence associated with the Islamic paradigm was detrimental to Arabs and Muslims themselves. The Arabs realized that a revolution could take place without violence as long as they could bring together enough people to voice their demands.

Although neither the socialist nor the Islamist paradigm of the good society has disappeared, a new paradigm has emerged during the Arab Spring and is being adopted by a whole new generation of Arabs as well as others throughout the Muslim world. This paradigm is that of a secular, democratic, nonviolent, nonideological society whose citizens are nationalist while maintaining their Arab and Muslim identities. This paradigm, in contrast to the two others, calls for a state that is governed neither by the military nor by religious authorities, but by civilians freely and fairly elected by the citizens of each country.

The Socioeconomic Context

So how did those revolutions in the Arab world come about? I contend that the popular outburst of anger that followed the young Tunisian's self-immolation in December 2010 and brought down the Tunisian regime was not a discrete event, but rather a continuation of such demonstrations and strikes, not only in Tunisia, but also in other parts the Arab world, including in Egypt, Libya, Syria, and Yemen, where the revolutions are taking place, as well as in Algeria, Morocco, Jordan, and elsewhere in the region where they have not yet come about.

The rallying cry of all these revolutions was the overthrow of the regimes in power and the setting up of free and fair elections and democratic institutions. The protesters also had economic demands, with the unemployed asking for jobs and the employed for higher pay. However, although the global economic downturn since 2008 affected North Africa, which had been growing at a vigorous 5 to 6 percent annually for more than a decade, the economic situation in Tunisia and Libya was not dire. In fact, according to CIA economic reports, unemployment in Tunisia in 2010 was about 13 percent, similar to that of Greece and Portugal that year, and much lower than that in Spain, whose unemployment rate reached 20 percent in 2010.[4] In Libya, after the United States had lifted its unilateral sanctions by 2006 (once Libya gave up its weapons of mass destruction and paid compensation to the families of the Pan Am 107 victims), investors poured into the country from around the globe with plans to develop the Libyan infrastructure. As a result, the service and construction sectors in Libya began to grow rapidly, creating jobs for young people in every field.

So why did people in Libya rebel in 2011 when their standard of living was steadily improving? Why did they not rebel earlier when they were much poorer? Crane Brinton, in his classic *The Anatomy of Revolution*, in which he compares the French, Russian, British, and American revolutions, helps us answer these questions. He explains: "Revolutions . . . clearly were not born in societies economically retrograde; on the contrary, they took place in societies economically progressive. . . . Thus we see that certain economic grievances— usually not in the form of economic distress, but rather [in] a feeling on the part of some of the chief enterprising groups that their opportunities for getting on in this world are unduly limited by political arrangements—would seem to be one of the symptoms of revolution."[5]

In Libya (as well as in other countries, such as Tunisia and Egypt), the perception of the young and educated, whose standard of living was much higher than that of their parents, was not only that the political elites in their country were politically oppressive, but also that the corruption that existed meant that the country's wealth was concentrated at the top and that they were being prevented from sharing in it.

When an Australian reporter visited Libya in 2004, he interviewed young people from all walks of life, asking them about their current lives and their dreams for their own and for Libya's future. The interviews revealed that young Libyans saw their country as "a land of opportunity" where they could build new lives not unlike the lives of young people in the Gulf Emirates. I argue that when this did not happen, Libyans turned against their government and rebelled, illustrating Brinton's principle that people rebel when they perceive "that their opportunities for getting on in this world are unduly limited by political arrangements."

Some of the statements the Australian quoted in his article in the *Sidney Morning Herald* reveal the expectations of the young. [6] "In the 1970s, Dubai was just a bunch of tents and we were booming," a Libyan student at the University of Tripoli told the reporter. "Libya is going to boom again, just wait and see."[7] "I'm not here for the scenery. I'm here because there are lots of opportunities," said one of the many young Libyans who returned from living abroad to take advantage of the country's new postsanctions business climate.[8] "They built Dubai in 10 years. . . . Give us 15 years and we will be bigger than Dubai," said another.[9]

But these dreams and hopes came to nothing. Instead, rampant corruption prevailed. Libyans saw Gadafi's family living extravagantly while they were forced to live frugally.[10] Consistent with Briton's analysis, those elites were perceived as siphoning the country's wealth and preventing ordinary Libyans from benefiting from it.

THE REGIONAL CONTEXT

There were also regional events that paved the way for the uprisings in the Arab world. Two examples will illustrate this point. In March 2005, Lebanon witnessed an unprecedented movement calling itself the "Cedar Revolution," made up of young men and women from all confessional groups who for an entire month after the assassination of former Lebanese prime minister Rafiq al-Hariri demonstrated peacefully, demanding the ouster of Syrian forces that had occupied Lebanon for thirty years. The outpouring was such that Syrian forces withdrew from Lebanon in April 2005. Young people across the Arab world watched and cheered as they witnessed military forces retreating before the peaceful, unarmed demonstrators. Robert Fisk, a foreign correspondent for *The Independent*, wrote an article that focused on the importance of this event as a turning point for the entire region. The article was entitled "The Arab Awakening Began Not in Tunisia This Year, but in Lebanon in 2005."[11]

Then there was the trial of Saddam Hussein in Iraq. Although Arabs had almost unanimously condemned the war on Iraq, the arrest and trial of Saddam, one of the most oppressive dictators in the Middle East, was another matter. Arabs watched the 2005–2006 trial on television, heard the witnesses testify against Saddam, heard him defend himself, and witnessed the team of lawyers that had been made available to him for his defense (including, apparently, Gadafi's daughter, Aisha). In contrast to the vociferous condemnation of the war, the reaction to the trial in the Arab world was subdued. Although Saddam had been caught by American forces, he was being tried in an Arab court by a panel of Iraqi judges. It was the first time that an Arab ruler had been asked to account for his misdeeds before his own people and that some of them were able to testify against him, freely, before a court of law and without fear of retaliation. To the rest of the Arab world, this meant that it was now possible to hold leaders accountable for their actions and that the leaders, their relatives, and their supporters were no longer above the law.

It is impossible to substantiate these claims directly for Libya because there was no free press under Gadafi and people were afraid to talk. However, these two events in the Arab world affected young people throughout the region, and we can assume that Libyans who watched the same television programs as their counterparts in other countries of the region were affected in the same way.[12]

WHO WERE THE REVOLUTIONARIES?

Since the beginning of his rule, Gadafi placed a high priority on developing the education system in Libya. By 2011, Libya had a higher literacy rate than Morocco, Algeria, and Egypt. According to a UNICEF report, Libya's adult literacy rate was around 60 percent in 2010, but 100 percent of Libya's youth, both male and female, between the ages of fifteen and twenty-four were literate.[13] With a population of around 6.7 million, Libya has more than twenty universities and thirty higher institutes of technology.[14]

The graduates of those institutions acquired the skills to use the Internet, including Facebook, YouTube, and Twitter. Through social media, they became even more aware of the need for freedom of speech, association, and the press, as well as for individual freedoms either curtailed or denied to them in their own countries.

Thanks to the communication revolution, it had become, among other things, more difficult to hide security crackdowns on dissidents, to pretend that elections were anything but charades, to block criticism by other countries of government policies, and to conceal scams and rampant corruption. Thus the new age of information technology both informed Arab youth of the ills of society and gave them the tools with which to address those ills.

But it was not only the graduates of the high schools, universities, and institutes of technology who were protesting. In Libya, as in Tunisia, Egypt, Syria, and Yemen, young military conscripts also joined the fray. In fact, thanks to compulsory military service in most countries of the Arab world, at least 60 percent of the armies are made up of conscripts who have no particular allegiance to the military and want to get out of it to pursue other careers. In Tunisia, General Rachid Ammar, the head of the Tunisian army, refused to follow the president's orders to shoot protesters, and he took the side of the people, thereby forcing President Ben Ali to resign, and no violence ensued. In Libya, the army was weak. Gadafi had undermined it from the start, fearing a military coup. When the uprising first took place in Cyrenaica, in eastern Libya, the army split. The military in that region joined the revolutionaries,[15] while Gadafi had to rely on militias led by two of his sons, Khamis and Mutassim, and on foreign mercenaries.

Another group that joined the rebels were civil servants and high-level professionals in almost all fields. "Regional governors, editors of government newspapers, prominent businessmen and senior members of the ruling party" quit their jobs in protest against the government actions and supported the revolutionaries, as did civil servants, university professors, school teachers, lawyer syndicates, journalists, members of human rights organizations, and women's associations.[16]

In Libya as in Tunisia, lawyers played a major role in the revolts. In December 2010, 300 lawyers took to the streets of Tunis to protest the unlawful arrests of people and their detention without trial. Later in January 2011, according to the National Bar Association of Tunisia, 95 percent of Tunisia's 8,000 lawyers went on strike to protest the unwarranted attacks on lawyers and the crackdowns on protesters. In Libya, organizations such as Lawyers for Justice in Libya helped build a network of human rights defenders and organized the NTC, which sought recognition from the West as the sole representative of the Libyan people. France and the United States did recognize the NTC and thus delegitimized Gadafi and his family.

There was another group that supported the revolutionaries in Libya, namely, the tribes of Cyrenaica. Those in the central part of Libya and those in Sirte supported Gadafi. The tribes of Cyrenaica had always resented Gadafi's rule, and he in turn often cracked down and tried to break up their organizations. It is interesting to note that throughout the fighting in 2011, on the very modern online site of the Libyan opposition, a very traditional phenomenon was videotaped and posted: tribal leaders in full regalia solemnly giving the *bayah* (paying allegiance) to the National Transitional Authority and cursing Gadafi and his progeny before the camera.[17]

Islamists also joined the fray during the Libyan uprising. Better armed and ready to fight, they played a very significant role in routing Gadafi's forces. This was not the case in Tunisia, for example, where there was little violence because the army as a unified body had refused to obey orders to shoot the demonstrators, and it forced the resignation of the president. In Libya, the government used force, unilaterally attacking protesters, hitting whole towns and villages with heavy weapons, and even bombing them from the air. It became clear to Libyans that even with NATO assistance, they could not easily dislodge Gadafi and his supporters in many areas of the country. They needed the assistance of the Islamists if they were to succeed in overthrowing the regime, and the Islamists were there to help. For example, as early as March 2011, members of the radical Libyan Islamic Fighting Group, which changed its name to the Libyan Islamic Movement (al-Harakat al-Islamiyah al-Libiyah) declared in Ajdabiyah, a key eastern town, that they were placing themselves under the leadership of the NTC and that they were ready to fight against Gadafi's forces. They also declared that they had 500–600 militants who were ready to fight.[18]

THE AFTERMATH OF GADAFI'S FALL

The transition to a new political system in Libya has proven to be more difficult than in Tunisia. According to a 2012 report by the *Washington Post*: "The economy has not recovered from the fighting, and government officials have not been paid for months. Despite repeated pledges by Libya's transitional government to find jobs for the rebel fighters who forced . . . Gadafi from power, tens of thousands of them are [without jobs and] operating in armed militia groups, patrolling streets and guarding buildings in Tripoli and other cities."[19]

According to another report, this one in the *Jerusalem Post*, an estimated 200,000 men are organized into as many as three hundred militias.[20] Some militia groups in the capital, Tripoli, have formed alternative committees to the NTC, while in Cyrenaica an estimated one hundred militia groups have joined forces and created a federation challenging the NTC.[21] In other words, the militias seem unwilling to recognize the legitimacy of the NTC, which in turn has created a power vacuum.

The International Commission of Inquiry on Libya reported in March 2012 that the Libyan rebels committed and continue to commit "serious violations, including war crimes and breaches of international human rights law . . . [such as] unlawful killing, arbitrary arrest, torture, enforced disappearance, indiscriminate attacks, and pillage."[22] In April, Amnesty International confirmed what everyone knew already: that abuses of prisoners were taking place in a number of regions in Libya. Since September 2011, the Misratah's Security Committee, a committee formed under the Misratah local council, held in its detention center numerous prisoners, many of whom were from Tawargha, a town located twenty-three miles southeast of Misratah on the road to Sirte in northern Libya. Many of the prisoners were reportedly tortured and killed at the hands of armed militias. The Tawargha were accused of having supported the Gadafi regime and been part of the armed forces that had fought the rebels in Misratah.[23] The entire population of Tawargha, made up of 30,000 men, women, and children, was expelled from the town, and it was looted and burned.[24]

In spite of these human rights abuses, the International Commission report also recognized the difficulties the transitional government was facing in investigating and bringing to justice the perpetrators of those crimes, and it praised the positive steps taken by the NTC to establish "mechanisms for accountability." Those included bringing back judges, reopening the courts, and restoring the judiciary. There also appear to be ongoing attempts at freeing some detainees held by militias and transferring them to central government control. Implementation of these first positive steps will go a long way toward establishing government legitimacy and credibility.

In early January 2012, the interim government took a first step toward the establishment of a new government by posting on its website a draft law laying out procedures for electing a planned constitutional assembly. The plan was to have legislative elections in June 2012 (postponed to July), after which the elected assembly is to form a representative cabinet and write a new constitution.

A draft constitution, entitled "Draft Constitutional Charter for the Transitional Stage," was passed by the NTC on August 3, 2011. It was publicly announced a week later by the vice president of the NTC, Abd al-Hafiz Ghoga. It consists of five sections: General Provisions, Rights and Public Freedoms, Form of State Governance During the Transitional Stage, Judicial Guarantees, and Conclusive Provisions. Although this document is intended to serve as an interim constitution until a new general assembly is elected, it establishes the basis upon which a new constitution can be written. For example, Article 34 states, "The constitutional documents and laws which were applicable before applying this Declaration shall be repealed."[25] That statement puts the last nail in the coffin of the Gadafi era. Article 4 declares, "The State shall seek to establish a political democratic regime to be based upon the political multitude and multi party system in a view of achieving peaceful and democratic circulation of power."[26] It is clear that the system that is currently envisaged is a multiparty democracy. Actually establishing a functioning one, however, is easier said than done. There continue to be internal antagonisms and political and social cleavages that will greatly complicate the process moving forward.

CONCLUSION

Were the events that brought about the downfall of the Gadafi regime a revolution, or were they just the ouster of an unpopular leader via a violent uprising? I contend that we witnessed a revolution. As Samuel Huntington puts it in his classic *Political Order in Changing Societies*, "A revolution is a rapid, fundamental, and violent domestic change in the dominant values and myths of a society, in its political institutions, social structure, leadership, and government activities and policies."[27]

With the ouster of Gadafi, the Great Libyan *Jamahiriyah* (Republic) came to an end. The socialist and somewhat esoteric values that were the foundation of the *Jamahiriyah* were swept away, and the political institutions such as the popular committees and the security apparatus, including the military and paramilitary state organizations, were dismantled or foundered. The Gadafi government activities and policies ceased to function or be implemented, as noted in the Constitutional Declaration.

Huntington continues, "A complete revolution, however, also involves a second phase: the creation and institutionalization of a new political order."[28] Interestingly, Huntington then goes on to contrast Western revolutions with Eastern revolutions, such as the Chinese revolution, noting that in the Western case the political institutions of the old regime collapse, after which new groups are mobilized into politics, and only then are new institutions created. In the case of Eastern revolutions, new groups enter the political arena first, create new institutions, and then overthrow the old order.

As we view the unfolding of the Libyan revolution, it appears to be following the Western model. Although the political institutions had not collapsed by the time the revolution began, they had become much weaker. Young people no longer believed in the socialist ideology of Gadafi, especially when his family lived so ostentatiously, enjoying the fruits of Libya's oil wealth and spending much of it in the West. The army was a hollow shell, having been undermined by Gadafi himself over the years, fearing that it might overthrow him. The popular committees, the revolutionary committees, and the General People's Congress were part of a state apparatus that had lost much of its credibility and legitimacy due to massive corruption.

It is clear that with the Arab Spring, new groups have entered the political arena in Libya—young, educated people whose worldview and values are much more attuned to the modern world of the Internet, cell phones, and social media. As in the rest of the Arab world, a generational conflict seems to be at work, one in which the young have opted to overcome the fears of their elders and defy those who wanted to keep them under the political yolk of a defunct ideology. Their view is much more open to the world, more global, and more optimistic.

Three other new groups have also entered the political arena The first is the Islamists, who had been kept out by Gadafi for fear that they might overthrow his regime, as they had tried on a number of occasions.[29] Some are more

moderate and have links to Tunisia's Islamists and Egypt's Muslim Brotherhood, while others are more radical and have roots in al-Qaida in the Maghreb
and the Wahhabis of Saudi Arabia.

The second group is made of the Arab tribes, the basic social organizational
unit of Libya since time immemorial. Those tribes, especially in Cyrenaica, but
in other parts of the country as well, were often attacked and undermined by
Gadafi's administration. They have now entered the political arena with a
vengeance.

The third group that actively participated in the revolution is the Berbers,
or Amazigh people as they call themselves, who fought actively against
Gadafi's forces in the western Nafusa Mountains. It is estimated that Berbers
constitute 5 to 10 percent of the Libyan population. As Libyans (and other
Maghrebeans) are of mixed Arab and Berber stock, it is sometimes difficult
to identify Libyan Berbers. I am therefore referring to those who identify
themselves as Amazigh, speak the Tamazight language, and act on behalf of
their community. It is unclear what their role is going to be in the new Libyan
republic, but Article 1 of the Constitutional Declaration states, "The State
shall guarantee the cultural rights for all components of the Libyan society
and its languages shall be deemed national ones."[30] It is interesting to note
that in the predominantly Berber town of Kabaw, the population was able to
celebrate Berber culture and fly a Berber flag in November 2011 without hindrance from any government agency. It is likely that Berbers will be represented in parliament at some point, as they are now in Morocco. They never
were recognized as a minority under the Gadafi regime, and therefore they
played no role on the political scene.

All these groups clearly will shape the future of Libya and each in its own
image. In the coming years, they must prepare themselves to take over power
in free and fair elections, to write a constitution that they will all agree to abide
by, and to introduce reforms in almost every sector of the society and the economy. The challenge will be the creation of viable political parties that have programs and platforms upon which the candidates for office can run. The urban
young people will have to connect with their counterparts in rural areas and
learn that they need to provide services in order to get the rural vote. The tribal
leaders will have to adapt to the ways of the new generation and give up some
of their power in order to continue to have influence on unfolding political
events. And the Islamists may have to adopt a more moderate platform if they
want to play a role in the new Libya.

The process will take time, as the various socioeconomic and ethnic groups, tribes, militias, and Islamic organizations negotiate a viable internal balance of power. The governing powers will also have to redistribute the oil wealth more equitably to the three regions that make up Libya in order to address the demands for development, employment, and rebuilding of the infrastructure. Despite the current chaotic conditions, the ouster of Gadafi and the success of the revolution have brought the majority of Libyans closer together and reinforced their sense of national identity. Consequently, I believe that the nation-state in Libya will survive and that the regional differences will subside in time.

NOTES

1. Adelle M. Banks, "Florida Pastor Oversees Quran Burning," *USA Today*, March 21, 2011.

2. Brian Murphy, "Islamic World Quiet as Bin Laden Age Closes," Associated Press, May 5, 2011.

3. Greg Miller, "In Videos, Bin Laden an 'Active' Leader," *Washington Post*, May 8, 2011.

4. http://www.indexmundi.com/tunisia/unemployment_rate.html; http://www.indexmundi.com/Spain/unemployment_rate.html.

5. Crane Brinton, *The Anatomy of Revolution* (New York: Prentice Hall, 1952), 36.

6. *Sidney Morning Herald*, July 17, 2004.

7. Ibid.

8. Ibid.

9. Ibid.

10. In 2004 unemployment was at 30 percent, and 33 percent of the population lived at or below the national poverty line. CIA, *The World Factbook, Libya, 2012*, https://www.cia.gov/library/publications/the-world-factbook/geos/ly.html.

11. Robert Fisk, "The Arab Awakening Began Not in Tunisia This Year, but in Lebanon in 2005," *The Independent*, April 15, 2011.

12. Ibid.

13. See the UNICEF report at http://www.unicef.org/infobycountry/laj_statistics.html.

14. http://www.chem.ru.ac.za/afuniv.html.

15. Report by an American correspondent, captured on YouTube, http://www.youtube.com/watch?v=ua39inwpIwQ.

16. Guardian.com, March 21, 2011; Ekram Ibrahim, "Professionals Coalition Requests Dialogue with Military," *Al-Ahram* (in English), February 15, 2011.

17. See http://www.ntclibya.org/english/allegiances/.

18. "Islamic Militant Group Pledges Support to Anti-Gadafi Rebels," *Irish Times*, March 29, 2011.

19. Alice Fordham, "In Libya, Jobs for Rebel Fighters a Distant Goal," *Washington Post*, January 28, 2012.

20. David Rosenberg, "Militias Turning Libya into Vigilante State," *Jerusalem Post*, February 19, 2012, http://www.jpost.com/LandedPages/PrintArticle.aspx?id=258479.

21. Ibid.

22. UN Human Rights Council, "Report of the International Commission of Inquiry on Libya," March 2, 2012, Summary, 2.

23. See Amnesty International, "Libya: NTC Must Investigate Death of Another Tawargha Man Under Torture," April 19, 2012.

24. UN Human Rights Council, "Report of the International Commission."

25. Constitutional Declaration, Art. 34, http://www.wipo.int/wipolex/en/text.jsp?file_id=246953.

26. Ibid., Art. 4.

27. Samuel P. Huntington, *Political Order in Changing Societies* (New Haven, CT: Yale University Press, 1968), 264.

28. Ibid., 266.

29. For a discussion of Islamic movements in Libya, see my "Great Socialist People's Libyan Arab Jamahiriya," in *The Government and Politics of the Middle East and North Africa*, ed. David E. Long, Bernard Reich, and Mark Gasiorowski, 6th ed. (Boulder, CO: Westview Press, 2011), 432–433.

30. Constitutional Declaration, Art. 1.

4

The Uprising That Wasn't
Supposed to Happen:
Syria and the Arab Spring

DAVID W. LESCH

SYRIAN PRESIDENT BASHAR AL-ASSAD officially took the constitutional oath of office and delivered his inaugural speech on July 17, 2000,
in Damascus. By Syrian standards, it was a remarkably enlightened speech, re-
plete with criticisms of certain policies in the past, even those of his predecessor
and father, Hafiz al-Assad, who ruled Syria from 1970 until his death in June
2000. The frankness of the speech confirmed the hopes among many in and
outside of Syria that indeed Bashar was a breath of fresh air who would lead
the country in a new direction.

His speech conveyed clear ideas on how Syria could move forward in terms
of economic reform and technological modernization, although it was ambiguous, even evasive, on the extent of political reform along a more democratic
model. Despite this, however, there was a genuine air of exuberance among
many who had longed for change in Syria. Bashar was the licensed ophthalmologist who had studied in London. He had nurtured a collaborative relationship
with elements of the intelligentsia after returning from London in 1994 upon
the death of his older brother, Basil, who had been the putative heir being
groomed to succeed the father. Bashar was chairman of the Syrian Computer
Society (SCS), something of a computer nerd himself who reveled in the technological toys of the West. He brought into the government a number of
members of the SCS, people who were generally thought to be reformers.

This added to the anticipatory environment, although the "reformers" were tasked with the job of modernizing Syria, implementing administrative reform in the ministries to which they were assigned, and examining the economic weaknesses of the Syrian system and devising ways to correct it. They were not there to enact political reform or diminish the monopoly of power of the ruling Baath Party. They had risen to their positions within this system; they were not about to substantially alter it.

Nonetheless, there was a noticeably more open political environment in the months after Bashar took office, leading many to call this period the "Damascus spring." The seven to eight months of the Damascus spring were marked by general amnesties to political prisoners of all persuasions, licensing of private newspapers, a shake-up of the state-controlled media apparatus, provision of political forums and salons in which open criticism and dissent were tolerated, and a discarding of the personality cult that had surrounded the regime of his father.

The regime appeared to be caught off guard by the precipitous growth of civil society organizations, prodemocracy groups, and the level of criticism directed at the government. It is generally believed that some of the stalwart elements in the regime—who were referred to at the time as the "old guard," those who had reached positions of power under and been loyal to Hafiz al-Assad, especially in the military-security apparatus—basically approached Bashar and warned him of the deleterious effects of his societal opening up on the regime's power base. As one diplomat who served in Syria at the time told me, "Probably some of the tough guys in the regime came to Bashar and essentially said, 'Hey kid, this is not how we do things here.'"[1]

As a result, most of the political and social reforms announced during the Damascus spring were reversed directly or indirectly, including the reimprisonment of a number of prominent prodemocracy activists. A winter of retrenchment set in, followed by years of primarily economic, monetary, and administrative reform, but scarcely a trace of real political reform away from the single-party system that dominated this neopatriarchal authoritarian state.

Fast-forward more than a decade later to 2011. Did history repeat itself in Syria, this time in a much more broad-based and lethal fashion? But on this occasion, the impetus for change emerged from the Arab Spring in other countries in the region, galvanizing the Syrian people themselves to act.

THE ARAB SPRING IN SYRIA?

By early 2011, despite the rumblings of change in Tunisia and Egypt, things in Syria seemed to be pretty stable, and Bashar al-Assad had reason to believe that his fortunes would continue to rise. As such, I can almost guarantee that Assad was absolutely shocked when the uprisings in the Arab world started to seep into his own country by March 2011. I believe he truly thought he was safe and secure and popular in the country, that he was beyond condemnation, which may have contributed to his belief that an uprising could happen only via conspiracy orchestrated by Syria's external enemies. But not in the Middle East of 2011, where the stream of information via the Internet, Facebook, and Twitter could not be controlled as it has been in the past. The perfect storm in the Arab world of higher commodity prices due to the 2008 global economic crisis that made basic items more expensive, a youth bulge that created a gap between mobilization (education and expectations) and assimilation (adequate jobs and a living), and even WikiLeaks, which revealed the profligate lifestyles of the ruling elite, bared for all to see the widespread socioeconomic problems, corruption, and restricted political space. In this Syria was no different. The number of people in the Syrian population of 22 million people below the age of twenty-five is about 60 percent. The unemployment rate, estimated at around 20–25 percent countrywide, is even much higher among those under age 25 at approximately 53 percent of females and 67 percent of males. The Corruption Perceptions Index for 2010, which rates the world's countries on corruption, transparency, accountability, and ease of doing business, listed Syria at 127 out of 178 countries, and in the Middle East and North Africa region, it came in 14 out of 19 countries, with states such as Iran, Libya, Yemen, and Iraq behind it.[2] And after the popular uprisings in Tunisia and Egypt led to the removal of the ancien régime in each country, the barrier of fear of the repressive apparatus of the state had been broken across the Arab world.

Assad, though, thought Syria was indeed different. In fact, calls for similar protests to be held in January and February in Syrian cities by anti-Assad elements in and outside of the country failed to produce much of a response, as only dozens, rather than thousands, showed up, usually fizzling out shortly or easily being dispersed by security.[3] There just didn't seem to be the same energy for opposition in Syria as in other countries, which only made the regime feel that much more secure. In January and February amid the uprisings in Tunisia, Egypt, Libya, Bahrain, and Yemen, Assad portrayed his country as almost immune from such domestic unrest.[4] The mouthpieces of the Syrian regime consistently echoed this view, even to the point of expressing support for the protesters in other Arab states.[5] It was pointed out that the septuagenarian and octogenarian leaders of these countries were out of touch with their populations. They were also corrupt lackeys of the United States and Israel. The implication, of course, was that Assad, a relatively young forty-five years old, was in touch with the Arab youth. He did not have to try to look young and vigorous, as many other leaders in the region attempted to do, mostly by dying their hair; he *was* young and vigorous. He had also consistently confronted the United States and Israel in the region and supported the resistance forces of Hamas and Hizbullah, thus brandishing credentials that played well in the Arab street. This may have bought him some time, but it was a misreading of the situation—or a denial of it. Syria was suffering from the same socioeconomic underlying factors existing in other non-oil-producing Arab countries that created the well of disenfranchisement and disempowerment, especially among an energized and increasingly frustrated youth.

However, there were indeed some differences between Syria and countries such as Tunisia and Egypt that led many to believe that the Syrian regime could weather the storm of the Arab Spring—or at least be one of the last to be subjected to it. Because of Syria's turbulent political development following independence, Syrians generally have had a disdain for engaging in activities that could produce instability and chaos. They only have to look across their borders on either side toward Lebanon and Iraq, two countries, like Syria, that are ethnically and religiously sectarian, to see how political disorder can violently rip apart the fabric of society. Of course, this trepidation was constantly stoked by the regime to reinforce the necessity of maintaining stability at all costs. It frequently portrayed itself as the only thing standing between stability and chaos. As long as Assad remained the only viable alternative in the minds of many Syrians, they were not going to participate in an opposition movement that could destabilize the country. For the many Syrians who were ambivalent, lack of support for the opposition was not necessarily a vote of confidence for the regime.

In addition, the fate of the Syrian military and security services is closely tied with that of the regime, so, unlike in Egypt, these institutions have not been as prone to separation from the political leadership; on the contrary, they aggressively led the violent crackdown against the protesters. Bashar al-Assad has carefully maneuvered his most loyal allies into the military-security apparatus over the years, as he has done in the government ministries and in the Baath Party. And the regime was careful to use the most loyal divisions in the military, particularly those made up mostly or entirely of Alawites, to spearhead the crackdowns in the cities and towns that generated the most unrest. The minority elements of the regime and the population as a whole (Alawites and Christians in particular) believed their fate rested with that of the regime; therefore, they would vigorously support the status quo. These elements in the military-security apparatus would not be able to survive the fall of the regime largely intact, unlike what happened in Egypt and Tunisia. The historical memory of Syrian military action ordered by Hafiz al-Assad in 1982 in Hama against Islamic militants (ironically, about the same lapse of time since he came to power as the current uprising from when Bashar took office), killing some 20,000 according to most reports, certainly weighed heavily on the minds of many Syrians. With the brutality of the crackdown, it appeared that the regime wanted to remind Syrians that it was willing to go to similar lengths as well to crush any resistance, and it had the necessary loyalty of military, party, and government to do it. The repressive apparatus of the state—military, *mukhabarat* (security/intelligence), paramilitary groups—was daunting to anyone contemplating taking it on.

On a related issue, the Syrian regime, dominated by the Alawite minority sect, had always portrayed itself as the protector of all minorities in a country that is 75 percent Sunni Muslim. In addition to the Alawites, there are various Christian sects in Syria comprising about 10 percent of the population as well as Druze (3 percent) and a smattering of Jews and other obscure Islamic sects. The Assads have skillfully played the minority card over the years, practically guaranteeing for themselves at least a 20–30 percent loyal support base in the country while playing on minority fears of the potential of repressive Sunni Muslim rule and/or instability in which minorities typically pay a high price. Then there are loyal Sunnis from the business class, part of the military-mercantile complex, as well as Sufi Muslims (mostly Sunni) in Syria, who tend to have a more eclectic and tolerant view of other Muslim sects and non-Muslim religions and who have been actively cultivated and supported by the Syrian government under the Assads (especially Bashar). The Assads have effectively employed a system of rewards that co-opts a critical mass into regime maintenance. The political and business elites do not want to bother having to renegotiate their privileged status with a new leadership and system. When we add all of these elements together, it probably is getting pretty close to half of the Syrian population. Through coercion, a pervasive spying apparatus, carefully constructed tribal and family alliances, bribery, and/or divide-and-rule tactics, the Assads maintained control over the remaining half of the population.

Bashar al-Assad himself was generally well liked in the country—or not generally reviled. He lives and acts humbly—there are no WikiLeaks reports detailing an extravagant lifestyle (as was the case with Tunisian President Zine al-Abidine Ben Ali)—because he did not have one. Stories of Bashar and his wife, Asma al-Assad, going out for dinner or shopping in Damascus and in other cities without bodyguards and the president driving his own car became urban legend. This did in fact occur on occasion, especially early on in Bashar's tenure in power, but soon enough the stories multiplied to the point where almost every Syrian claimed to have seen them. The image, of course, was that he and his family were normal people, not distanced from the masses, but engaged with the public and therefore knowledgeable of and concerned about the problems of the masses. His supporters would talk about him in reverential terms, almost as if he were a prophet delivered to Syria to bring the country forward and claim its rightful place of importance in the region.

By becoming president, Bashar gained a good bit of credit in the eyes of the Syrian public for giving up his passion, ophthalmology, to serve the country when it needed him most. Of course, this was also promoted as regime propaganda and in a way may have bought Bashar a long learning curve and more public patience with his incremental reform efforts for the very fact that he was not groomed from the beginning to be president. His is the image of a good family man with a beautiful, cosmopolitan, and civically active wife. Despite the fissiparous pressures both in and outside of his country, he kept it together for a decade despite all odds, to no small level of gratitude from the Syrian people. And through it all, there had been some economic growth, if uneven.

The Syria opposition, in and outside of the country, was for most of 2011 and into 2012 uncoordinated and often divided, without any generally recognized—or effective—leadership. The Syrian regime had done a good job over the years at making sure this was the case. There have been various attempts by Syrian opposition groups in exile during the uprising to come together in order to present a unified, inclusive front, which at first was more important in terms of attracting international support but also was meant to offer a real alternative to those Syrians who supported the regime simply because there was no legitimate alternative. In addition, in Syria, as happened in Iraq following the U.S. invasion in 2003, there was general feeling that the exiled opposition was illegitimate. Opposition groups have also been tainted, whether legitimately so or not, by their oftentimes close relationship with the United States and some European countries. With antipathy toward U.S. policy at an all-time high during the first decade of the twenty-first century and into the second, opposition groups associated too closely with the United States, or any other country doing so only out of what was seen as self-interested rapaciousness, would have a very difficult time gaining traction with most Syrians. It was easy for the regime to paint the opposition inside and outside of the country as tools of the imperialists because this sort of thing was commonplace in Syria during the first couple of decades after independence. On the other side of the coin, the Syrian regime understood that it had the support of some important regional and international allies, most particularly Iran and Russia. This would play out considerably as the uprising endured: Iran provided material support in the form of much-needed financial aid while much of the international community deepened economic sanctions against the Syrian regime. Teheran also provided surveillance and cyberwarfare equipment to use against the opposition, an area of technology in which Iran has excelled. Russia (and China) provided crucial diplomatic support for the Syrian regime in international forums, persistently preventing more concerted UN action against Syria, as happened with Libya, primarily by frequently utilizing the veto in the UN Security Council against resolutions designed to tighten the noose on and possibly authorize military action against Damascus.

Despite all of this, however, many of the underlying socioeconomic and political factors at the root of the Arab uprisings were also present in Syria: unemployment and underemployment, poverty, massive corruption, and an unequal distribution of wealth. The political, social, and economic gaps between the rural areas and lesser cities of Syria, on the one hand, and the two main cities in the country, Aleppo and Damascus, on the other, had become pronounced, as Bashar had effectively applied a complex patronage system in each. This in part explains the rural origins of the uprising, as opposed to the relative quiescence in Aleppo and Damascus until mid-2012. Ironically, the Baath Party came to power in the early 1960s in large measure due to the support from the rural population in Syria against what was considered the exploitative urban notables in the major cities who had monopolized money and power. The Syrian regime today seems to have come full circle in this regard.

In addition, there was little political space; indeed, Syria has been a politically repressive state. Not only is this system oppressive, but also the repressive activities of the *mukhabarat* are oftentimes quite arbitrary. Preemptive fear and intimidation are useful tools frequently employed by security agents as a deterrent against potential unrest. A certain level of countrywide paranoia exists as a result, which the regime uses to maintain control over the population. As one Syrian man bemoaned, "The garbage collectors are intelligence agents. Sometimes we think even our wives are working with the intelligence. All phones are monitored. We live in hell."[6]

The *mukhabarat*'s accumulation of empowerment over the years, overseen if not sanctioned by the government, led to systemic recklessness that obviously backfired against the regime. After all, it was their collective hubris in arresting and roughly handling schoolchildren who had written antiregime graffiti in the Syrian southern town of Deraa that launched the uprising. It is interesting that the graffiti on the wall read, "Down with the system [*nizam*]" instead of "government [*hukuma*]." This may indicate that the protesters agitated more for social justice and against corruption than called for democracy. It also indicated that graffiti—and ultimately revolution—were the only ways to enact change to the system, since there are no real elections in Syria to effect political turnover. If a Syrian wanted complete change, there was no choice but revolution.

I have seen this phenomenon up close and personal a number of times in Syria—and several times with President Assad himself. On one occasion in late 2007, when I was traveling to Syria for a scheduled meeting with President Assad, I was detained at the airport, my passport was confiscated, and I was interrogated for three hours. The security officer, a colonel, tried to intimidate me mostly by twirling what I assumed was a loaded pistol around the table in front of me, almost as if we were playing Russian roulette. I was released only after I convinced the colonel to call the president's office to confirm the meeting. The right hand did not know what the left hand was doing, nor did either seem to care about being on the same page, a disconnect that is at one and the same time both an abdication of authority and a potential danger for almost anyone in Syria.

When I met with Assad, I expressed my anger at being detained. I told him that upon my return to the United States a few days later, I was scheduled to give testimony promoting a U.S.-Syrian dialogue in front of the Senate Foreign Relations Committee. I asked him what would have happened had I not convinced the officer to make the call? What if I had been incarcerated or even tortured? It could have instantly turned someone considered a friend of Syria at the time into an enemy. I strongly suggested to him that he needed to rein in the security forces because the freedom he allowed them could come back to haunt him.

Syrians have faced this sort of arbitrary repression on a daily basis. Most Syrians know someone who has been arrested, tortured, or interrogated by the *mukhabarat*. Most Syrians know where the red lines are in terms of what not to say or do, but the *mukhabarat* appear to have no red lines, and Bashar al-Assad, who seems to have viewed them as a necessary evil, has been reluctant, if not completely unable, to control them.

Syrians grew tired of the *mukhabarat* state, especially when they saw in early 2011 the popular revolts in Tunisia and Egypt seemingly throw off the yoke of repression and move against the police and security services. They saw regular people in other Arab states say "no" to presidents having lifetime guarantees to rule. Gone are the days when presidents and prime minister rule for decades. Hafiz and Bashar al-Assad have ruled Syria for forty-two years. People want to be able to choose their rulers, hold them more accountable, and have some sort of say in the future of their countries. Political space is so restricted in Syria, and after having witnessed the Arab Spring in Tunisia, Egypt, and elsewhere, many Syrians began to think, "Why not" in their own country? The power of the street—buoyed by the instruments and technology of social media—was on full display, knocking out one authoritarian leader after another. Of course, there are numerous questions now about what exactly will emerge in the aftermath of the Arab Spring. Will it indeed be better—and better for whom? But back in the volcanic and hopeful period of the movement in early 2011, its galvanizing effects were incalculable. Anything was possible. Or so it seemed.

BASHAR'S WORLD

It is not the purpose of this chapter to examine the nature of the Syrian uprising in detail. It is still history in the making. It is enough to know that the uprising happened, and there was a vicious government crackdown against the protesters that, as of this writing in June 2012, has resulted in more than 11,000 Syrians killed, according to a number of estimates. The international community, hoping to avoid having to take assertive action against the Syrian regime, particularly of the military kind, prevaricated at first, hoping Bashar al-Assad would finally be the reformer many had hoped he would be and implement the necessary changes. It was hoped that the uprising would then simply fizzle out as a result. But as the regime vigorously held on, as the protests continued, and as the violence escalated, the international community, led by the United Nations and the Arab League, attempted to resolve the issue through negotiation one way or another, preferably by compelling Assad and his cronies to step down.

By early 2012, calls for direct military action by some conglomeration of the international community, similar to what happened in Libya, in support of the protesters/rebels grew. As the Syrian leadership tenaciously held on, as many of the factors that convinced analysts Syria would not be hit by the Arab Spring came into play in keeping the regime in power, the international community was eager to somehow curtail the violence, even if it meant Assad staying in office, in order to prevent an all-out civil war that could spiral out of control into a regional conflagration. This would also put off the difficult decision of whether or not to more vigorously support the uprising, including with military intervention. Eventually though, as the violence escalated by the summer of 2012, many countries in the international community, led by the United States, the European Union, Turkey, and Saudi Arabia, sanctioned more assertive support of the Syrian opposition amid more aggressive attempts by the United Nations and the Arab League to diplomatically resolve the crisis. But to all too many, it seemed that Bashar had become the prototypical Middle East tyrant. He unleashed the dogs on his own population and at the end of the day reminded Syrians that he was more like his father than the reformer many hoped he would be when he assumed the presidency in 2000.

Much of the disappointment in Bashar, particularly in the West, is based on the conceptual gap between the Syrian leadership and much of the rest of the world. For instance, early in Bashar al-Assad's presidency he decreed the elimination of military uniforms in primary and secondary schools. At the time, Western media, officials, and analysts dismissed, even ridiculed, the change as virtually worthless. It was emblematic, they said, of how little Assad was actually doing to reform his country. This added to the growing disappointment in what was supposed to be a different type of Syrian ruler.

However, when examined more closely, there was more to the decree than met the eye. Where Assad could in a system almost immune to change and at a time when his authority was less than what it would soon become, he tried to redirect Syria's operational philosophy away from the symbols and trappings of martial indoctrination to a more normal educational environment that focused on developing useful skill sets. Ironically, this may have contributed to a new generation of youth thinking not of battling against real and imagined foes but of securing a sociopolitical milieu more conducive to a better life. In any event, the conceptual gap on the utility and effectiveness of this decree between the West and Syria was quite wide. On another visit with Assad, this one soon after the withdrawal of Syrian troops from Lebanon in April 2005 due to the international pressure on Syria after the assassination of former Lebanese Prime Minister Rafiq al-Hariri, he expressed anger that the West, especially the United States, did not appreciate the "enormous" concession he had made by agreeing to withdraw. The implication, of course, was that he could have made a lot more trouble had he wanted to or even kept Syrian forces in Lebanon. He felt he received no credit for his supposed magnanimity. These are but two examples of the conceptual gap between Syria and the West in general. When Assad spoke in his first speech to the nation on March 30, 2011, in reaction to the growing protests in his country, he branded terrorists, conspirators, and armed gangs as the primary reasons for the unrest—he still does at the time of this writing. Most of those outside of Syria scoffed at such blatant misdirection from the real socioeconomic and political problems that brought the Arab Spring to Syria. But many Syrians, even Assad himself, readily believe such claims. Their perception of the nature of the threat is vastly different from what we see outside of Syria. Blame it on Syrian paranoia bred by imperialist conspiracies of the past, Arab-Israeli conflict, and/or regime brainwashing to consecrate the necessity for the security state, but it is in large measure a function of living in a dangerous neighborhood where real threats are indeed often just around the corner.

It is the conceptual and perceptual gap that is at the root of the impasse between what much of the international community demands of the Syrian regime and what Assad is actually doing (or feels he should do) to end the violence against protesters and enact far-ranging reform. This could be seen in Assad's (now infamous) televised interview with ABC's Barbara Walters in Damascus broadcast in early December 2011. In the interview, Assad was ridiculed in the Western press for saying some rather strange things, one State Department official remarking that the Syrian president appeared to be "utterly disconnected with the reality that's going on in his country." Commenting on

Assad's response to one of Walters's questions in which he said that he would be "crazy" to order his forces to kill his own people, one analyst cleverly said, "It's now clear that Assad meets his own definition of crazy."[7] When asked by Walters, "Do you think that your forces cracked down too hard?" Assad replied, "They are not my forces; they are military forces belong [sic] to the government. . . . I don't own them. I am president. I don't own the country, so they are not my forces."[8] In the West, of course, Assad seemed totally out to lunch or, possibly even worse, not in control.

I do not think this is the case at all. I have been with Assad on numerous occasions where he said something similar. First, although his command of English is impressive, it is very much incomplete and a work in progress. He has difficulty conveying the nuances of what he means in a medium that in effect is his third language (after Arabic and French). What he most likely meant by this is that he is not all-powerful in Syria—and he is correct. He has to constantly manage competing interests and listen to powerful voices on different issues. Although he has a great deal of power, by far more than anyone in Syria, he often cannot act in an arbitrary manner. He has also pummeled me over the years with the idea that Syria has viable institutions, ones that he had been in the process of reshaping and revitalizing. Assad never liked to portray himself as acting outside the framework of these institutions, even though he did so quite frequently; indeed, on one occasion he admitted his frustration to me that he had signed a thousand decrees but only a few had been implemented, thus forcing him to go outside of the purview of government ministries to get things done. For whatever reason, it is important to him that it does not seem as if every aspect of Syria is under his watchful eye. I do not think it is to avoid responsibility. I believe it is more him trying to depict his country as a modern, working state that functions like others. He does not want to appear to be the king who inherited the throne. I am also sure that if I had met with Assad at any time during the uprising, he would have pointed out to me that he had made extensive concessions and enacted dramatic reforms. He would have again complained that he was not receiving any recognition or credit for this, and as such, he would have concluded, as he has done in the past, that the United States and the West have it out for him, that no matter what he does, it will not be enough. And I think he would sincerely believe this.

Assad is the product of an authoritarian system, one that is a paradigm of stagnation and control. The Syrian system is not geared to respond to people's demands—it controls people's demands. It is not geared to implement dramatic reform—it is constructed to maintain the status quo and survive. At any other time, the reforms thus far announced—lifting the emergency law in place since 1963, providing for Kurdish citizenship to those Kurds designated stateless since the early 1960s, creating political parties in what has been in essence a single-party political apparatus dominated by the Baath since coming to power in 1963, having officials write a new constitution that would sanctify political pluralism—would be viewed as significant. Now, however, they are seen as self-serving, after the fact, and insufficient. In any event, to reform more deeply and rapidly is anathema to the Syrian system simply because doing so would spell the end of the regime itself. This level of reform is counterintuitive to the basic instincts of an authoritarian, neopatriarchal system.

I got to know Bashar al-Assad fairly well. I do not see him as either an eccentric or a bloodthirsty killer along the lines of Muammar al-Gadafi or Saddam Hussein. People I know who have met all three readily agree with this assessment. There are those, however, who differ (sometimes vehemently), viewing Bashar as a corrupt tyrant from the very beginning. They oftentimes base their position on the evidence of continued repression and delayed reform. This is understandable, and if they said that the Syrian system was corrupt and repressive from the beginning of Assad's rule, then I would wholeheartedly agree.[9] If they said that he would eventually succumb to this system even if he were altruistic in the beginning, then they would be correct. But Bashar was different from the typical Middle East dictator, which led many people, including me, to hope for the best—and maybe even engage in wishful thinking. That Bashar was perceived by most who met him to be a relatively ordinary person who then sanctioned a brutal crackdown of the uprising in what may have been a very matter-of-fact manner says something about human behavior and how even normal people can devolve under the pressure of power and delusion. He learned soon enough that to succeed in the Syrian system, he had to conform to it.

Somewhere along the road, Assad lost his way. The arrogance of authoritarianism will do that; indeed, power is an aphrodisiac. Either he convinced himself or was convinced by sycophants that his well-being was synonymous with the well-being of the country, and that what he was doing in terms of violently putting down protests and not meeting the demands for change was both necessary and correct. A self-reinforcing alternate reality was orchestrated and constructed around him, and there was no way of testing it against what was real.[10] A friend of mine, Ayman Abd al-Nour, is a prominent voice on things Syrian. He went to college with Bashar in Syria and got to know him well as a friend. Ayman was forced into exile several years ago because of his criticisms of the regime on his blog, All4Syria. On Assad he said the following: "After he became president, when people showered him with compliments and inflated his ego, he became totally different—as if he was chosen by God to run Syria. He believed he was a prophet and started to build his own world."[11] This is human nature in all walks of life, from kings, presidents, and politicians to corporate heads.

While the rest of the world thinks Assad has been delusional (or at the very least trying to deflect attention from the real causes of the uprising) ever since his March 30, 2011, speech, when he blamed foreign conspiracies for the unrest in Syria, it is my contention that he and his inner circle really believe—more than most people can imagine—that there indeed have been foreign conspiracies from the very beginning. It is simply the very different way the Syrian leadership perceives the nature of threat based on its own history, one in which, as stated earlier, Syria has been subject to conspiracies by external enemies just enough to lend credence to such exhortations to many Syrians. The Syrian leadership just has a different conceptual paradigm regarding threat. From the point of view of the West, this paradigm appears to be extremely paranoid; from the perspective of Damascus, however, it is prudent and based on historical circumstances. And the violence Assad unleashed has helped create the circumstances in Syria whereby external forces in fact involved themselves in the uprising more extensively, so it became a self-fulfilling prophecy.

The Syrian government's crackdown was a push-button, convulsive response to domestic threat. It was business as usual. It is not as though Assad does not control the security forces. It is that this has been the way Syria works under the Assads. They reach into their historical pocket and pull out what worked for them in the past and what they found was much closer to Hama in 1982 than anything else. And to date, as indicated earlier, Bashar has not been willing to reduce the tremendous amount of leeway he has given the security forces to deal with threats, both domestic and foreign, with the latter often seen as causing the former. In my view, this has empowered thuggish security forces that know only one way to deal with threats. Bashar simply went along with business as usual instead of understanding the new circumstances created by the Arab Spring. In addition, the regimes of Hafiz and Bashar al-Assad simply do not make concessions from a perceived position of weakness. They will make concessions only from a perceived position of strength, so cracking down hard on demonstrators while offering political reforms are two sides of the same coin. This is the Syrian way—under the Assads.

In *The New Lion of Damascus: Bashar al-Asad and Modern Syria* (2005), I wrote the following in the final pages of the book: "Bashar cannot become a modern reincarnation of his father. If he does, he would indeed become the new lion of Damascus, but this is exactly what Syria does not need." And I posed the following questions: "Will the shell of the dictatorship molded by his father, the repressive and controlling institutions of the state, transform Bashar into a reluctant dictator? Or will Bashar, the president of Syria, eliminate the institutional basis of Syrian dictatorship?"[12]

From my meetings with Assad and other Syrian officials in conducting research for the book, I came away with a sense of hope that perhaps he could initiate a period of real reform in Syria. Of course, I was not alone. Many in and outside of Syria were energized in a positive way by the new young president. In retrospect, I do not necessarily think that the feeling of hope was misplaced or that somehow we were all falsely led astray. I do believe that at first Bashar was truly interested in serious reform. But he soon realized what he could and could not do, not unlike U.S. presidents who upon coming to office soon find that they are unable to implement the sweeping changes typically promised during their campaigns. There are established interests and established ways of doing things that stifle attempts at change. In Syria, politics is more of a life-and-death game. Soon enough Bashar found that all he could do at first was to make some cosmetic changes and institute in-depth reform in areas such as education, which did not threaten the cozy socioeconomic and political positions of the establishment.

Hafiz al-Assad did his job well. He constructed an airtight but stultifying array of family, tribal, and sectarian-based patronage systems that produced loyalty and stability, but little else. As Peter Harling, an astute Syria observer on the scene in Damascus, writes: "For the regime, its supporters and its allies, Syria's is an immature, if not disease ridden society. They posit—with evidence both real and invented, and generally blown out of proportion—that Syrian society shows sectarian, fundamentalist, violent and seditious proclivities that can be contained only by a ruthless power structure."[13] Ultimately, Bashar and his cohorts could not trust anyone else in Syria. He had little faith that anything or anyone other than his presidency could lead the way forward. The Assad regimes simply were not geared to implement change in anything close to an expedient or a dramatic fashion, which is exactly what was needed at the beginning of the uprising. Bashar's initial strategic vision for an internationally respected and integrated Syria became consumed by a Syrian paradigm of political survival. He was either unwilling or powerless to stop what in Syria is a reflexive response to perceived threat. He retrenched into a typically Syrian authoritarian mode of survival, an Alawite fortress to protect the sect's chokehold on power. In the end, when the pressure was greatest, Assad was not the enlightened, Western-educated ophthalmologist. He returned to his roots as a child of the Arab-Israeli conflict, the superpower cold war, and Hafiz al-Assad, which appears to have shaped the nature of his response more so than anything else. Many of us hoped Assad would change the system. What seems to have happened is that the system changed him.

Assad desperately needed to break out of the stifling, anachronistic box of Syrian politics as usual and embrace a transformational role in his country. No one denies the difficulty of doing so, especially with powerful pockets of resistance to any significant change to the status quo arrayed against him and little international support. But he was not up to the task. He was shortsighted and deluded. He failed miserably. The ability of the Syrian regime to meet the demands of the protesters and the international community all along was slim or none. If the protests miraculously stopped at any point, the reforms announced to that time, without the internal and external pressure that generated them, would most likely have been diluted to insignificance or revoked altogether. After all, Assad has not inspired confidence in terms of his ability or even his willingness to actually implement reform beyond their mere promulgation. Some of this is him, some the inert Syrian system.

The Syrian leadership is also tremendously suspicious of any brokered agreements, especially if they are mediated by the Arab League, United Nations, or some other manifestation of what it views as organizations controlled by anti-Syrian states. As Bashar confided to me some years ago (following the Hariri assassination), he was (and probably still is) convinced that the West and its regional allies are "out to get him" one way or another, either through force or diplomacy. While the Syrian opposition, its Arab supporters, and the West see Assad as untrustworthy and prevaricating, especially when he, in essence, conditionally accepted internationally brokered agreements to end the violence and did relatively little to implement the accords, the Syrian leadership viewed these exact same organizations and countries and their diplomatic efforts as pernicious attempts through diplomacy to buy time for the opposition to regroup and rearm. Syrian leaders, in my opinion, believe that if they do not maintain unrelenting pressure on the rebels, then they will have time to strengthen their position and possibly even establish safe havens from which they can be supported from the outside. From the beginning, Bashar and his loyalists always saw and pursued a security solution to the uprising. But in the process he lost his legitimacy and mandate to rule, and ultimately this will erode his base of power politically, economically, and militarily, especially if outside support for the rebellion increases. Unfortunately, one way or another, whether the regime does or does not fall, this likely means continuing bloodshed and potential regional instability.

NOTES

1. David W. Lesch, *The New Lion of Damascus: Bashar al-Asad and Modern Syria* (New Haven, CT: Yale University Press, 2005), 92. For a more extended discussion of the Damascus spring and subsequent events, see 81–97.

2. Transparency International, "Corruption Perceptions Index 2010," www .transparency.org. By comparison, the top three (that is, the least corrupt) in the Middle East/North Africa were Qatar, the United Arab Emirates, and Israel. The top three on the global list were, in a tie for first, Denmark, New Zealand, and Singapore. The United States came in at twenty-two on the list.

3. Even as late as March 15 an antiregime rally demanding reforms to be held in Damascus and organized by a London-based opposition group called the Syrian Revolution Against Bashar al-Assad attracted only some two to three hundred protesters. James Gelvin, *The Arab Uprisings: What Everyone Needs to Know* (London: Oxford University Press, 2012), 75.

4. See, in particular, an interview Assad gave to the *Wall Street Journal*: Jay Solomon and Bill Spindle, "Syrian Strongman: Time for Reform," January 31, 2011.

5. For instance, see an essay written by Bouthaina Shaban, the media and political adviser to the Office of the President and one of Assad's closet advisers: "The Real Evils Plaguing the Region," *Forward Magazine* (Damascus) 48 (February 2011): 16. In the same issue, see also an essay by Sami Moubayed, a leading commentator and analyst in Syria who often reflects regime exhortations, entitled "Lesson from Egypt: West Is Not Best," 4.

6. Bassem Mroue and Elizabeth A. Kennedy, "120 Dead After 2 Days of Unrest in Syria," April 23, 2011, www.seattletimes.nwsource.com/html/nationworld /2014859099_syria24.html.

7. Bruce Bueno de Mesquita and Alastair Smith, "Assessing Assad," *Foreign Policy*, December 20, 2011, http://www.foreignpolicy.com/articles/2011/12/20/is_assad_crazy_or_just_ruthless?page=full, accessed December 21, 2011.

8. Ibid.

9. And as I wrote on two separate occasions in 2005 and 2007 in chapters on Syria in the annual *Freedom House* volume that rates countries worldwide on such indices as corruption, transparency, and political freedom, I gave Syria some of the lowest scores in the volume on each occasion. People used to ask me how I could give Syria such low ratings and still maintain access to the president of Syria, who they naturally thought would cut me off because of my criticisms. I told these people—and it is the truth—that I actually sent a copy of the volumes to President Assad as well as the Syrian ambassador to the United States, Imad Moustapha.

10. My thanks to Middle East scholar Roger Owen for suggesting this language to me at a conference at UCLA in May 2012.

11. Quoted in Massoud A. Derhally, Flavia Jackson, and Caroline Alexander, "Assad Detachment from Syria Killings Reveals Life in Cocoon," Bloomberg, December 14, 2011, http://bloomberg.com/news/2011-12-12/assad-s-detachment-reveals-life-in-cocoon.html, accessed December 14, 2011.

12. Lesch, *The New Lion of Damascus*, 240–241.

13. Peter Harling, "Beyond the Fall of the Syrian Regime," *International Crisis Group Report*, February 24, 2012.

5

Oil, Saudi Arabia, and the Spring That Has Not Come

STEVE A. YETIV

W HEN THE ARAB SPRING started to catch fire at the regional level, concerns existed around the world that Saudi Arabia might also face serious instability. Unlike in Tunisia, Egypt, or even Libya, trouble in the Kingdom created the specter of much higher oil prices, which could send the American economy into a double-dip recession and tip the rest of the world that way as well. Eyes were focused on even minor events in Saudi Arabia, such as a proposed rally in the eastern al-Hasa oil province that never materialized after gripping the attention of oil markets and global purveyors. And Riyadh was not without its problems. On October 4, a brief, ominous release came from the state-controlled Saudi Press Agency in Riyadh acknowledging that there had been violent clashes in the eastern city of Qatif between restive Shiites and Saudi security forces. It reported that "a group of instigators of sedition, discord and unrest" had assembled in the heart of the Kingdom's oil-rich region, armed with Molotov cocktails. As authorities cleared the protesters, eleven officers were wounded. The government made clear it would respond to any further dissent by "any mercenary or misled person" with "an iron fist." Meanwhile, it pointed the finger of blame for the riots at a "foreign country," a thinly veiled reference to archrival Iran.

Why did the Arab Spring not come to Saudi Arabia in 2011 and 2012, even though real pressures for reform have mounted over the past two decades at least?[1] After all, even before the September 11 terrorist attacks, which raised serious questions about Saudi stability, intelligent analysts and scholars argued

97

that the Saudi regime could, or was likely to, fall eventually. Osama bin Laden was born and raised in Saudi Arabia, as were fifteen of the nineteen hijackers and hundreds of Afghan Arabs trained in Bin Laden's terrorist camps. They were uneasy products of the Saudi cultural, political, and religious milieu, a milieu largely shaped, controlled, or tolerated by the Saudi royal family. These realities made it easy to conclude that the profound anti-Americanism of the September 11 attackers had deep roots in a state that the United States considered an ally and on which the world counted for oil stability.

And there were certain signs of domestic problems, apart from the implications of 9/11. In the 1990s, domestic instability was compounded by unprecedented economic strains. The 1991 Persian Gulf War temporarily bankrupted the state, though not its wealthy princes. In the past, the regime had copious monies to keep its domestic allies and adversaries happy. But financial problems and a corresponding need to cut back on the services provided to a growing population accustomed to the quintessential welfare state contributed to domestic discontent and Islamist violence against the regime.[2]

Decreasing oil revenues in the 1990s, combined with high defense expenditures, further forced the regime to reduce the size of the welfare state, thus making it harder to keep political opponents from arising.[3] For a state whose oil revenues made up approximately 90–95 percent of its total export earnings and 35–40 percent of its GDP, falling oil prices took a serious toll. In some countries, fiscal problems can be addressed through tax increases, but not in Saudi Arabia, where the norm is that the government doles out money rather than rakes it in; the religious establishment in particular sees taxes as a sacrilege, which would make such a move in the future even more difficult.

In addition to the impact of economic problems on political stability, the regime has had to deal with a growing population that is better educated and more connected to the world, especially the Arab world, through the Internet and television. This creates greater potential for political activism and antiregime sentiment. The disparity between the beliefs of the ruling family and those of the educated middle class, especially the younger Saudis, was growing slowly. That Saudi domestic reforms were not major also inflamed opposition groups, which consisted chiefly of Sunni religious militants, disgruntled Shia, and antiregime groups stationed abroad. Most political groups have simply wanted the Saudi regime to reform itself, and to become less corrupt, but others seek its outright overthrow. Indeed, until the Gulf War, most Islamists refrained from directly challenging the government and instead attacked liberal officials.

However, the war revealed core dependence on the West and Saudi weakness relative to Iraq, which focused greater attention on the government.

After 9/11, concerns about Saudi stability were raised anew and with added strength.[4] While some scholars tried to explain why regimes have been stable in the Gulf, it became more common among scholars and analysts to predict trouble for the House of Saud, wondering if the regime would follow the path of the shah of Iran.[5]

ARGUMENT OF THE CHAPTER

For a variety of reasons, I argue that the Arab Spring was "springless" in Saudi Arabia in 2011 and 2012. Saudi Arabia is a rentier state that uses its oil monies in various ways to bolster its regime. Saudi Arabia has also been more stable than most observers believe, and these elements of stability helped anchor the regime through these stormy times. We should also consider that King Abdullah is much more popular than other Arab autocrats, that the Saudis have strong control of their institutions, and that they were not under much pressure by the United States and other countries to democratize in any serious way. Quite the contrary, the West probably prefers a slow or even no evolution over any destabilizing changes. In addition, Iran and al-Qaida and the radical forces that may sympathize with them became less—not more—able to undermine the Al Saud over time and were largely neutralized in the Arab Spring.

This chapter first develops the oil argument and then proceeds to identify these elements of stability to which I refer. The thrust of this argument is not that the Kingdom has been immune to domestic and international instabilities, but rather that it appears to have coping mechanisms that heretofore at least have worked.

THE OIL DIMENSION

Oil has suppressed democratic sentiment, probably helping explain why non-oil-rich states in the Middle East faced the most serious uprisings. The modern state of Saudi Arabia, founded in 1932 by Abd al-Aziz al-Saud (also referred to as Ibn Saud), has managed a major transformation, after the territory of the present-day country was carved out largely through war and conquest in the eighteenth and early nineteenth centuries. Saudi Arabia is the only state with proven oil reserves at one-quarter of the world's total, the potential to produce consistently above its market production, and the field production and pipeline capacity to add significant amounts of oil to the world market, especially in a fairly short period of time. It is therefore especially interesting in terms of the oil-nondemocracy connection.

Democratic theorists have long struggled to explain what facilitates and sustains democratization. They have identified many variables, ranging from education, political culture, levels of hierarchical government, war, regime type, and elites. Most explanations of democratic reforms in the Middle East link the process of political change to economic crises, but wealth is one of the general conditions viewed as favorable to democracy worldwide. Yet the monarchies of the Middle East are oil rich. Based on the variable of wealth, we would expect them to tend toward democracy, all other things being equal. How can we explain that they are oil rich and democracy poor?

Many scholars have found that oil is an impediment to democratization.[6] This literature can help illuminate how oil has impeded the Arab Spring. Terry Karl has argued that oil wealth in particular, and natural resource wealth more generally, leads almost inexorably to authoritarian or autocratic government or at least is negatively correlated with "democracy," "democratization," or, more broadly, political participation and accountability.[7] Using pooled time-series cross-national data from 113 states between 1971 and 1997, political scientist Michael Ross has supported this general finding via the use of regression analysis.[8] Meanwhile, economist Kevin K. Tsui, using a different methodology based on actual oil resources, has found that states that discover 100 billion barrels of oil (approximately the initial endowment of Iraq) achieve a level of democracy that is almost 20 percentage points below trend after three decades. Tsui also varied the size of oil fields and the quality of the oil discovered to see if either affects democratization. He found that the estimated effect is larger for oil fields with higher-quality oil and lower exploration and extraction costs. However, he believes that the estimates are less precise when oil abundance is measured by oil discovery per capita, and he interprets this finding to mean that politicians may care about the raw level instead of the per capita value of oil wealth.[9]

The Arab world experienced a liberal phase in the nineteenth and early twentieth centuries, which may well have reversed, in part due to increasing oil discoveries, in the 1950s and 1960s.[10] The biggest oil producers in the region have the worst records on democracy. Freedom House, a nonpartisan

American human rights group, ranks only Kuwait as partially free and the United Arab Emirates, Iran, Iraq, and Saudi Arabia as not free or as absolute dictatorships.[11] Kuwait has the best record among these countries, but it ranks lower on the democratic rankings than a number of Muslim states that lack oil, including Turkey, Bosnia, Albania, and resource-poor Bangladesh.

Oil is not necessary for autocratic government in the Middle East—or elsewhere, for that matter. For instance, former Syrian President Hafiz al-Assad and his son, Bashar, who succeeded him, would have gone to great lengths to have Kuwait's oil but had no problem dominating their people. The father was infamous for crushing a revolt in the city of Hama in 1982, where his soldiers wiped out an estimated 10,000 to 20,000 people in a few days, and Bashar al-Assad has shown little mercy against those seeking to bring the Arab Spring to Syria.

Several explanations exist for the oil connection to nondemocracy. Economists have pointed to the notion of "Dutch disease," whereby major revenue in a single sector of the economy can raise the exchange rate, which reduces the competitiveness of other sectors of the economy and impedes diversification. It has also been argued that dependency on a single commodity is an unsustainable route to development because of the likelihood of declining terms of trade.

Beyond economics, a common explanation for why Gulf states like Saudi Arabia lack parliaments is encapsulated in rentier state theory. The theory, which predicts that oil states will not democratize, appears to be borne out by some important surveys and studies. The basic assumption is that wealth generated from rents, which can come from oil or any other good, produces a negative and different impact on democracy than wealth generated by a diversified economy.[12] Nathan Jensen and Leonard Wantchekon point out that a rentier state is characterized by high dependence on external rents produced by a few economic resources, not from production (labor), investment (interest), or management of risk (profit).[13] Rentier economies obtain most of their monies from foreign sources based on one good, which they sell at a much higher price than it costs them to produce. A minority of their people generates the rent and also controls it, while the majority is involved only in its distribution and use.[14] Some democracies also benefit from external rents from energy and other exports, but these funds are treated differently. They are often managed professionally and are not used for political means. By contrast, in authoritarian regimes most of these rent monies are controlled by and bolster the elites.

A prominent version of the theory posits that these states lack parliaments because their enormous oil resources free them from having to tax their citizens and also allow them to provide major services to their citizens free of cost.[15] As a result, they do not have to bargain with their citizens, which is the purpose of parliaments and which is one of the main reasons that they arise in the first place. These states are not accountable to the citizenry, which cannot demand representation.[16] Without the need for accountability to the wider population, they solidify their autocratic control, with the state surviving on "rents" captured from the oil industry.

Oil rents can also be used by oil-rich regimes to placate dissent, thus stifling democratic impulses, as some scholars have found in earlier studies. Oil monies can help obtain allegiance from individuals and groups that otherwise would be much more unpredictable and even volatile. They may even block the formation of independent social groups that can become the bedrock of democratization. For instance, facing rigid state control, organized labor groups have been destroyed in the Persian Gulf due to the oil boom, whereas once they were the backbone of nationalist movements.[17]

Beyond suppressing democratic sentiments from which an Arab Spring could spring, oil monies also allow for controlling and cracking down on dissent, if it does start to develop. In fact, the Saudi regime drew on oil monies to placate potential dissenters who sought to join their Arab brethren in challenging autocratic rule in Saudi Arabia. King Abdullah reacted to the Arab Spring by ordering spending of $130 billion on social benefits, housing, and jobs, in efforts to quell dissent, especially from the Shia minority. Such "riyal" diplomacy has been the modus operandi for the royal family, and it has probably placated at least some of the regime's most serious detractors, if not hard-core elements such as al-Qaida. For example, in 1979 the Saudi regime was threatened. It faced a massive Iranian-inspired Shiite uprising in the oil-rich eastern province and the seizure by Islamic zealots of the Grand Mosque at Mecca. The Saudis suppressed the revolt and then appeased the Shiites with riyal diplomacy, as they are doing now to preserve stability.

As Michael Ross has pointed out, oil-rich regimes were more effective at deterring attempts to unseat them, and that had to do with oil.[18] On the whole, the Arab Spring unseated just one oil-rich ruler—Libya's Muammar al-Gadafi—and he might well have succeeded in suppressing dissent were it not for his clumsy threats to wipe out the dissenters and NATO's decision, behind the United States and France, to intervene on behalf of the rebels.

PREVENTING CONTAGION TO SAUDI ARABIA
BY SUPPRESSING BAHRAIN

The international community, dependent on oil and fearing a double-dip global recession or worse, was far more likely to support the Al Saud than any other regional autocrats. This is true not only with regard to the Saudi domestic context, but also with respect to the Al Saud's efforts to cauterize the Arab Spring in Bahrain, thus preventing any contagion to Saudi Arabia.

Saudi Arabia played an unprecedented role as an interventionist state throughout the Arab Spring, working hard to manage events across the region.[19] In no place was this clearer than in Bahrain. Indeed, Saudi forces under the rubric of acting on behalf of the Gulf Cooperation Council moved into Bahrain. Why did Saudi tanks roll across the border to help put down the mass uprising that threatened the powers that be in neighboring Bahrain? It lent the Saudi-backed, Sunni monarchy in Manama the muscle it needed to keep control of its Shia-majority population and, in turn, its hold on power. More importantly, Saudi intervention stifled momentum in Saudi Arabia's oil-rich eastern province among the newly restive Shia minority, who might have sought a repeat performance of what was occurring in Bahrain. This province had been the locus of several massive demonstrations against the regime, especially in 1979 when it appeared as if the regime were unstable enough to fall.

Could the Saudis have intervened with force in an unprecedented manner had Riyadh not been oil rich? Possibly, but they most probably would have faced global pressure not to do so, and the Saudis might well have faced their own internal insurrection, which they would have had a harder time suppressing without the requisite oil resources and largesse.

THE LACK OF EXTERNAL PRESSURE

We have much to learn about the United States and the Western role in the Arab Spring, and it will take years to gain a sound understanding. However, it is clear that the United States and its allies played a major role in some Arab revolts but not in Saudi Arabia or Bahrain. Libya is the most obvious case. The NATO allies mounted a rather large military intervention, and some Western states were at the forefront in recognizing the Libyan transitional government, with France taking the lead. For many reasons, such action would never have been launched in Saudi Arabia or Bahrain. Nor would the United

States have seriously criticized these governments for crackdowns on protesters, unless they had become truly grotesque, in which case such verbal attacks
might have been launched.

To be sure, the Arab Spring generated Saudi-American tensions because
the Saudis were furious when Washington failed to support Husni Mubarak
of Egypt, and Washington raised issues when Saudi tanks rolled into Bahrain,
despite the fact that such action helped stabilize global oil prices. Nonetheless,
in December 2011 in what was hardly a show of disdain, Washington announced an agreement to sell F-15 fighter jets valued at nearly $30 billion to
the Royal Saudi Air Force as part of a broader ten-year, $60 billion arms pack-
age that Congress had approved in 2010.

But can the absence of external pressures explain why the Arab Spring did
not take off in Saudi Arabia? That's a tough question to answer with any
specificity, but it is fair to argue that local dissenters may take cues or gain
ballast from outside powers. They may also receive material support and information as well as communications support. Local actors don't act in a vacuum. Conflicts do not occur in isolation in an interconnected world. Local
actors see what others think of their plight, and those others can engage in
the conflict, even as third-party actors or even bystanders. Even if military
support or other forms of assistance are absent, third-party actors can affect
the discursive environment in which local actors perceive their fight. And they
can also use various levers to try to influence the government directly.

LEADERSHIP

Another key reason that the Saudis did not face an Arab Spring movement
has to do with leadership. The Saudis have faced myriad domestic problems,
and the royal family is highly disliked in some quarters. However, it is clear
that King Abdullah is far more respected than was Egypt's former President
Husni Mubarak or many other leaders in the Middle East, for that matter. Indeed, a survey conducted May 18 to June 16, 2009, by the Pew Research Center's Global Attitudes Project found him to be the most popular leader in
Muslim countries. About 92 percent of Jordanians and 83 percent of Egyptians
said they had complete confidence that King Abdullah would do the right
things in international affairs. King Abdullah received positive ratings outside
the Middle East as well, especially in largely Muslim Asian nations, such as
Pakistan (64 percent) and Indonesia (61 percent). The survey was conducted

in six predominantly Muslim nations—Egypt, Indonesia, Jordan, Lebanon, Pakistan, and Turkey—as well as in the Palestinian territories, among the Muslim population of Nigeria, and among Israel's Arab population.[20]

Moreover, even though Abdullah is aging and a nasty and destabilizing struggle for succession is possible, Saudi norms militate against internal dissension, the likes of which could produce openings for regime critics. And there do not appear to have been such serious differences either in terms of succession struggles or within the ranks of the royal family that could be exploited by domestic opponents. Differences have usually been reconciled within the ruling elite of the royal family, divided between the Sudeiri family and the others sons of Ibn Saud. In essence, the country is governed by key senior royal family members—and not just the king—with varying levels of importance, depending much on their lineage, position, and access. Decisionmaking has rarely been unilateral, but rather has been done through a custom of consensus and consultation, which play a central role in most serious matters of domestic as well as foreign policy.

In addition to such norms, the royal family has a good sense of how to survive. Although it was split on certain issues ranging from how to deal with domestic turmoil to managing relations with the West, the longevity of the regime has remained enviable by almost any standard. Despite some serious domestic problems, the Saudis have faced real difficulties in the past as well.

In addition to traditional forms of oppressive state control, the regime has used a variety of strategies to quell domestic opposition and decrease potential internal conflicts. King Fahd, for instance, took effective steps to shore up his relations with the other tribal leaders from the Nejd, his historical base.[21] Abdullah has been well situated to reconcile tribal and traditional pressures with the pressures of modernization and Western ties. This results from a combination of factors: his command of the National Guard, strong support among the large Bedouin tribes of the Nejd, a reputation as potentially critical of Western intervention in the region although not ideologically so, and powerful tribal connections. In the view of one Saudi official, "Critics underestimate us. Unlike the Shah, we know how to modernize without excessively Westernizing, to handle relations with religious forces, to accommodate our critics, and to have evolution and not revolution."[22]

Indeed, the Saudis have adopted a number of "evolutionary" strategies designed to accommodate various critics of the regime. These efforts have included since 2003 the convening of a series of "National Dialogues" designed to foster increased tolerance and rights, including for ethnic and religious minorities; widespread educational reform; enhanced rights for women in a number of areas; and an antiterrorism campaign aimed at delegitimizing violence.[23]

In addition, unlike in Iran in 1979, the Saudis also have benefited from the fact that geography makes it hard for a large opposition to unite. The Shias of the eastern al-Hasa province have been a source of anti-Western fervor, but they represent 10 percent of the population and are not only religiously but also geographically distant from other Saudi groups.[24]

It certainly doesn't hurt that the royal family sits above the world's largest proven oil reserves. Riyadh faces short-term and possibly longer-run economic problems, but these reserves can work in its favor over time. In addition, deposits in Western banks are enough to allow Riyadh to guarantee its external financial obligations, and the government ministry could also draw on the royal family's massive, undisclosed international investment portfolio, which may exceed one-half trillion dollars. The Saudis, despite their economic problems, have amassed major financial reserves. The purpose of the fund is to allow the country to weather any period of low oil prices and can help stabilize domestic politics through such difficult times.

Opponents and even lukewarm supporters of the royal family also must consider that toppling the regime could leave them even less able to realize their goals. They could face internal chaos, be outmaneuvered by other forces filling the void, and lose present contacts with the regime. It is one thing to topple a regime and another to create a workable alternative. Democratic forces must fear that nondemocratic forces could hijack any movement toward greater democracy, and each segment of society, including competing factions within the religious establishment, must wonder how its interests will fair in such an upheaval.

Concerns about what type of regime would replace the royal family, and the absence of any clear and preferred alternative, create a serious logic of vested interests that works against significant shifts in the status quo. Bin Laden may have had the sympathies of a dangerous number of Saudis, but it is hardly clear that many of them would have wanted him, a violent man with no experience in governance and with a price on his head globally, running their lives.

The regime has also been careful not to threaten the interests of substantial segments of the population. This has made it harder for an antiregime coalition that crosses tribal, class, and religious boundaries to arise. Key religious, technocratic, and tribal leaders and factions have been allowed to maintain their positions of influence and to offer informal input into the decisionmaking structure. The September 11 attacks and the campaign on terrorism, however, have forced the regime to confront the trade-offs between cracking down on those suspected of supporting al-Qaida and losing political support in some circles that are sympathetic to al-Qaida and between curbing religious extremism and maintaining good relations with some key mullahs.

The pressure for political reform will undoubtedly continue, as will the challenges of dealing with such questions. Such pressures can produce the positive outcome of forcing the regime to liberalize slowly without threatening a violent and destabilizing upheaval. But in any case, the Saudis do not have to be as concerned as in the past that such political challenges will be stoked and intensified by revolutionary Iran.

ROYAL FAMILY CONTROL OF INSTITUTIONS

Ousting the royal family would require a revolution or coup. Yet as suggested above, the military, like all institutions in the country, is penetrated and controlled by the thousands of princes who constitute the broader backbone of the royal family; more than seven hundred are direct descendants of Ibn Saud, and approximately four hundred are key. Revolutionaries must penetrate that hierarchical structure and develop serious alternatives to it for governance at the same time. It may well be that al-Qaida sympathizers exist in the military, but penetrating it enough to gain any influence is no easy feat. It is doubtful, in any case, that the foot soldiers of revolution currently even exist, despite rising socioeconomic and political dislocation and despite the fact that 50 percent of the Saudi population is under age eighteen.

A new generation of more politically active and disgruntled Saudis has emerged, but even many of them have shown limited enthusiasm for radical or violent change.[25] Even if they did fathom such scenarios, it is not clear that they could muster the numbers to make a difference. In that respect, Saudi Arabia is not Iran. While the forces of extremism are afoot, regimes are not overthrown by rhetoric, demonstrations, or even terror alone. Mass grassroots activity is needed, or military officers must coordinate if the deed is to be done by military coup. And for grassroots activity to emerge, the regime usually has to be widely viewed as illegitimate at the core. And unlike the shah of Iran, who was viewed as enabled, controlled, and propped up by the United States, the Saudi royal family, as I noted at the outset, has the dubious distinction of having forged the state on the bloody anvil of brutal conquest.

Saudi Arabia is also different from Egypt and other Arab countries in that its institutions are not equally penetrated by royal families or the families of their current or former dictators. Mubarak had influence with the military, but his family did not run it, which was also true, for instance, of Gadafi.

IRAN LESS ABLE TO EXPLOIT THE ARAB SPRING TO UNDERMINE SAUDI ARABIA

Iran was more able to stir discontent in the Kingdom in the past than it was in 2011. Were the opposite true, Iran could have stoked antiregime sentiment that may well have contributed to Arab Spring–like behavior in the Kingdom.

The 1979 Iranian revolution increased the internal threat to Saudi stability, partly by bedeviling Saudi-Iranian relations. Relations were complex at many levels, but at the core Saudi Arabia's monarchical form of government, generally pro-Western tilt, and conservative outlook clashed with Iran's postrevolutionary clerical rule, anti-Western bent, and revisionist foreign policy. Indeed, the Saudis viewed Ayatollah Rouhollah Mousavi Khomeini as a heretic, with a proclivity for violence.[26] Saudi legitimacy rested on the regime's role as the guardian of the two most holy sites of Islam, namely Mecca, the birthplace of Islam, and Medina, where the prophet Muhammad launched his mission in God's service. Unlike Pahlevi Iran, revolutionary Iran challenged Riyadh's claim as the champion of Islam by offering an alternative Islamic model that rejected the monarchical, Islamic state and offered a theocratic one in its place. The clash between these two approaches to Islamic governance created frictions in Saudi-Iranian relations that were dramatized by the Iran-Iraq War and erupted in earnest in July 1987 over the annual pilgrimage to Mecca.

Several notable efforts were made to undermine Saudi authority in 1979. The first was in November 1979 when the Grand Mosque in Mecca was seized by several hundred armed zealots, who launched an Islamic uprising to protest the corruption in the royal family. The protests were small but important in that they represented the first open attack on the credibility and improper conduct of the royal family since the reign of Ibn Saud in 1927.[27] That prompted predictions of the fall of the royal family. With outside assistance, the Saudi National Guard successfully suppressed these zealots. But the Al Saud were concerned enough over the Mecca fallout to agree to a set of resolutions condemning the United States for its role at Camp David, in the hope that this would bolster the Kingdom's credentials in the Muslim world.[28]

Eight days after the seizure of the Grand Mosque, while the Saudi National Guard was still battling the zealots at Mecca, disturbances erupted in Saudi Arabia's oil-rich eastern province. They constituted the first political challenge posed by the Shia to the Sunni Saudi regime and were viewed as serious enough by the royal family to prompt the dispatch of 20,000 troops to the area. The Mecca incident further cast Saudi stability and the Kingdom's role as a pillar of Gulf security into doubt.[29]

Further clashes broke out in September and October 1981 in Medina and Mecca, respectively, between Iranian pilgrims and Saudi police. Iranian officials claimed that these disturbances were indeed an export of the Iranian revolution, aimed at destabilizing the Saudi regime. Shortly thereafter, in December 1981, Bahraini authorities arrested and subsequently convicted seventy-three individuals for plotting a coup against the regime. Bahrain charged that the coup was part of a broader strategy to overthrow the House of Saud as well and that the coup plotters at a minimum had direct connections to Tehran.[30] This came as no great surprise since Khomeini repeatedly assailed the Gulf monarchies for being illegitimate and corrupt.

Riyadh faced the ongoing potential for Iranian-inspired subversion, but it was not until 1987 that this was manifested in stark relief. The annual pilgrimage to Mecca was disrupted by a riot touched off when Saudi security units moved in to stop a forbidden political demonstration by Iranian pilgrims in front of the Grand Mosque. Despite considerable evidence to the contrary, Iran's president, Hashemi Rafsanjani, a close friend of Khomeini's from his early days in exile and later a key adviser, denied that Iran instigated the subversion. He asserted that the Saudis were to blame and called on Iranians as "the implementers of divine principles" to overthrow the Saudi royal family in revenge.[31] This caused alarm across the Gulf and in certain Western quarters. Iran, which competed with Saudi Arabia for leadership of the Islamic world, wanted once again to destabilize Saudi Arabia and challenge its rule over Islam's holy places. The Mecca crisis pushed the Saudis to sever relations with Iran and nearly put the two states in military conflict.[32]

Over time, Iran lost the ability and will to foment instability in Saudi Arabia, partly due to the Iran-Iraq War. Iran's war failures gave moderate elements in Iran a chance to advance their political agenda. By arousing fear and focusing attention on Iran's revolution, the war made it more difficult for Khomeini to spread Islamic fundamentalism without provoking considerable alarm. Had Iraq not attacked Iran in 1980, Tehran could have spread Islamic fundamentalism in a nonmilitary and less provocative fashion, behind the tacit threat of its feared military hand. The war forced Iran to play this hand and to deplete its military arsenal.

By 1987, Iran was more concerned with consolidating and protecting the revolution within its own borders than with exporting Islam, and the Saudis were clear beneficiaries of that trend. By the late 1980s, Iran's political and economic agenda was dominated by talk about the importance of attracting foreign investment, enhancing foreign trade, and improving relations with the West.[33] These concerns were driven by the imperatives of postwar reconstruction and by Iran's dependence on oil revenues.

To be sure, Riyadh still views Iran as a serious, subversive threat. This can explain why it was so quick, as noted earlier in the chapter, to help Bahrain deal with its internal instability, from which Iran may have benefited. The Saudis have also been concerned about the so-called Shia arc of crisis, or rising Iranian influence in the Middle East, and according to reports, Iran has increased its arming of rebels in Yemen, which the Saudis no doubt view as a threat. Concern about Iran also helps explain why the Saudis have supported protesters in Syria but not in Egypt. Since Iran is aligned with Syria, if President Bashar al-Assad were to fall, Iran's regional influence would likely be weakened, which could benefit Saudi Arabia. Of course, Mubarak was pro-American and not anti-Saudi, and Saudi Arabia had no interest in undermining him—in fact, Washington's lack of commitment to Mubarak raised questions about Washington's commitment to the Al Saud.

Still, despite the ongoing Iranian threat, Riyadh arguably has less to worry about now in terms of Iran's internal subversion than in the decade following the Iranian revolution. In those times, many analysts thought that the regime could fall altogether.

AL-QAIDA DIMINISHED

Anti-American views were prominent in Saudi Arabia well before 9/11, but it highlighted them. The attacks threatened to reveal growing fissures in Saudi society and accentuate antiregime fervor. But much has changed since then, and al-Qaida and those who sympathize with it appear to have been weakened in the past decade, perhaps significantly.

Osama bin Laden, for his part, had repeatedly asserted his diatribe against the presence of "infidel" forces in the land of Mecca and Medina. In his words, it was "not permitted for non-Muslims to stay in Arabia."[34] That the Saudi regime allowed U.S. forces entry in 1991 and let some forces stay thereafter motivated Bin Laden and other Saudis who opposed the regime.

Throughout history, Islamic rulers have faced the potential of being challenged by those who portray themselves as better or purer Muslims. Bin Laden's austere existence, his invective against Western corruption, and his puritanical position on excluding infidels from Saudi land contrasted sharply with the profligacy of Saudi princes, the royal family's connection to Washington, and the allowance of U.S. forces on Saudi territory. It is no doubt true that his sentiments struck a chord in the Saudi body politic, which exhibited quite negative views of the United States. Such views are not surprising given that most Saudis are nursed on a strict diet of religious education anchored in the extremist Wahhabi sect of Islam, sometimes referred to as Saudi Islam, an education that is perpetuated and enforced by the state. This extreme sect draws inspiration from the teachings of Muhhamad bin Abd al-Wahhab, who spread his message throughout the eighteenth century until his death in 1787.

Wahhabism takes different forms, but prominent among them is the notion that non-Muslims should not be present on Saudi soil and that aggressive jihad against them can be justified, even mandated. This does not mean that Wahhabism should necessarily spawn terrorism, a notion widely rejected by Saudi authorities, whose brand of Wahhabism differs from that of Bin Laden, but it could have done so.

Transnational terrorism and the appeal of Islamic extremists like Bin Laden probably represent an ongoing risk factor. Of Saudi Arabia's estimated 21 million people, more than half are under eighteen. In June 2003, Saudi security forces discovered a plot to attack Mecca. Half of the twelve suspected al-Qaida militants were minors, who are more susceptible to recruitment and manipulation through the Internet, mosques, and other venues. Rocked by the May 12 al-Qaida suicide bombings on Western residential compounds in Riyadh that killed thirty-five people, as well as by the Mecca plot, Saudi authorities initiated a crackdown on militants. They more zealously sought a dozen prominent Saudis suspected of giving al-Qaida millions of dollars. Riyadh, which in the past had stonewalled U.S. intelligence agencies whenever such support could embarrass it at home, continued its crackdown on terrorists in July and August, arresting sixteen al-Qaida-linked terror suspects and uncovering a network of Islamic extremists so large that it surprised Saudi officials.[35]

However, the al-Qaida movement has weakened. Systematic polling data from 2002 to 2008, as well as surveys in 2011 from the Pew Research Center's Global Attitudes Project,[36] showed that confidence in Bin Laden and al-Qaida had waned in the Muslim world, well before his assassination by U.S. Navy Seals in 2011. Despite his death, this data can tell us something about transnational terrorism. These surveys strongly suggest that the message of al-Qaida and Bin Laden was increasingly ignored. The data are also important inasmuch as they may well indicate that radicals in the Muslim world, beyond just the terrorists, have lost influence relative to moderates. In turn, this suggests that the uprisings and revolutions in the Middle East, even if fraught with setbacks in the coming years, may have a greater chance of success than would otherwise be the case.

It appears as well that al-Qaida increasingly has faced financial stress, albeit it has also shown signs of adaptation. Witness the moves toward a partial diversification of income, including drug money, and toward the partial morphing of the organization into various local affiliates. While al-Qaida continued to gain monies in the oil-rich Persian Gulf, global cooperation in shutting down its funding also improved. Adding to its problems, al-Qaida also largely lost its base in Afghanistan and has been on the move, with many of its senior leaders killed by American forces and drone attacks.

What these developments suggest is that al-Qaida was not in a good position to stoke the Arab Spring in Saudi Arabia for purposes of undermining the regime. Had it been stronger in 2011, it may well have added some impetus for more serious uprisings against the Al Saud or at least contributed to the seeds of domestic discontent or indirectly encouraged other antiregime forces to take a stronger role.

CONCLUSION

The question of why the Arab Spring was springless in Saudi Arabia in 2011 and 2012 is of interest, even though we cannot predict the future and cannot tell what will happen in the coming months and years. It would, in fact, be surprising if Saudi Arabia escaped the buffeting winds of Middle East change and did not see some increased domestic upheaval. Yet, whatever does occur in the future, the issue of why Saudi Arabia was immune to the Arab Spring while other countries were not is notable.

What I argue is that oil wealth was an important factor. Even though other factors were in play, such as the popularity of King Abdullah, even that cannot be disconnected from oil wealth, which helped him placate and suppress adversaries. This finding means something for the broader literature. Many scholars have found that oil impedes democratization, and this study fits into that genre. Insofar as oil monies helped insulate the Kingdom from the impulses of the Arab Spring, it helped the Al Saud prevent various manifestations of democratization that other Arab countries experienced, including freedom of expression and assembly, public rallies, antiregime statements and fervor, calls for greater suffrage and human rights protections, and uproar against ingrained and unjustified institutions of repression or status quo maintenance. Future work might do well to consider more methodically the relationship between oil wealth or oil trade as a percentage of GDP, on the one hand, and levels of democratization or antiregime activity during the Arab Spring, on the other. That could further test the oil-nondemocratization link and what it means for Middle East politics and security, and for America's foreign policy toward the region and that of other outside powers as well.

NOTES

1. As one report shows, Saudi Arabia is not immune to protest and dissent, but it is striking how little the Kingdom has faced in the way of major challenge to government. See Anthony H. Cordesman, "Saudi Stability in a Time of Change," April 2011 (Washington, DC: CSIS, April 2010), http://csis.org/files/publication/110421_saudi_stability_change.pdf. See Mai Yamani, "The Two Faces of Saudi Arabia," *Survival* 50 (February-March 2008): 143–156.

2. On such challenges, see Leigh Nolan, "Managing Reform," Policy Brief (Doha, Qatar: Brookings Center, May 2011). For explanations of antiregime sentiment, see Thomas Hegghammer, "Islamist Violence and Regime Stability in Saudi Arabia," *International Affairs* 84 (2008): 701–715.

3. See Rachel Bronson, *Thicker Than Oil: America's Uneasy Partnership with Saudi Arabia* (New York: Oxford University Press, 2007).

4. See John E. Peterson, *Saudi Arabia and the Illusion of Security* (London: Oxford University Press for the International Institute for Strategic Studies, 2002).

5. See Jill Crystal, *Oil and Politics in the Gulf: Rulers and Merchants in Kuwait and Qatar* (New York: Cambridge University Press, 1995), 75–78. For a discussion of

these views, see Nawaf E. Obaid, "In Al-Saud We Trust: How the Regime in Riyadh Avoids the Mistakes of the Shah," *Foreign Policy*, January-February 2002; Eric Rouleau, "Trouble in the Kingdom," *Foreign Affairs*, July-August 2002, 75–89; and Robert Baer, *Sleeping with the Devil* (New York: Crown, 2003).

6. One problem with the theory is that in some cases, such as in Malaysia, Norway, Chile, and Indonesia, natural resource wealth has not impeded democratization. The theory cannot account for these cases.

7. Terry Lynn Karl, *Paradox of Plenty: Oil Booms and Petro-States* (Berkeley and Los Angeles: University of California Press, 1997).

8. Michael Ross, "Does Oil Hinder Democracy?," *World Politics* 53 (April 2001): 325–361. Using different data and methods, Michael Herb questions the extent of the oil-democracy connection. See Michael Herb, No Representation Without Taxation? Rents, Development, and Democracy," *Comparative Politics* 37, 3 (2005): 297–316.

9. Kevin K. Tsui, "More Oil, Less Democracy: Evidence from Worldwide Crude Oil Discoveries," *Economic Journal* 121 (2010): 89–115.

10. Saad Eddin Ibrahim, "An Open Door," *Wilson Quarterly* 28 (Spring 2004): 36–46.

11. See www.freedomhouse.org.

12. Herb, "No Representation Without Taxation," 300.

13. Nathan Jensen and Leonard Wantchekon, "Resource Wealth and Political Regimes in Africa," *Comparative Political Studies* 37 (September 2004): 816–841.

14. Hazem Beblawi and Giacomo Luciani, eds., *The Rentier State* (New York: Croom Helm, 1987), esp. 11–16.

15. On rentier theory and challenges to it, see ibid., esp. 298–299.

16. On how oil made Kuwait and Qatar less accountable to the merchant class, see Crystal, *Oil and Politics in the Gulf*. For evidence on lack of accountability, see Kristopher W. Ramsay, "Revisiting the Resource Curse: Natural Disasters, the Price of Oil, and Democracy," *International Organization*, Summer 2011, 507–529.

17. F. Gregory Gause III, *Oil Monarchies: Domestic and Security Challenges in the Arab Gulf States* (New York: Council on Foreign Relations, 1994), 70–75.

18. Michael L. Ross, "Will Oil Drown the Arab Spring?" *Foreign Affairs*, September-October 2011, 2–7.

19. See John R. Bradley, "Saudi Arabia's Invisible Hand in the Arab Spring," *Foreign Affairs* online, October 13, 2011, http://www.foreignaffairs.com/articles/136473/john-r-bradley/saudi-arabias-invisible-hand-in-the-arab-spring.

20. See Pew Global Attitudes Project, "Little Enthusiasm for Many Muslim Leaders," February 4, 2010, http://www.pewglobal.org/files/pdf/268.pdf.

21. Ibid.

22. Ibid.

23. On these strategies, see Mark L. Haas, *The Clash of Ideologies: Middle Eastern Politics and American Security* (New York: Oxford University Press, 2012), 260–264.

24. Obaid, "In Al-Saud We Trust."

25. See Mai Yamani, *Changed Identities: The Challenge of the New Generation in Saudi Arabia* (Washington, DC: Brookings Institution Press, 2000).

26. Ayman Al-Yassini, *Religion and State in the Kingdom of Saudi Arabia* (Boulder, CO: Westview Press, 1985), 123.

27. Madawi Al-Rasheed, *A History of Saudi Arabia* (Cambridge: Cambridge University Press, 2002), 144.

28. Nadav Safran, *Saudi Arabia: The Ceaseless Quest for Security* (Cambridge, MA: Harvard University Press, 1985), 358–359.

29. For details on Saudi instability during this period, see *Middle East Contemporary Survey* 3 (1978–1979), 358–359, 736–755.

30. See Manama WAKH, Foreign Broadcast Information Service: MEA, February 25, 1982, C-3.

31. Quoted in John Kifner, "Iranian Officials Urge 'Uprooting' of Saudi Royalty," *New York Times*, August 3, 1987.

32. Ibid.

33. Anoushiravan Ehteshami, "The Foreign Policy of Iran," in *The Foreign Policies of Middle East States*, ed. Raymond Hinnebusch and Anoushiravan Ehteshami (Boulder, CO: Lynne Rienner, 2002), 288–292.

34. This section is based on several Osama bin Laden videos shown on CNN in the period September 15–October 15, 2001.

35. Faiza Saleh Ambah, "Saudis Arrest al-Qaida Suspects in Crackdown," Associated Press, July 22, 2003.

36. Pew Global Attitudes Project, "Osama bin Laden Largely Discredited Among Muslim Publics in Recent Years," May 2, 2011, http://pewglobal.org/2011/05/02/osama-bin-laden-largely-discredited-among-muslim-publics-in-recent-years/.

6

Jordan and the Arab Spring

Curtis R. Ryan

A S THE WINDS OF CHANGE of the "Arab Spring" swept the region in 2011 and 2012, many wondered which country would be next. Popular revolutions had ousted dictators in Tunisia and Egypt. Turmoil in Yemen led to a carefully negotiated departure for the incumbent president. Civil war and foreign military intervention toppled the Gadafi regime in Libya, and Syria threatened to descend into perhaps the most violent civil war of them all. Yet Jordan at least appeared untouched. The dogs bark, as the old saying goes, but the caravan rolls on. Was this the case for Jordan, however? Was it indeed a kind of Arab exception to the Arab Spring? Might it in fact carve out a more unique niche, navigating the Arab Spring through its own reform program, and hence avoiding the revolutionary—or worse—turmoil that had engulfed so much of the region? Or is it merely a matter of time before Jordan too experiences revolutionary change?

This chapter explores these questions and will offer some tentative conclusions regarding the present and future of politics in the Hashemite Kingdom. For despite the lack of Jordanian revolution thus far, politics within the kingdom has been anything but docile or silent. Jordanians had, in fact, participated in political demonstrations and rallies every Friday since the very start of the Arab Spring. These demonstrations actually predated—by a few weeks—the larger mass movements that emerged in both Tunisia and Egypt. In the Jordanian case, however, demonstrations numbered in the hundreds and sometimes in the thousands (in a country of approximately 6 million people) and thus did not really echo the massive gatherings of millions across Egypt. In addition to the smaller numbers, most demonstrations were also different in terms of their aims. Unlike their counterparts in Tunisia and Egypt, most Jordanian protesters called for reform, not revolution. They called for the ouster of the prime minister and his government, but not for the ouster of the king.

Yet the demonstrations were nonetheless intense in tone and called for a return to reform. The implications seemed clear: if the kingdom did not return to genuine reform on its own, then the demonstrations could easily change in both size and focus, taking Jordan in a more volatile direction than the regime—and indeed most Jordanians—wanted it to go. In 2011–2012, the demands were therefore not yet revolutionary, but they were certainly real, and it would be a mistake for government or opposition to assume that the winds of change had swept by Jordan. They had not. They had, however, simply taken a more reformist turn. But the future of the Hashemite Kingdom hinged on the decisions taken in response to these reform pressures. Could the country reform itself, or would the process fail, leaving the country open to far more revolutionary pressures?

Proregime Jordanians are often quick to acknowledge that reform remains the central point of discussion within Jordanian politics, and that this is not actually new. Nor did it begin with the Arab Spring. Jordanians have been debating these issues for decades. This very fact, however, can be taken in at least two very different ways. For more conservative Jordanians, this indicates that the kingdom is far ahead of the rest of the region and that revolutionary fervor has not reached Jordan itself precisely because the country has been slowly but steadily following a path of reform since at least 1989. For more progressive or reform-oriented Jordanians, the point of departure is the same: 1989. They too point to the inauguration of the much-heralded reform process from that era, but often with nostalgia for a more reform-oriented moment in Jordan's history. Reformers therefore almost lament the comparison of 1989 to the present, noting that this means that the kingdom has advanced little since that promising beginning or that it has perhaps regressed in the reform process over the years. Before returning to the present, then, we must explore a key part of the past. Why exactly is 1989 so often invoked in these debates by both pro- and antireform constituencies in Jordanian politics?

1989 AND AFTER: STRUGGLES FOR REFORM

Jordan had certainly come to a crossroads by 1989. The Jordanian economy was in very poor shape, leading the government to turn to the International

Monetary Fund (IMF) for help. But IMF loans always come with conditions. In Jordan, as in most cases, the conditions included a financial austerity program of the type that rocked countries like Greece as recently as 2012. In April 1989, the government cut subsidies on basic foods, leading to massive price increases just as most Jordanians were having an especially difficult time making ends meet. The result was volatile. In the more impoverished south of Jordan, Jordanians protested the austerity measures and also launched demonstrations against political and financial corruption in government. The demonstrations soon turned into riots.

Protesters called for the ouster of Prime Minister Zayd al-Rifai and for a greater role for citizens in political life and in public policy. Their demands, in short, sounded very similar to those that rocked much of the Arab world in 2011 and 2012. In Jordan in 1989, what was especially disturbing to the regime was the fact that most demonstrators were of East Jordanian background. That is, their family origins were east of the Jordan River, unlike those of Jordan's many Palestinian citizens. The unrest, in other words, came not from Palestinian camps or urban neighborhoods, but from the bedrock communities on which the regime itself was based. These were East Jordanians, many with tribal, and some with Bedouin, backgrounds.

The ethnic dimension of the riots certainly caught the attention of King Hussein. The king quickly sacked the prime minister and his government and announced that Jordan would embark on a major program of reform. This reform would include both political and economic liberalization, shifting Jordan toward a more privatized market economy while also opening the political system to greater public participation, competitive elections, a loosening of government restrictions on the media, and a lifting of martial law (which had been in place since the 1967 war with Israel).[1]

Parliamentary elections were held in November 1989, as promised, and yielded a parliament that included not only conservatives and royalists, but also large numbers of Islamists (mainly affiliated with the Muslim Brotherhood) and leftist activists. By 1991, the process took another step by creating the National Charter, calling for greater pluralism and participation in governance in Jordan but in return for loyalty to the Hashemite monarchy. Following the establishment of the National Charter, political parties were legalized for the first time since the 1950s, and soon more than a dozen were officially registered, including the Islamic Action Front (IAF), the political party associated with the Muslim Brotherhood, Jordan's largest Islamist movement, and one that has historically been socially and religiously conservative, but also democratic and reformist.

By the mid-1990s, however, the reform process seemed to have stalled or perhaps even regressed. The key factor here was King Hussein's signing of the 1994 peace treaty with the state of Israel. While the treaty secured peace between the two countries, it left the future of Palestinians very much in doubt. Economic liberalization continued, but the political reform process effectively stalled in an effort to thwart domestic opposition to the unpopular peace treaty.[2] By 1999, however, Jordan had reached a turning point of another kind, as King Hussein died after many years of battling cancer. In the weeks before his death, the king also shifted the line of succession from his long-serving brother, Hasan, to his eldest son, Abdullah. Educated largely in British and American schools, and with a strong military background, the new king ascended the throne with little personal political experience.[3]

Nevertheless, King Abdullah II reiterated his father's commitment to the liberalization process and pursued the economic dimensions of the program even more aggressively than his father had. The new king was determined to modernize Jordan's infrastructure, from roads and utilities to communications, Internet access, and cell phone networks. In both domestic and foreign relations, the king emphasized the importance of trade and foreign investment in the kingdom and made sure to solidify relations with the United States, the European Union, and global financial institutions.

In terms of political reform, the king had ruled by decree for two years, having dismissed the previous parliament. By 2003, the political part of the reform process appeared to return, with new elections to parliament. Other elections followed in 2007 and 2010. But the latter two episodes were marked by widespread allegations of election rigging (especially the 2007 polls).[4] Each election, going back to 1989, has been conducted under a new temporary election law. In 1989, Islamists and other opposition forces had done so well that together they controlled more than half the parliament. In many ways, the opposition has been trying to reachieve that level of success ever since, while the regime has experimented with numerous different electoral systems, each designed to ensure that the 1989 outcome is not reproduced.

In general, it is fair to say that political reform has long lagged behind the greater priority of economic reform. This neoliberal economic model, however, was criticized within Jordan for creating greater wealth for some but also greater levels of impoverishment for others. The privatization process, while lauded by external economic and political actors, left many former employees of the public sector unemployed or underemployed, and many of these were from the East Jordanian communities that had always acted as the main pillars of support for the regime, and indeed as the main sources of recruiting for its police, armed forces, and intelligence services. The economic changes, in other words, have been disorienting for many Jordanians and have led to widespread charges that the process is not only uneven but also corrupt. Indeed, charges of corruption echo across Jordanian political debates and only escalate as Jordanians see the vast levels of wealth on display, and the massive construction projects (for new malls, five-star hotels, villas, high-rise luxury apartments, and so on) that they themselves cannot patronize.

The real gap here, then, is between rich and poor, with a dwindling middle class. Yet these complaints too often take a more ethnically oriented tone, as many reactionary social forces attempt to sharpen the divisions in society between Jordanians of Palestinian and of Transjordanian origin; that is between those "West Bankers" whose origins are historically in Palestine and those "East Bankers" whose families, clans, and tribes hail originally from east of the Jordan River. Yet the recurrent ethnic politics card played so often by conservative and even chauvinistic elements in Jordan (and not, therefore, by most Jordanians regardless of background) is especially effective and even dangerous in harsh economic times. Times like today.

Rising Domestic and Regional Tensions

There is no question that ethnic identity tensions within Jordan have dramatically increased over the last ten years. This is due, in part, to the severe economic hardships, but also to the kingdom's extreme vulnerability to regional tensions. These include Israeli discussions of Jordan as an "alternative homeland" for Palestinians, to war in Iraq and massive Iraqi refugee flows into Jordan (after 2003), and now to fears of complete civil war and even collapse of Syria to the north. By 2012, Jordanian officials argued that more than 120,000 Syrian refugees had crossed the northern border of the already small and economically poor kingdom.

Each of these external strains has had a harmful impact on Jordan's own internal identity politics. These identity dynamics have been most clear in the strong nativist trend that has emerged to "protect" Jordan for "real Jordanians." This has even included unprecedented levels of criticism of the regime and of the monarchy (including of the king's Palestinian wife, Queen Rania) for allegedly selling Jordan to a Palestinian economic and now increasingly governmental elite. Tensions have abounded in the largely East Jordanian southern cities and towns and between and among Jordanian tribes. High-profile criticism of the monarchy has emerged from tribal leaders and from retired military officers.[5]

Public questioning now crosses red lines that would have been unthinkable under King Hussein, including now even open criticism of the king himself. For King Abdullah, as one Jordanian analyst noted, "all his choices are contested; his choice of prime minister, his choice of crown prince, his choice of wife. All are contested."[6]

Media accounts of Jordanian politics tend to pick up on these tensions, but they too often mistake the more polarized views of particular extreme Palestinian and East Jordanian political figures for the views of most Jordanians. Jordan is actually a diverse country and should not be confused with the ethnic caricatures that both Palestinian and East Jordanian chauvinists use for each other. Jordan is not the country that these more chauvinistic elements suggest. It is not, for example, a nation of tribal bigots or of disloyal rich Palestinians. Rather, it is predominantly an Arab state with a significant Circassian minority. It is a predominantly Muslim country with a large Christian minority. Some Jordanians have tribal backgrounds, but many do not. And regardless of the exclusivist and nativist trend supported by some in Jordanian politics today, all Jordanians actually have ties across one or more of the kingdom's borders. Not least among these is the Hashemite royal family itself (a point often made by former crown prince Hasan), since it hails originally from Mecca and the Hijaz region of Arabia. While political tensions in Jordan frequently manifest themselves in ethnic, tribal, or identity terms, they are more often than not more deeply about class divisions between rich and poor and between haves and have-nots. And these cut across ethnic lines.[7]

Still, violence across Jordan's borders has greatly exacerbated internal tensions. The collapse of Syria into civil war, for example, is of great concern to the Jordanian regime, but it has also caused the kingdom's own broad-based reform movement to splinter in its responses. The large Islamist movement, based in the Muslim Brotherhood and Islamic Action Front, has called for the ouster of the Assad regime and broken from many secular left opposition parties that have stood by Damascus. Some of the latter parties, originally allied with the Islamists as part of a broad reform coalition in Jordan, now fear that the Arab uprisings have led only to Islamist empowerment and a weakening of the political left across the Arab world.

As one democracy activist suggested, even within Jordan "there is also a certain sense of waiting for what will happen in Syria. It divided the opposition. Some of the Jordanian opposition backed Bashar al-Assad, because he and they take an anti-U.S., anti-Israel, and anti-capitalist stance. This includes the old socialist Baath Party or Arab left. Their main focus isn't necessarily prodemocracy, but antiprivatization and Jordanian foreign policy." The same activist noted the contradictions in both leftist and Islamist positions regarding each other. "The secularists are sometimes so terrified that they end up supporting an authoritarian regime, while the Islamist discourse links secularism and liberalism, as though Ben Ali and Mubarak were liberal."[8]

Yet despite the various ethnic and ideological fault lines that exist in Jordanian politics, proreform and prodemocracy demonstrators (including leftist, nationalist, and Islamist parties and also nonpartisan youth movements across the country) have marched and protested against corruption and for reform almost every Friday throughout 2011 and 2012.

THE 2011 AND 2012 PROTESTS

In January 2011, as protests rocked both Tunisia and Egypt, Jordanians too formed mass demonstrations calling for the ouster of the executive and his government. The executive in question, however, was the prime minister, not the king. Prime Minister Samir al-Rifai had just been sworn in for his second term as prime minister, but regional and domestic politics had taken a decidedly populist turn. Rifai was seen by many Jordanians as a neoliberal technocrat, and he became the focal point of antigovernment demonstrations. Clearly influenced by rapidly changing regional events, the regime dismissed Rifai and his government in February 2011, appointing instead Marouf al-Bakhit, a former prime minister, former general, and former head of the intelligence services—the General Intelligence Directorate (GID), or *mukhabarat*.

For conservative East Jordanian nationalists who had railed against the allegedly Palestinian Rifai government, Bakhit was a conservative East Jordanian from a major tribe, and in many ways the opposite of Rifai—save that they were both loyalist regime insiders. But for the many reform activists who had marched in the streets calling for change, they had hoped for reform and instead got a conservative member of the old guard. Youth activists were at once flush with the success of triggering a change in government yet disappointed with its replacement.[9]

Still, King Abdullah argued that the Arab Spring was not a challenge to the Hashemite monarchy, but rather a necessary wake-up call to Jordan and the whole region. The king suggested that the waves of change be welcomed as an opportunity for Jordan to forge a more unique path—one very different from the revolutions, civil wars, and international interventions that had changed regimes elsewhere. Jordan, he argued, would forge a path—perhaps similar to Morocco—in which a monarchy reformed itself.[10]

The king called for a new national dialogue committee, comprising elements from both government and some parts of the opposition, to forge a new set of reforms to the kingdom's laws on elections and political parties and even to the constitution itself. But the regime also lobbied hard for international support from its Western allies and from Gulf oil monarchies, noting the geostrategic importance of the kingdom and the severe economic hardship it was undergoing in 2011 and 2012. The regime recognized that, although many grievances were social and political, the danger of a real spark toward a more volatile situation probably lay in economic grievances and hardship. Jordan therefore lobbied urgently for increased aid to weather the storms of the Arab Spring.

Jordan even explored a tentative offer by Saudi Arabia and the Gulf Cooperation Council (GCC) to join the GCC. For critics of the kingdom, this amounted to a counterrevolutionary alliance of well-to-do monarchies, effectively shoring up the Hashemite monarchy and perhaps stifling domestic hopes for reform. For Jordanian government officials, however, being more explicitly tied to the region's wealthiest alliance was potentially an economic lifeline that could transform the kingdom's future and had no necessary bearing on the domestic reform process.

In a June 12, 2011, speech to the nation about the kingdom's reform efforts, King Abdullah ended his remarks by thanking Saudi Arabia for its invitation to Jordan to join the distinctly non-reform-oriented GCC. But the Jordanian king also called for strengthening the party system and shifting from governments that were royally appointed to those drawn from the majority bloc in a democratically elected parliament. This was a surprise. If implemented, it would meet a major opposition demand and suggest at least tentative moves toward a more constitutional monarchy.[11] Most opposition activists, however, met the speech with skepticism. As one activist put it, summarizing the general view, "It's a good idea . . . if it happens."[12]

The tepid response to the royal reform initiative is indicative of a more pervasive pessimism across the reform movement—a pessimism that has been well earned. Jordan's broad-based proreform constituency has clearly gotten tired of promises, slogans, government reshuffles, and new national committees for reform. They are suspicious, in short, of cosmetic reform and seek instead clear and irreversible steps on the ground. In the words of another opposition activist, "The whole region is moving at high speed like a BMW while we are riding donkeys . . . *donkeys*, not even horses."[13]

But regardless of the regime's ultimate intentions or level of commitment to reform, the spirit of 2011 and 2012 across the Arab world remains a major point of departure in Jordanian public life. Jordan has seen the rise of extensive levels of youth activism, both in the streets and in cyberspace, from blogs to Twitter to Facebook groups. It has seen a revitalization of old political movements, from leftist parties to the better-organized Muslim Brotherhood and its party, the IAF (but interestingly none of these seem to be of interest to Jordan's energized youth). It has seen a rise in public sphere discussions on virtually all topics, in cyberspace, in print, and in person. Young Jordanians, for example, host various discussion sessions and public debates, livestreaming the events, and taking questions and comments from Twitter as well as from the local audience. The constituency for real reform in Jordan therefore stretches across Jordan's generation, class, ethnic, and gender divides. In many ways it represents the exact "modern Jordan" that the regime itself helped to create since 1999. Yet proreform Jordanians continue to feel thwarted by entrenched antireform elites.

In some respects, these various forces ran headlong into one another at a critical moment within Jordan's version of the Arab Spring—specifically on March 24 and 25, 2011. The reform movement had continued its weekly demonstrations and had been boosted by its own success in achieving the ouster of the Rifai government. The demonstrations thereafter continued every Friday, calling for an end to perceived endemic corruption, for greater inclusion in public life, and for a return to political liberalization and democratization. Specifically, demonstrators called for major changes in the electoral and political party laws, leading ultimately to a governing system characterized by checks and balances between a more constitutional monarchy and a more powerful, effective, and representative parliament.

Organized online as the March 24 Movement, Jordanian democracy and reform activists gathered at the Ministry of Interior Circle in the capital, Amman, for perhaps their most important demonstration yet. Despite the presence of myriad East Jordanian nationalist symbols, including red-checked East Jordanian *keffiyas* (head scarves), Hashemite and Jordanian nationalist songs, and a clearly peaceful protest, the demonstrators were attacked on March 25 by *bultajiyya* (thugs). Calling themselves the Dawa al-Watan (Call of the Nation) and believing they were saving the monarchy from "Palestinian" revolutionaries who were "occupying" their capital, they stormed the peaceful demonstration, leading to the death of one participant.[14]

In many respects, March 24 represented a high point of democracy activism, while March 25 marked a low point, as peaceful democracy activists were dispersed by reactionary antireform zealots. The question then and now, of course, is, who sent the *bultajiyya?* Was the monarchy itself implicated, or was it thwarted once again by its own increasingly independent security services? Both the monarchy and the democratic opposition complain of the excessive role of the GID in public life, so suspicion naturally fell on the *mukhabarat*.

Despite such incidents, most Jordanians remained strongly in favor of reform rather than regime change. Meanwhile, outside Jordan, the extreme violence of the latter round of Arab uprisings—in Libya, Yemen, and, especially, Syria—may actually have helped the Hashemite monarchy, at least temporarily, since no Jordanian wants to see the country take those routes. It bought the monarchy at least some more time, and most Jordanians seemed willing to give the king a chance to join and even lead the reform effort.

For many, another decisive moment for reform then occurred in October 2011, when King Abdullah dismissed the government of Prime Minister Marouf al-Bakhit. Given the pattern of previous government reshuffles, most Jordanians expected another neoliberal technocrat or a member of the East Jordanian tribal old guard and presumably someone with a background in the army or intelligence services. The new appointee, however, was not really a politician at all. New Prime Minister Awn Khasawneh was instead a judge on the International Court of Justice. As an internationally respected jurist, Khasawneh returned to Jordan to accept the position of prime minister, signaling perhaps a new era in Jordanian politics.

The new prime minister completed the process of presenting parliament with new laws on elections, on parties, and on the establishment of a constitutional court and an independent electoral commission. But he sparred with the monarchy over the nature of governance itself, arguing that Jordan had a parliamentary—not presidential—political system and that therefore the prime minister was the head of government, not to take directives from another executive once in office. But the *diwan* (the royal palace) did indeed make clear its views and wishes, while the Khasawneh government attempted to forge ahead on its own. The king argued that the new government was moving too slowly, dragging out the reform process.

While Khasawneh accepted the end of parliament's term in office, hoping for a newer and more effective one after national elections were held, the monarchy called for an extension of parliament in order to complete the reform process by passing the remaining reform laws. That, it turned out, was the final straw. Parliament's session was extended by royal decree while the prime minister was abroad, on a state visit to Turkey. In an unprecedented move, and after a mere six months in office, Prime Minister Khasawneh resigned while still abroad. Both prime minister and king issued letters that politely but clearly implied that the palace or the government was (respectively) to blame. But however blame is apportioned for the sudden end to the Khasawneh government, Jordanians were suddenly confronted with a fourth government in the sixteen months since the start of the regional Arab Spring.

The new government looked far more familiar, as Fayez Tarawneh, a conservative former prime minister from a powerful East Jordanian family, took office. If the reform process were to continue, it would now be led, once again, by a conservative not known for his reformist sympathies. But Tarawneh was also an economist by training and came to office at a time of severe economic hardship. Even before returning to the prime ministry, Tarawneh had noted that economic pressures were perhaps even greater than political or social strains and that the government's options were severely limited. "The demands on government are unbelievable," he noted. "People have legitimate demands for a better quality of life, but the budget deficit makes this very difficult."[15]

Within weeks, in response to a first series of austerity measures that included an increase in some electricity prices, the new government faced street demonstrations and even parliamentary demands for it to step down, Given the tense social and political climate in Jordan and across the region, the timing was precarious, to say the least, for economic austerity measures. Indeed, most Jordanians seem to want no economic austerity measures whatsoever and desire instead a shift toward deeper and extensive political reform.

Yet the stakes are very high for real reform in Jordan, since the new rules are intended to set the stage for new elections and a new parliament, and both the monarchy and opposition forces have suggested that (for the first time in modern Jordanian history) future governments will be drawn from parliamentary majorities, rather than by royal appointment.

But the stakes are also high in the broader regional sense. As these debates over the nature and parameters of reform, political participation, and governance in Jordan proceed, the Arab uprisings continue to transform the region. Jordan is not in any way immune to these pressures. As a small state, in terms of both geography and population, and with a weak economy, Jordan is especially vulnerable to regional pressures and violence. Unlike its monarchical neighbors to the south, Jordan does not have a massive oil income to co-opt opponents and buy off its own population. Meanwhile, as civil war rages in Syria and tens of thousands of Syrian refugees cross the border into Jordan, the pressures on state and society—and indeed even pressures on its already limited economy—only increase. As a recent detailed report by the International Crisis Group suggests, the internal and external pressures for change show no sign of abating.[16]

For proregime conservatives, these dangerous domestic and regional currents signal a need to be slow and methodical or perhaps to stop the talk of reform and change entirely. But for reform activists, they signal a desperate need to move faster, and more thoroughly, to transform Jordan via reform, before it is too late. The question, as always in Jordanian politics, is where the king himself is in this polarized atmosphere.

Clearly both the opposition movement and the general public are frustrated with the pace of reform and frequently cite 1989 as a benchmark of hopes that remain unfulfilled, even so many years later. Others cite the 1999 monarchical transition and yet make a similar argument: that reform should have been achieved by now.[17] But proregime officials and supporters argue that the problem is not the monarchy or the king, but a resistant old guard, an antiquated antireform elite, and an interventionist GID that thwarts not only the will of the people but also the will of the Hashemite monarchy itself. Still, whether sympathetic or not, neither pro- nor antireform elements seem to have much faith in the regime or the reform process. To say there is a crisis of confidence would be an enormous understatement.

Even reform measures are still often met with reserve rather than applause and with suspicion about motivations rather than praise. A profound lack of trust pervades Jordanian politics, and this includes a lack of faith in the regime. This does not mean looming revolution or civil war. Jordan is likely to muddle through, as it has through past challenges dating back to the birth of the state itself. And, indeed, most Jordanians still support the monarchy and want it to lead the country to genuine reform. But the depth of suspicion and lack of faith can be seen in virtually every government move. Even reform moves, in other words, are met with suspicion. Does reform really mean reform, or is it merely more cosmetic political change? And when the regime moves against corruption, a key opposition demand, the inconsistency of who are arrested and whether they come to trial or not leads to still more questions. For Jordanian royalists, these types of questions are infuriating. The regime, they argue, can't seem to get any credit no matter what it does. Regime critics, in contrast, argue that the cynicism comes from experience and a litany of disappointments.[18]

CONCLUSIONS

So far, Jordan has managed to avoid the revolutionary change of Tunisia and Egypt, the violent civil wars of Libya and Syria, and the counterrevolutionary violence of Bahrain. Instead, the regime argues that it is embarking on an alternative path toward methodical homegrown reform and toward a greater pluralism and liberalization aimed at preserving the monarchy and the state, rather than replacing either. This process has a chance of succeeding, and indeed the monarchy would actually be stronger if it took a few steps back, curbed the power of the GID, and allowed parliamentary governments to emerge. Yet the GID itself sees the kingdom's large Islamist movement as the real threat to Jordan's future and fears that greater democratization would empower Palestinians at the expense of East Jordanians and Islamists at the expense of conservative secularists. The security services fear an Islamist takeover of Jordan, with democracy as a onetime ticket to an Islamic republic and an end of the Hashemite regime.

The Muslim Brotherhood and the Islamic Action Front, of course, make precisely the opposite argument: that the largely East Jordanian security forces are controlling the state, that the tribes have too much power, and that they therefore thwart democracy to preserve their own privileges. Secular proreform forces make similar arguments. Some activists and analysts even fear that the security services themselves would force a change in monarch if they felt it would help secure the monarchy and their own privileges. To be clear, neither a coup d'état nor a revolt is likely in Jordan, but neither are they impossible. The outcome of the Arab Spring for Jordan will depend on the influence of regional events and on the kingdom's own domestic reform efforts.

Lost in much of this, as usual, is Jordan's large and well-educated youth population, who seem to have little faith in the political motivations of the regime, the GID, the Islamist movement, or the old opposition political parties. Jordan's youth, in short, are really the key to Jordan's future, but their more genuinely democratic and less partisan inclinations may be thwarted by one or more of the older social forces noted above. The stakes, to repeat, remain high. For they include nothing less than the future of the monarchy, the state, and the nation, as the winds of change continue to buffet Jordan and the entire region.

NOTES

1. Rex Brynen, "Economic Crisis and Post-Rentier Democratization in the Arab World: The Case of Jordan," *Canadian Journal of Political Science* 25, 1 (1992): 69–97; Malik Mufti, "Elite Bargains and the Onset of Political Liberalization in Jordan," *Comparative Political Studies* 32, 1 (1999): 100–129; Glenn E. Robinson, "Defensive Democratization in Jordan," *International Journal of Middle East Studies* 30, 3 (1998): 387–410.

2. Laurie A. Brand, "The Effects of the Peace Process on Political Liberalization in Jordan," *Journal of Palestine Studies* 28, 2 (1999): 52–67; Jillian Schwedler, "Don't Blink: Jordan's Democratic Opening and Closing," MERIP Press Information Note, July 3, 2002, http://www.merip.org.

3. For details on the monarchical transition and changes in Jordanian politics, see Curtis R. Ryan, *Jordan in Transition: From Hussein to Abdullah* (Boulder, CO: Lynne Rienner, 2002).

4. Asher Susser, "Jordan: Preserving Domestic Order in a Setting of Regional Turmoil," Middle East Brief No. 27 (Waltham, MA: Crown Center for Middle East Studies, Brandeis University, March 2008), 4–5.

5. Curtis R. Ryan, "'We Are All Jordan'... but Who Is We?," *Middle East Report Online*, July 13, 2010, http://www.merip.org/mero/mero071310.

6. Author interview, Amman, Jordan, June 2010.

7. This section draws on Curtis R. Ryan, "Identity and Corruption in Jordanian Politics," Middle East Channel at *Foreign Policy*, February 9, 2012, http://mideast .foreignpolicy.com/posts/2012/02/09/identity_and_corruption_in_jordanian _politics.

8. Author interview, Amman, Jordan, December 2011.

9. Author interviews with youth activists. Amman, Jordan, May 2012.

10. Author interview with His Majesty King Abdullah II, Basman Palace, Amman, Jordan, May 21, 2012.

11. Curtis R. Ryan, "The King's Speech," Middle East Channel at *Foreign Policy*, June 17, 2011, http://mideast.foreignpolicy.com/posts/2011/06/17/the _kings_speech.

12. Author interview, Amman, Jordan, June 2011.

13. Author interview with Jordanian democracy activist, Amman, Jordan, June 2011.

14. See the account by democracy activist and blogger Naseem Tarawneh, "The Quick Death of Shabab March 24th and What It Means for Jordan," Black Iris of Jordan (blog), March 26, 2011, http://www.black-iris.com/2011/03/26/the-quick -death-of-shabab-march-24-and-what-it-means-for-jordan/.

15. Author interview with Dr. Fayez Tarawneh, Senate, Amman, Jordan, December 13, 2011.

16. International Crisis Group, "Popular Protest in North Africa and the Middle East (IX): Dallying with Reform in a Divided Jordan," *Middle East Report* No. 118, March 12, 2012, http://www.crisisgroup.org/en/regions/middle-east -north-africa/iraq-iran-gulf/jordan.aspx.

17. Marwan Muasher, "A Decade of Struggling Reform Efforts in Jordan: The Resilience of the Rentier System" (Washington, DC: Carnegie Endowment for International Peace, 2011).

18. Ryan, "Identity and Corruption."

PART II

The Regional and International Context of the Arab Spring

7

The Gift and the Curse:
Iran and the Arab Spring

Reza Marashi and Trita Parsi

Though leaders of the Islamic Republic of Iran had long predicted that pro-Western Arab dictatorships would soon fall, the Arab uprisings took them by surprise. Their initial hope that shifts in the region would be a major challenge to the West while providing Iran with unprecedented opportunities has yet to materialize. Instead, the regional flux has created potentially existential risks for the regime in Tehran. A discernible strategic logic to address these dangers is, however, slowly emerging.

The Islamic Republic's top priority is regime survival. A second objective, which also serves as a means to achieve the first objective, is to gain an undisputed leadership role in the region. As a Persian and Shiite power in a region dominated by Sunnis and Arabs, Iran has long faced complicating natural barriers in its quest for leadership. These are complications that, Iran has learned, cannot be overcome through military means. The soft-power component of the Islamic Republic's strategy for leadership—the utilization of political Islam to bridge differences with Iran's Sunni/Arab environment—has been essential. While the Arab uprisings have weakened Iran's key competitors, including the United States, it has also severely challenged Iran's source of soft power in the region, at least in the short and medium term.

Through this prism, it is clear that—more than religion or ideology— geopolitics, hegemony, and survival have come to the fore as central factors shaping how Iran is responding to unprecedented regional unrest. Ideology is, first and foremost, a pivotal instrument for Iran's geopolitical maneuvering. It is a tool that provides Tehran with both internal and external legitimacy and enables it to expand its influence (through soft power) well beyond its borders. To the Islamic Republic, recent developments have shaken up not only existing political systems (including its own), but also its rivalry for regional influence with Israel, Saudi Arabia, the United States, and Turkey. Iranian decisionmakers see this shock as changing the context of the rivalry rather than ending it, and creating challenges and opportunities for all sides.

Overall, Iran's geopolitical strategy aims to consolidate the Islamic Republic as a regional power. The cornerstones of its strategy are (1) managing and balancing its ties with immediate neighbors and key Islamic countries—relations with Turkey and Saudi Arabia are key factors in Iran's regional positioning for influence in Iraq, Lebanon, Palestine, and elsewhere; (2) consolidating Iranian regional preeminence with indigenous technical capabilities—the country's nuclear program, missile tests, weapons purchases, and satellite launch are all facets of this strategic track; (3) standing up to the West—in the words of Supreme Leader Ayatollah Ali Khamenei, Iran intends "not to give in" to Western pressure.[1] Iran's approach in the nuclear standoff is a good example of this conviction.

Historical precedent has shown Iran that Western powers tend to accept the status of a regional power when that power becomes formidable. China, India, and Brazil are often cited as examples. The Islamic Republic is counting on such an eventual acceptance. The key virtue from Iran's perspective has been patience. Decisionmakers in Tehran know that the cost of this strategy is high—sanctions, isolation, and threats of war are not negligible—but they believe that Iran must assume the role of an accepted regional power. If the West insists on making Iran yield on issues of contention through pressure—in particular its nuclear program, support for Hizbullah and Hamas, and human rights violations—Iranian strategy will continue to be predicated on patience and a conviction that it can eventually succeed by playing the long game. If nothing else, this serves as a sober reminder to its rivals that Tehran will not capitulate in its standoff with the West, as Iranian decisionmakers believe that if the Islamic Republic does not "give up," the other side will do so in due course.[2] As this regional rivalry unfolds, the changing Arab political landscape has demonstrated both the relevance of the Arab street and its ability to play a decisive role in the region's future—something Tehran has long trumpeted in opposing the regional status quo. Thus, Iran sees a continuation of

Arab political upheaval as a challenge not only to the status quo powers investing in an order that suppresses the streets, but also to the powers that claim to champion them. (Iran is a status quo power in Syria, so this dilemma applies to Tehran in this case, as we discuss more fully below.)

Tehran has identified this paradox as the new fault line in the region, one that will be under increasing strain as each of the players in this regional rivalry positions itself to address a growing vacuum left by a deteriorating status quo. In the past, this rivalry has played out in both hard- and soft-power arenas, but as Arab political upheaval persists, a third war front in the region becomes untenable without exacerbating an already combustible security environment. As a result, it is sustained soft power—the battle for hearts and minds over the medium to long term—that is becoming increasingly important to decisionmakers in Tehran for achieving the three cornerstones of its grand strategy.

To that end, Iran faces a question, as by extension do its rivals: If Iran's main instrument for building its regional leadership position has been its soft power among the region's populations—rooted in a rejection of the status quo guarded by the United States, Israel, and Saudi Arabia, combined with the ideology of political Islam and financial and political investment in political factions across the region—will the regional shifts continue to enable the Islamic Republic to exploit popular Arab frustrations? Or will the emergence of a more empowered Arab street undermine the foundation of Iran's soft power, thereby allowing its rivals to exert greater influence? And how much short- and long-term damage will Iran's support for the Assad regime's brutal crackdown do to Tehran's soft power?

More than a year after a young Tunisian street vendor lit the match that set both himself and the region aflame, Tehran's strategy—cautious and reactive due to internal political infighting and predicated on the perceived limitations of its rivals—has taken shape. To be sure, Iran is not happy. Its short- to medium-term gains from regionwide upheaval have not cemented its longer-term regional standing, and Iran's overall limitations have come into sharper focus. However, decisionmakers in Tehran are not panicking either. Regional flux has also complicated the long-term interests of Iran's rivals, thereby exacerbating an already tense strategic rivalry and conflict for supremacy in the Middle East. As the actors trade moves on this complex regional chessboard, Iran perceives a good defense as its best offense.

Iran's Relations with America, Israel, and Saudi Arabia

A crucial question is how Iran regards the informal U.S.-Israeli-Saudi "alliance" as it struggles to adjust to a region in flux. Tehran has long viewed the alliance as an unsustainable force in the region, and the changing Arab political scene has provided an opportunity to act on this perception. The Iranian government's skepticism regarding negotiations with the United States is not necessarily rooted in an ideological opposition to the idea of improving relations with Washington. Instead, hard-liners in Tehran fear that any relationship with the United States would require Iranian acquiescence to status quo regional policies, thereby stripping Tehran of its independence and forcing it to follow America's investment in Arab dictatorships rather than the Arab street.

Since its inception, the Islamic Republic has calculated that the Arab street would ultimately overthrow pro-American dictatorships and the balance of forces that favored Israel. Iran's long-term regional security calculation has thus been predicated on championing the Arab street and rejecting any engagement with Washington designed to rehabilitate Iran as a compliant U.S. ally. Iranian decisionmakers see no example in the Middle East—past or present—of relations with the United States that are based on equal footing. Patron-client relations are an unpopular and inconvenient regional truth.

Decisionmakers in Tehran now think that Israel and Saudi Arabia are also faced with strategic challenges, which in turn limit U.S. flexibility to address regional upheaval. Israel has seen the interests of two of its foremost regional allies diverge from its own. Turkish-Israeli ties reached an all-time low after Israel's incursion into Gaza in 2008 and its attack on the Turkish Flotilla of Freedom in 2010. In the view of many analysts, these ties cannot be fully resurrected. Israel has also lost its most senior and strategically important Arab partner, the Mubarak government in Egypt, with no subsequent clarity on how future governments in Cairo will frame ties. U.S. diplomatic cables released by WikiLeaks revealed the extent of collaboration between Israel and Mubarak's Egypt against Iran.[3] The September 2011 attack on Israel's embassy in Cairo by Egyptian citizens and the Egyptian government's April 2012 decision to scrap a gas supply deal with Israel are ominous signs reflecting short- to medium-term turbulence—likely years, rather than weeks or months.[4]

The challenge for Saudi Arabia was crystallized when the House of Saud drew a line in the sand as protests swept through neighboring Bahrain. Its objection to U.S. support for revolts in Tunisia and Egypt unheeded, Riyadh feared that American "betrayal" could inevitably reach the Persian Gulf. The prospect of a Sunni monarchy on its border being overthrown, or even entering a power-sharing arrangement, and Shiite communities being empowered as a result hit too close to home for Saudi decisionmakers, who have long repressed their own restive, oil-rich, Shiite-dominated eastern province. Saudi Arabia has flatly rejected American efforts to negotiate peaceful reform in Bahrain. Instead, Riyadh ignored U.S. pleas for calm and invaded the Sunni minority-led nation with the Bahraini ruling family's consent, using force to crush a popular uprising.

Iran thus sees a unique imbalance of interests between Washington and its allies compounding the challenges facing their informal alliance. While the United States has recognized that the regional status quo is untenable and is struggling to balance its values (democratization) and its strategic interests (support for Israel, secure access to energy, military dominance in the Persian Gulf), Israel and Saudi Arabia view regional developments differently. Martin Kramer of Israel's conservative Shalem Center put his finger on the central point of contention during the February 2011 Herzliya Conference. Questioning America's conclusion that the regional status quo is unsustainable, Kramer was unabashed: "In Israel, we are for the status quo. Not only do we believe the status quo is sustainable, we think it's the job of the U.S. to sustain it."[5] Concern in Riyadh is no less palpable. The *New York Times* has reported that according to an Arab official who was briefed on talks between President Barack Obama and King Abdullah bin Abd al-Aziz al-Saud, the Saudi monarch was unwavering: "King Abdullah has been clear that Saudi Arabia will never allow Shia rule in Bahrain—never."[6]

Iran's perception of the U.S.-Israeli-Saudi alliance as an unsustainable regional power, unwilling or incapable of shifting its policies in accordance with a new power distribution (see below for details), has thus held firm. This includes Tehran's perception of a relentless American hostility toward the Islamic Republic. The proverbial screws have been tightened through sanctions to increase Iran's political and economic international isolation, and Washington is doing all it can to help Tel Aviv and Riyadh box in Tehran—short of military conflict. But developments pre– and post–Arab Spring have provided Tehran with some added maneuverability to counter Washington's pressure: the wars in Iraq and Afghanistan have significantly weakened the United States and by extension its allies, volatility across the region that has destabilized numerous pro-American outposts; empowered pro-Iranian political factions in Iraq and Lebanon; a belief in Iran's indispensable role in any long-term solution to stabilize U.S. national security interests in nonproliferation, terrorism, energy security, Afghanistan, Iraq, and even the Israeli-Palestinian conflict; and the fall of pro-American autocrats and continued instability in Egypt, Libya, and Tunisia.

From the outset of the Obama administration, decisionmakers in Tehran have reiterated that tactical changes in America's posture were insufficient to realign relations between the two countries. Changes in rhetoric, tone, and multilateral diplomatic participation were noted throughout the Islamic Republic. For the Iranian government, only a strategic shift by Washington that accepted Iran's role as a regional power within a broader collective security framework—unlikely in Iran's view, given concerted pushback by Israel, the U.S. Congress, and the Saudis—could break the U.S.-Iran stalemate.[7] Thus, going forward, Iran sees more short- to medium-term value in shelving the notion of full-scale rapprochement with America that Iranian reformists had entertained and instead pursuing the strategic objective of hastening Washington's military exit from the region. Barring an unforeseen increase in U.S. strategic flexibility, Iranian hard-liners seek a "codified rivalry"—one that will enable Iran to continue building soft power on the Arab street by maintaining its role as the region's leading critic of America and Israel (the status quo), while ensuring that the rivalry does not spill over into open military confrontation. Within the context of this codified rivalry, Tehran's interest in tactical collaboration with Washington may actually increase, as it perceives greater strategic parity with the U.S.-Israeli-Saudi status quo. Sanctions—both UN Security Council measures and American-led "coordinated national measures"—have hurt Iran's economic health writ large, yet decisionmakers in Tehran maintain their refusal to capitulate. As sanctions alone have failed to change Iran's strategic calculus, the Islamic Republic views greater parity in its rivalry vis-à-vis the United States—largely due to regional unrest and a demonstrated ability to indigenously enrich uranium to the 20 percent level. In this ongoing game of brinkmanship, Iran's hardened stance has involved trading escalatory measures with the United States.

Iran correctly estimated that Russia and China would not support additional UN Security Council sanctions in the short to medium term. Consequently, the U.S. and European Union strategy has focused on expanding coordinated national measures or sanctions by a "coalition of the willing" in an effort to show

Iran the cost of its policies. Convincing an already hesitant set of allies with long-standing economic ties to Iran—including Japan, South Korea, India, and South Africa—to adhere to another round of unilateral sanctions inevitably required the United States to strike diplomatic quid pro quos, reinvigorate direct diplomacy with Iran, and demonstrate a willingness to compromise on the nuclear file, all despite the domestic political constraints that a hostile Congress presents.[8] Against this backdrop, decisionmakers in Tehran are pushing a public narrative that frames recent popular protests in the Middle East as an Iran-inspired "Islamic Awakening." Privately, they acknowledge that the regional dynamic is far more fluid than their public narrative suggests and works against a status quo that produced tangible benefits for both Iranian and American interests. The Iranian government does see increased instability throughout the region as a way to deflect pressure and exploit fissures within the international community. To that end, Iran's stance toward the United States reflects how Tehran is simultaneously more worried than its public narrative conveys, but less isolated than the U.S.-led narrative of sanctions, Stuxnet computer virus, and secret assassinations suggest.[9]

IRANIAN SELF-PERCEPTION

While decisionmakers in Tehran see regional unrest (with the notable exception of Syria, as we discuss more fully below) as providing challenges and opportunities in the short to medium term, they remain cautious of their ability to draw long-lasting profit from the fall of pro-American dictatorships. In Iran's view, the U.S.-Israeli-Saudi alliance is in a decline set in motion by the invasion of Iraq and increasingly evident through regionwide protests, thus creating a power and leadership vacuum that the Islamic Republic seeks to fill. Although Iran has long anticipated this moment, it knows that there are additional contenders for power. It also understands how its ambitions could be thwarted both by the nature of the vacuum and by its own position in the region. As the only majority Shiite, Persian state in a region dominated by Sunnis and/or Arabs, Iran has historically suffered from an acute sense of strategic loneliness: it considers none of its regional allies to be "natural," and its experience with extraregional superpowers has left its decisionmakers convinced that their security depends on self-sufficiency. The notion that Iran is destined to be *primus inter pares* (first among equals) in regional decisionmaking is deeply ingrained in its identity, regardless of the system of governance or political leadership of the day. Iran sees itself as the odd man out in a region that it nevertheless seeks to lead.

Modern history has taught Iran that hard power alone will not facilitate regional leadership. Even though Tehran's Arab neighbors recognized Iranian military superiority in the 1970s, the late shah understood that he could neither obtain nor maintain a preeminent position in the Persian Gulf through arms and oil alone; Iran needed to be seen as a legitimate power in the eyes of the Arab street as well. The shah also realized that Iran could not forever treat the Arabs as enemies and counterbalance them through Iranian military dominance. Not only was a more conciliatory policy necessary to gain legitimacy for Iranian domination, but also befriending the Arabs was the most efficient way to guarantee Iran's long-term security. By the mid-1970s, Iran was at its peak. It had befriended Egypt, neutralized Iraq, quadrupled its oil income, and established its regional preeminence. Yet the shah never managed to bridge the Sunni-Shiite and Persian-Arab divides. To achieve that, soft power was needed, of which the shah's Iran was in short supply.[10]

The Iranian revolutionaries who took power in 1979 recognized this and sought to bridge the divide between Persians and Arabs through the ideology of political Islam. Although this strategy has been abysmally unsuccessful with ruling Arab elites, who feared the ideological force of the clerics more than the military force of the shah, Iran's promotion of political Islam and its anti-imperialist posture have won it respect on the Arab street. As such, Iran's self-perception of regional leadership is not based on military superiority, but rather on its political and financial investment in various regional movements and its ability to exploit popular frustration over domestic political issues and injustices in the region, such as the Israeli-Palestinian conflict.

RELATIONS WITH TURKEY

A significant challenge that Iran sees going forward is the emergence in the region of a foreign policy realignment by states that have traditionally followed America's lead. The impact of Turkey's shift is evident to Tehran: Turkish Prime Minister Recep Tayyip Erdoğan was the only world leader to poll higher among Arabs than Iranian President Mahmoud Ahmadinejad.[11] Despite growing economic and political cooperation, decisionmakers in Tehran know that competition over regional clout will test Turkish-Iranian ties in the long run. Thus, as the situation on the Arab street remains fluid, Iran has

prepared itself for the possibility that the balance of its competition and collaboration vis-à-vis Turkey may tilt toward the former.[12] Ankara and Tehran
both seek to become the preeminent arbiter in the region, and key differences
in their respective soft-power strategies are clear to each side. In contrast to
Iran's approach of exploiting popular frustration over regional injustices and
engaging political proxies, Turkey employs trade, investment, and a consistent
emphasis on diplomacy and international integration. Privately, Iranian officials acknowledge that Ankara's soft-power strategy is more appealing in the
long term: it serves Turkish national interests by securing new markets for
the country's growing economy without compromising the Islamic sentiment
of the ruling Justice and Development Party's political base; and it provides
Turkish decisionmakers with greater flexibility to use backroom or mega-
phone diplomacy, depending on the circumstance, in support of the current
push for peaceful democratic transitions.[13]

Postwar Iraq provides a compelling example of the growing competition between Iran and Turkey for regional influence. Policymakers and pundits in the
West regularly refer to Iran as the big winner of the Iraq War. Overthrowing
Saddam Hussein has removed a historical barrier to Iran's regional ambitions
and all but guaranteed a Shiite-dominated and Iran-friendly government in
Baghdad. It has also given Tehran a freer hand in the region and created a lucrative market for Iranian goods. Less noticed are the near-identical geopolitical
benefits that Turkey has gained since the American invasion. Turkey's significant political, economic, and cultural influence has steadily increased in Iraq,
as it rebalanced its strategic approach and maneuvered to fill the power vacuum
created by the United States.[14] Unlike Iran, however, Turkey has been able
to increase its influence in Iraq—and by extension work against the U.S.-
Israeli-Saudi status quo alliance without the burden of historical mistrust
(the Iran-Iraq War), international hostility (sanctions, the nuclear impasse),
or democracy deficits (Turkey's democratic model versus Iran's model of mil-
itaristic theocracy). Unsurprisingly, Iranian decisionmakers have been somewhat irritated by Ankara's ability to "hijack" the anti-status-quo mantle of
change.

In addition to Turkey's more balanced projection of soft power, Erdoğan's
public criticisms of Israel—and concrete Turkish efforts to put Israel on the
defensive—have won the Turks strong admiration on the Arab street. One
observer in Tehran quipped to one of the authors that Iran had done all the
groundwork "in the resistance against Israel," but that at the last minute the

Turks stole the show. Turkey's comprehensive soft power in the region, including cultural affinity, economic ties, a balanced approach toward Israel,
and the example of a democratic government that allows for the assertion of
Islamic identity, presents Iran with a major challenge in any future competition for leadership in the region.[15] Insofar as Turkey's new assertive foreign
policy continues to challenge the U.S.-Israeli-Saudi alliance in the long run,
Iran will feel the uniqueness of its regional position—and its source of soft
power—to be increasingly at risk.

Nevertheless, although Turkey's brand of Islamic democracy and its "zero
problems" regional policies provide an appealing model for many Arabs,
Tehran is not entirely convinced that Ankara's soft-power strategy is trans-
ferable beyond the short to medium term. Turkey may be limited to solu-
tions that play to its strengths (diplomacy, business, NATO membership)
rather than competing in the spheres of its rivals in the United States, Israel,
Saudi Arabia (military superiority, maintaining the status quo), or Iran (political proxies, championing the disenfranchised). It is also open to accusations of hypocrisy. Turkey was one of the first countries to call for Husni
Mubarak's resignation, urged dialogue and restraint in dealing with a recal-
citrant Muammar al-Gadafi, and has suffered from a degree of strategic
paralysis on the upheaval in Syria. It remains to be seen how perceived Turkish double standards will play on the Arab street. But Iran sees a Turkish
rival that will face the increasingly difficult challenge of balancing its interests
with its values—a challenge not entirely different from the paradigm that
has seemingly trapped the Islamic Republic's rivals in Washington, Tel Aviv,
and Riyadh—while trapping Iran in the same problem in Syria.

RELATIONS WITH EGYPT

As Iran jockeys for regional preeminence, Egypt will become a new geopolitical
battlefield for its soft-power projection. Widely regarded as the beacon of the
Arab world, Egypt is also the wild card that can potentially tip the scales in
favor of any one of these three aspiring regional hegemons (Iran, Egypt, and
Turkey). It is already being pulled in three very different directions. Egyptians
took an important step toward democracy with the toppling of Mubarak, but
many daunting challenges remain—not least of which is the fact that each of
the key Egyptian leaders serving in the Supreme Council of the Armed Forces
was a high-level member of the Mubarak regime.[16] A transition to democracy

through free and fair elections was promised, but concerns linger regarding the demonstrably nondemocratic behavior exhibited by the council on issues including freedom of the press, freedom of assembly, and unilateral decrees limiting the power of the parliament and the presidency. Precisely because Egypt remains in flux, and domestic stability in the short to medium term is unlikely, Iranian decisionmakers see an opportunity to exert regional influence while capitalizing on Egypt's inward orientation.

Following Mubarak's fall, Egypt's status as "bulwark of the regional status quo" shifted to "foreign policy in flux" almost overnight. That alone has created new challenges for the U.S.-Israeli-Saudi alliance, each of which Tehran readily appreciates. Once the trio's most staunch regional partner, Egypt is now transitioning in such a way that its inward focus does not allow for the diplomatic bandwidth to comprehensively address the myriad issues it faces; and the shifting trajectory of post-Mubarak Egypt does not track entirely with Egypt's Mubarak-era foreign policy preferences. In an effort to keep any future Egyptian government as a close ally, the United States has pledged more than $2 billion in debt relief and investment assistance in addition to the mammoth yearly aid package of approximately $1.5 billion.[17] Conversely, the Egyptian government banned numerous American nongovernmental organizations and indicted their employees—many of whom were American citizens.

The Saudi government had also provided the Mubarak regime with a steady flow of aid. After Mubarak's overthrow, the House of Saud announced a $4 billion aid package for Egypt—a not-so-subtle reminder to the Mubarak-era officials still in power that patronage is readily available and that it can be withdrawn just as easily as it is offered if future Egyptian policies stray too far from the status quo.[18] For its part, the Supreme Council has pledged to honor all regional and international obligations and treaties (read: Egypt's peace treaty with Israel). Israeli Prime Minister Benjamin Netanyahu welcomed this announcement. Thus, it may seem that Egypt has changed leaders rather than policies, but politicians know that policy differences with their population were the impetus for Mubarak's demise—thus making the status quo policies dangerously unsustainable.

Iran views various decisions made by Egypt's post–Arab Spring government as improvements over the entrenched Mubarak-era antagonism. Opening the Rafah crossing into the Gaza Strip, allowing Iranian warships to pass through the Suez Canal, working gradually toward improving Iran-Egypt relations, and enabling an increased presence of the Muslim Brotherhood in

Egypt's parliament are four notable policy shifts that, if nothing else, demonstrate an Iran that faces less isolation to its west. The Islamic Republic benefits from any degree of independence in Egyptian foreign policy. Moreover, despite Egypt's status as the beacon of the Arab world, its current instability prevents it from exercising its full influence in the region. Before Egypt can recalibrate, a sustainable domestic political homeostasis must be achieved. Until then, Iran will try to foster relations with new political actors and in turn increase the likelihood that one less regional actor conforms to U.S.-Israel-Saudi efforts to contain it. Still, initial expectations in Tehran that Egypt would restore diplomatic relations with Iran have yet to materialize.

Taking a page from its rivals' playbooks, Turkey is trying to split the difference between monetary and political support for post-Mubarak Egypt. Iran believes that Turkish policymakers are both worried about the economic repercussions that widespread regional unrest can cause and confident about the opportunity to enhance their regional influence. While Turkey's peaceful approach to resolving regional unrest is genuine, decisionmakers in Tehran also see Ankara's strategy as politically and economically expedient. For Turkey's impressive economic growth to persist—and Erdoğan's Justice and Development Party to remain popular at home—regional unrest and conflict must abate to maintain an environment conducive to low political and economic risk. If instability intensifies and oil prices remain over $100 a barrel, Turkey's economy might suffer as foreign and domestic investors move their money to safer locations. To that end, Iranian decisionmakers see their Turkish counterparts trying to balance interests and values as part of a longer-term strategy. The Iranians themselves are not overly concerned with Ankara's efforts in the near term, given Tehran's cautious and reactive approach and its dependence on the limitations of others.

RELATIONS WITH SYRIA

Where Iran's regional strategy runs into the most trouble is in Syria, as the mass protests and human rights abuses there are shaking the stability of Iran's closest regional ally and undermining support for Iran among the Arab masses. The theocratic Islamic Republic of Iran has maintained a three-decade-long alliance with secular, socialist, Baathist Syria—perhaps the most enduring alliance between Middle Eastern countries since the end of World War II. There is perhaps no better demonstration of Iranian readiness to sacrifice ideology in favor of more practical strategic interests. Iran sees its relations with Syria as a marriage of convenience with a fellow authoritarian country that is willing to assume steep political and economic costs to maintain domestic control and independence from foreign powers. To that end, as the Syrian government faces an unprecedented uprising, it has used brute force in an effort to force protesters into submission. This use of force has been even more oppressive than the Iranian government's suppression of protests that followed the country's contested 2009 presidential election.

In the context of Tehran's geopolitical rivalry, the case of Syria reveals a strong measure of hypocrisy—and a battle over regional positioning. Prior to the Arab Spring, Tehran watched as the U.S.-Israeli-Saudi alliance forged a cold peace with Damascus over the five years following Syria's 2005 withdrawal from Lebanon. There were significant changes after Obama took office: America slowly engaged the Syrian government and reinstated its ambassador in Damascus; Israel participated in Turkish-mediated peace talks with Syria, only to have Syria withdraw to protest Israel's 2008–2009 bombardment of Gaza; and Saudi Arabia repaired its strained relationship with Syria in an effort to ensure that differences over Iran and Lebanon did not impede cooperation in Iraq, Yemen, and elsewhere in the region.

In the wake of regional unrest, however, Tehran has seen notable shifts in each actor's strategy. Washington has all but abandoned its efforts to engage the Syrian government, with Obama saying in no uncertain terms, "President [Bashar al-]Assad now has a choice: he can lead that transition [to democracy], or get out of the way."[19] Accusations of hypocrisy have been heard at home and abroad due to America's comparative silence toward Saudi-supported repression in Bahrain—with Tehran leading the charge (and with no regard for Tehran's own hypocrisy in supporting protesters in Bahrain while supporting the oppression in Syria). Iranian decisionmakers see their Israeli and Saudi counterparts following America's lead and pushing a regime change policy in Syria to strengthen the containment of Iran and weaken its regional standing.

A key component of Iran's deterrence vis-à-vis a military attack on its nuclear facilities and its foothold in the predominantly Arab Middle East revolves around supporting the Assad regime, which has long served as a political, financial, and military hub for Hizbullah, Hamas, and Palestinian Islamic Jihad. When the Arab Spring hit Syria, Iran's support for the regional uprisings reached its red line, and the U.S-Israeli-Saudi alliance has since sought to take advantage. In an attempt to weaken Iran's regional standing—and by extension, its deterrent capabilities—Saudi Arabia and Israel have declared their support for the prodemocracy movement in Syria.[20] As the Saudis and Israelis ramp up their overt and covert regime change activities in Syria, Iran will likely pursue much more aggressive regional policies—particularly in Iraq, Bahrain, and Lebanon—to rebalance its regional power networks and deterrence infrastructure. Iran will go to great lengths to work against international intervention and democratic transition in Syria. Decisionmakers in Tehran would prefer that Assad remain in power, but for reasons predicated on Realpolitik, they will settle for preserving Syria's governing elite and security forces should Assad fall.

Iran's own hypocrisy when it comes to Syria has rendered it difficult for the Islamic Republic to fully capitalize on American, Israeli, and Saudi policies toward the Arab Spring. The United States has been at the forefront of crying foul, accusing Iran of aiding Syrian government repression.[21] On this point, Obama did not mince his words: "And this speaks to the hypocrisy of the Iranian regime, which says it stands for the rights of protesters abroad, yet represses its own people at home. Let's remember that the first peaceful protests in the region were in the streets of Tehran."[22] The postelection protests in Iran served as an unexpected precursor to the Arab Spring, because they highlighted the indifference of regimes throughout the region to the long-standing political, economic, and social aspirations of the people. Just as geopolitical concerns have determined Iran's response to uprisings across the region, political realism limits Iran's ability to win hearts and minds on an Arab street that seeks an end to the authoritarian governments that the Iranian regime itself resembles in many respects.

At best, Iran sees an opportunity to maintain a semblance of the status quo in its alliance with Syria: together they stand a better chance to survive and achieve their long-term goals. Syria wants to regain the Golan Heights from Israel and maintain its influence in Lebanese politics, both goals that are aided by Iranian support for Hamas and Hizbullah, which maintain instability on Israel's flanks and increase the costs of Israel's occupation. In return, Syria aids the Islamic Republic's quest to assume preeminence in the Persian Gulf by helping to neutralize Israeli capabilities and American encroachment. Any change in Syria's governing elite increases the likelihood that Damascus will adopt regional policies more in line with those of its Arab brethren, such as support for Sunni political forces in Iraq. It could also lead to Syria becoming a full-fledged Saudi client. That could strip Iran of its strongest Arab ally. The Islamic Republic would prefer to see a weakened version of the Assad regime remain in power; such a scenario hedges against Damascus swinging toward the United States and increases Syrian dependence on Iranian support.

For decisionmakers in Tehran, there is perhaps no greater long-term challenge to the stability of their Syrian alliance than Turkey. While the U.S.-Israeli-Saudi alliance is limited in its capacity to influence events on the ground in Syria, Iran sees neighboring Turkey as uniquely able to leverage the Assad regime's strategic calculus—and being increasingly willing to do so. Prior to the Arab Spring, Syria epitomized Turkey's zero problems foreign policy in the region. Political cooperation between the neighboring countries facilitated substantial trade relations, including the construction of infrastructure to cement long-term connectivity. Nevertheless, after protracted shuttle diplomacy, Ankara's efforts to utilize its soft power in Syria have been unable to foster a nonviolent compromise solution. Now, Tehran sees a heavy expenditure of political capital—and inevitable accusations of hypocrisy—taking a toll on Turkish decisionmakers and causing them to shift strategies. Just as Turkey eventually came to support NATO intervention in Libya, the Erdoğan government has recalibrated the balance of its interests and values in a shift away from the Assad regime. To that end, Ankara has publicly pronounced its willingness to take in Syrian government defectors, deliver relief aid to protesters inside Syria, and consider a military-enforced humanitarian buffer zone on the Syrian side of the border.[23] Herein lie the limitations of Tehran's strategy: as Turkey attempts to shift the region's balance of power, Iran's cautious and reactive approach and its increased economic dependence on Ankara restrict it from taking innovative countermeasures.

However, the geopolitical paradox on Syria cuts both ways: sustained violence by the Assad regime benefits neither Iran, Syria's closest regional ally, nor its rivals. An increased degree and duration of regime brutality damages Iran's soft-power standing on the Arab street—and increases the likelihood of foreign intervention that would further Iran's isolation. Conversely, Tehran sees a gap between the discourse of its rivals and their willingness to act. Both Washington (and thus by extension, Riyadh and Tel Aviv) and Ankara are reluctant to take action in Syria without UN consent that provides multilateral support and international legitimacy.

Barring a strategic shift (far from guaranteed at the time of this writing), the United States prefers to "lead from behind," Turkey does not want to "own" the Syrian crisis and the bulk of any military operations, and both are reluctant to confront Russian patronage to Syria for fear of geopolitical retribution—Russia is critical to both America's efforts to curb Iran's nuclear program and Turkey's natural gas imports. In an effort to maintain this delicate balance, Tehran will likely stress to its counterparts in Damascus the need to reduce violence and engage in United Nations–led peace efforts—where Russia and China can help prevent the kind of foreign intervention that would tip the scales against Iran's interests.

HIGH STAKES

While Iran has longed for the decline of American preeminence in the Middle East, this moment has paradoxically presented a more arduous challenge than Tehran anticipated. Despite showing significant ideological flexibility in the past, Iran knows that its ability to adjust to new realities over the long term is limited. A more democratic Middle East would highlight Iran's own political, economic, and social shortcomings; a more autocratic region would continue using Shiite Iran as a pretext for its own domestic crackdowns. In the short to medium term, however, regional unrest puts Iran's adversaries on the defensive and plays to one of Iran's demonstrated strengths: the ability to exploit instability and division. After revolution, eight years of war with Iraq, and international isolation, the Iranian government has an inclination for managed disorder that tends to hamstring its rivals. Iran is seeking to leverage new working relationships with the Arab street that capitalize on both the declining U.S.-Israeli-Saudi status quo and Turkey's newfound balancing act. Serious complications in Syria, however, demonstrate the limitations in Tehran's approach beyond the interim. Iran's geopolitical strategy— to consolidate the Islamic Republic as a regional power undaunted by Western objections—has taken one step forward and two steps back, despite opportunities provided by the challenges facing its rivals. Iran has marginally improved ties with Egypt and haphazardly managed its working relationships with most others in the Muslim world, even if Saudi Arabia and Bahrain remain fearful of Shiite power. Iran's nuclear program continues to make slow but steady progress, and its satellite launches have demonstrated its missile capabilities—but at no small cost to its overall economic health. Iran shows no sign of capitulating to the West's pressure-based approach to relations, but it remains open to negotiating incentives, and decisionmakers in Tehran are trying to leverage the Arab Spring to reduce pressure. For example, by indigenously enriching uranium to the 20 percent level, Iran has raised the stakes. The West is also faced with confrontation at a level that it does not have the ability to address easily, particularly at a time of widespread regional unrest. To that end, the Islamic Republic does have leverage in its quest for regional influence.

For Iran, winning the Arab street—and by extension, regional dominance—will require a projection of soft power that advances aspirations for political, economic, and social freedoms. Real-time developments in Egypt and Syria provide compelling opportunities that Iran would do well to seize. Decisionmakers in Tehran think that the U.S.-Israeli-Saudi alliance still lacks the ability to adapt to fast-paced transition but maintains enough military and economic clout to decelerate changes that many nevertheless consider inevitable. Iran acknowledges that Turkey possesses a more compelling political and economic model for the Arab street, but it is betting (precariously) on Ankara's status as an emerging power to force it to balance—and in more complex scenarios choose between—interests and values. In this high-stakes game of geopolitical poker, Iran's rivals have a better hand, but the better hand does not always win.

The Islamic Republic's strategy is reactive in nature and predicated on patience, largely because its ability to be proactive is limited. Because the primary concern for decisionmakers in Tehran is regime survival, they fear the unpredictable consequences of proactive decisionmaking at home and abroad. Iran's own internal challenges reinforce its reactive posture. It displays less foresight than cognizance. The Islamic Republic is not happy with how its geopolitical battle for the Arab street has played out thus far—but it is not panicking either. Its rivals also face long-term challenges with little indication of having sustainable answers.

As the regional political climate changes, so too must the various actors trying to shape its future. Legitimate regional preeminence can be achieved only if popular will allows it to be. To date, neither Iran nor its rivals have effectively championed—in both words *and* deeds—the political, economic, and social freedoms sought by the majority of the region's populations. Unless one or more of the actors in this rivalry shifts its strategy accordingly, competition in the region will likely intensify. Asserting power will increasingly involve protecting interests and blocking perceived enemies. With no discernible shifts in the offing–and decisionmakers in Tehran prioritizing their own survival above all else—Iran will likely continue to operate on the premise that its best offense is a good defense.

NOTES

1. Islamic Republic News Agency, "Text of Khamenei's Speech to Iranian Government Officials," August 19, 2009.

2. Reza Marashi, "Why Sanctions Against Iran Won't Work," *Salon*, June 4, 2011, http://www.salon.com/news/politics/war_room/2011/06/04/iran_sanctions.

3. Reuters, "WikiLeaks: Iran Tried to Recruit Sinai Bedouin to Smuggle Arms into Gaza," *Haaretz*, December 16, 2010, http://www.haaretz.com/news /diplomacy-defense/wikileaks-iran-tried-to-recruit-sinai-bedouin-to-smuggle -arms-into-gaza-1.330983.

4. Barak Ravid, Jack Khoury, and the Associated Press, "Israeli Diplomatic Staff and Families Evacuated After Egyptians Storm Embassy in Cairo," *Haaretz*, September 10, 2011, http://www.haaretz.com/news/diplomacy-defense /israeli-diplomatic-staff-and-families-evacuated-after-egyptians-storm-embassy -in-cairo-1.383588. Avi Bar-Eli and Reuters, "Egypt Cancels Natural Gas Deal with Israel," *Haaretz*, April 23, 2012, http://www.haaretz.com/news/diplomacy -defense/egypt-cancels-natural-gas-deal-with-israel-1.425883.

5. Matthew Duss, "Letter from Herzliya, Neocon Woodstock," *The Nation*, February 14, 2011, http://www.thenation.com/article/158547/letter-herzliya-neocon -woodstock.

6. Helene Cooper and Mark Landler, "Interests of Saudi Arabia and Iran Collide, with the U.S. in the Middle," *New York Times*, March 17, 2011, http://www .nytimes.com/2011/03/18/world/18diplomacy.html.

7. "Text of Khamenei's Speech to U.S. President," BBC, March 22, 2009.

8. Reza Marashi, "The Political Psychology of Obama's Iran Policy," *Muftah*, January 6, 2012, http://muftah.org/?p=2505.

9. Reza Marashi, "Iran Raises the Stakes: The Istanbul Talks and Iran's Political Psychology," NIAC Iran Working Paper Series, February 23, 2011, http:// www.payvand.com/news/11/feb/1236.html.

10. Trita Parsi, "Whither the Persian-Jewish Alliance?," bitterlemons -international.org, December 16, 2004, http://www.bitterlemons-international .org/inside.php?id=263.

11. Shibley Telhami, "2011 Annual Arab Public Opinion Survey," Brookings Institution, November 21, 2011.

12. Interview with Iranian-government-affiliated think tank, May 28, 2011.

13. Ibid.

14. Anthony Shadid, "Resurgent Turkey Flexes Its Muscles Around Iraq," *New York Times*, January 4, 2011, http://www.nytimes.com/2011/01/05/world /middleeast/05turkey.html.

15. See, for instance, the effect of Turkish soap operas on the Arab population. Nadia Bilbassy-Charters, "Leave It to Turkish Soap Operas to Conquer Hearts and Minds," *Foreign Policy*, April 15, 2010, http://mideast.foreignpolicy.com/posts /2010/04/15/leave_it_to_turkish_soap_operas_to_conquer_hearts_and_minds.

16. "Egypt's Military Leadership," Al Jazeera, February 11, 2011, http://www .aljazeera.com/news/middleeast/2011/02/201121185311711502.html.

17. Helene Cooper and Ethan Bronner, "Focus Is on Obama as Tensions Soar Across Mideast," *New York Times*, May 18, 2011, http://www.nytimes.com /2011/05/19/world/middleeast/19diplo.html.

18. Una Galani, "Saudi $4 Bln Lifeline to Egypt Won't Come for Free," Reuters, May 23, 2011, http://blogs.reuters.com/columns/2011/05/23/saudi -4-bln-lifeline-to-egypt-wont-come-for-free/.

19. "Obama Speech Text: Middle East Has 'A Choice Between Hate and Hope,'" *Los Angeles Times*, May 19, 2011, http://latimesblogs.latimes.com/washington /2011/05/obama-israel-mideast-speech-text.html,

20. For Saudi Arabia, see Joseph Logan, "Saudi Switch Against Syria's Assad Is Blow to Iran," Reuters, August 9, 2011, http://www.reuters.com/article/2011 /08/09/us-saudi-syria-idUSTRE7781QS20110809. For Israel, see Associated Press, "In Shift, Israeli Leaders Say It Is Time for Syria's Assad to Step Down," *Washington Post*, April 27, 2012, http://world.foxnews.mobi/quickPage.html ?page=26154&content=71099572&pageNum=-1.

21. Ariel Zirulnick, "U.S. Officials: Iran Helping Syria's Assad Put Down Protests," *Christian Science Monitor*, April 14, 2011, http://www.csmonitor.com /World/terrorism-security/2011/0414/US-officials-Iran-helping-Syria-s-Assad -put-down-protests.

22. "Obama Speech Text."

23. Borzou Daragahi, "Turkey Breaks with Syria over Crackdown," *Los Angeles Times*, June 17, 2011, http://articles.latimes.com/2011/jun/17/world/la-fg-turkey -syria-20110617.

8

Turkey and the Arab Spring: Ideological Promotion in a Revolutionary Era

MARK L. HAAS

A LTHOUGH TURKEY DURING the Arab Spring did not experience the domestic upheaval that many of its Middle Eastern neighbors did, the revolutionary developments of 2011 and 2012 did result in major changes in Turkey's international relations.[1] Most notably, Turkish leaders' Middle Eastern policies became increasingly ideological as the Arab Spring progressed, with a growing focus on democracy promotion in the region as a central strategy for promoting Turkey's interests. This objective, among other important outcomes, led to major frictions with Syria and Iran and to a tightening of relations with key allies, especially the United States.

The primary objective of this chapter is to explain these developments. My analysis will proceed in two main steps. First, I will provide a theoretical argument that accounts for why leaders often believe that the spread of their ideological principles to other countries is likely to benefit their interests. Second, I will detail how Turkey's policies in response to the Arab Spring largely support this analysis, thereby demonstrating the frequent centrality of ideologies to states' most important international decisions. I will conclude the chapter with a summary of major findings.

Ideological Exportation and States' Security

Turkish leaders' policies during the first few months of the Arab Spring were inconsistent. After large-scale popular protests began in Egypt in January 2011, Prime Minister Recep Tayyip Erdoğan was one of the first foreign leaders to call for Husni Mubarak's resignation and for the initiation of major political reforms. President Abdullah Gül was also the first head of state to meet with the Egyptian Supreme Council of the Armed Forces, which governed the country after Mubarak's ouster, and other Turkish leaders after the revolution promised close strategic ties with the new government. Foreign Minister Ahmet Davutoğlu, for example, asserted that Turkey wanted to create an "axis of democracy" with Egypt as it transitioned from an authoritarian to a democratic regime.[2]

Turkish leaders' reactions to the Libyan uprisings that began in February 2011 were, however, much different. The Turkish government did not cooperate with UN-mandated efforts to freeze Muammar al-Gadafi's assets, and in February and March Turkish leaders openly opposed the creation by NATO forces of a no-fly zone designed to protect Libyan civilians from their government. Turkey, as Prime Minister Erdoğan put it, rejected "the foreign intervention in friend and brother Libya."[3] Even after NATO air strikes began in March, Ankara continued to argue against the use of force and instead pushed for a cease-fire so that Gadafi could implement political reforms. Only in May 2011 did Erdoğan advocate that Gadafi surrender power and leave Libya. This position came well after almost all other governments in the region had adopted this position.[4]

Turkey's leaders demonstrated a similar reticence to support the uprisings in Syria, at least during their first few months. These policymakers originally opposed international intervention in Syria on behalf of the protesters and instead recommended that any reforms be initiated and controlled by the Bashar al-Assad regime. The Turkish government even put its prestige on the line by sending senior officials to Damascus to meet with Assad. These officials subsequently vouched for the Syrian dictator's reformist intentions and credentials.[5] Turkey's politicians, in sum, sometimes were in the vanguard advocating regime change during the Arab Spring and other times were openly opposed to revolutionary forces, especially during the early stages of protests.

By August 2011, however, Turkey's leaders had become much more consistently and forcefully supportive of democracy promotion in Syria. This
change contradicted a number of contemporaneous predictions. Prominent
analysts in the summer of 2011 forecasted that Turkey would not pursue
ideology-based policies in cases, like Syria, that would jeopardize major material
interests.[6] Outcomes, though, turned out to be very different from these predictions. As scholar of Turkish politics Tarik Oğuzlu explained, "As the crisis
deteriorated in Syria [over the summer of 2011], Turkish leaders made it clear
that Turkey desires to see a more democratic, representative and plural order
taking root." Importantly, this preference was part of a regional strategy that
placed renewed emphasis on the spread of democracy as a key precondition for
positive relations with Turkey: "The discourse adopted by Turkish statesmen
suggests that Turkey's neighbors need to transform in a way to respond to the
society's demands and, most importantly, search for good governance if they
want to earn Turkey's friendship and cooperation."[7] Şaban Kardaş expressed
similar analysis (writing in the fall of 2011): "A conspicuous aspect of Turkey's
response [to the Arab Spring] has been the increasing salience of democratic
principles in the making of Turkey's regional policy.... Turkey over time abandoned its resistance to regime change and embraced and even openly advocated
a democracy promotion agenda."[8]

Why would Turkey's leaders pursue increasingly ideology-based foreign
policies when the costs of these actions were likely to be quite high (as I detail
below)? What, in other words, were the likely benefits for Turkey of democracy promotion? In order to answer these questions, we must first understand
how political ideologies systematically shape states' security interests. I will
then demonstrate how Turkey's foreign policies as the Arab Spring progressed
were consistent with these fundamental patterns.

I define ideologies as leaders' preferences for ordering the political world.
Ideologies, in other words, reflect the core institutional, economic, and social
goals that politicians try to realize or preserve in their states.[9] Do politicians,
for example, advocate for their country the creation or continuation of representative or authoritarian political institutions? Capitalist or socialist economies? Theocratic or secular values? Full rights of citizenship for some or full
rights for all groups in their state? Prominent ideologies include communism,
fascism, liberalism, monarchism, and religious fundamentalism.

Leaders' ideological beliefs have major implications not only for domestic
politics, but also for foreign policies. The literature on ideologies and interna-

tional relations indicates that significant ideological differences dividing states' leaders can affect their international decisions by shaping their *understandings of the threats* that they pose to one another's interests.[10] Ideological differences shape leaders' threat perceptions and consequent foreign policies by two main pathways. First, ideological differences play a key role in affecting *how leaders assess one another's international intentions.* The greater the ideological differences dividing decisionmakers, the more likely they are to assume the worst about one another's objectives. Ideological enemies tend to believe that conflict between them is in the long run inevitable. Even if ideological rivals in the present exhibit no hostility toward one another—or are even currently cooperating with one another—leaders will often assume that such amicability is temporary and is bound to be replaced eventually with overt animosity.

Second, large ideological differences are likely to shape leaders' threat perceptions by *affecting their understandings of the dangers to their most important domestic interests*—namely, the preservation of their political power and the regime type they support. The greater the ideological differences dividing decisionmakers in different states, the greater their fears of domestic subversion are likely to be. Leaders will tend to worry that the success of ideological enemies abroad will be contagious, ultimately boosting the political fortunes of like-minded individuals at home, even to the point of revolution. The tendency for developments in one country to spur or inspire similar outcomes elsewhere is known as "demonstration effects." This tendency helps explain why revolutions often cluster in time, including those in Europe in 1848 and the "color" revolutions in Eastern Europe in the 2000s, as well the Arab Spring. Reinforcing the fears of subversion due to the power of demonstration effects is the proclivity for politicians to assume that international ideological rivals will provide aid to the latter's ideological allies throughout the system in an attempt to promote political change in targeted states. In these ways, international ideological competitions tend to be translated into domestic struggles for power and legitimacy.

The opposite threat relationships often hold for states' leaders who are dedicated to similar ideological beliefs. Policymakers who share core ideological principles are likely both to interpret one another's international intentions in a mostly favorable light and to believe their domestic interests to be interconnected. On this last point, leaders will often view the success of ideological allies abroad as a boost to their domestic interests; success of particular ideological beliefs in other countries will likely increase their legitimacy and popularity at home. Conversely, when co-ideologues are weakened abroad, this development increases the likelihood of similar outcomes domestically. Trust in others' international intentions and beliefs in the interconnectedness of domestic interests have often resulted in significant cooperation among proponents of multiple ideological groups, including among liberals, monarchists, fascists, religious fundamentalists, and even communists.[11]

The preceding effects of ideologies on leaders' threat perceptions shape their foreign policies in key ways. Among the most important of these is an enhanced, security-based interest in ideological exportation. Because leaders tend to believe that hostilities with ideological enemies is in the long run unavoidable and cooperation with ideological allies likely, they will view the conversion of ideological rivals to their own legitimating principles as a way of reducing the number of enemies in the system and increasing the number of allies. Fears of subversion to the principles of international ideological enemies add domestic incentives to work for the spread of one's principles abroad. Taken together, these beliefs explain why politicians of virtually all ideological beliefs—monarchical, liberal, fascist, communist, and religious fundamentalist—have attempted to export, including by force, their defining ideological principles and institutions.[12]

The incentives for regime promotion abroad are likely to be particularly powerful during periods that John M. Owen labels ones of high "ideological polarization," which he defines as the "progressive segregation of a population into two or more [ideological] sets, each of which cooperates internally and excludes externally."[13] Ideological polarization is most likely to occur when elites in various countries are dedicated to different ideological beliefs (i.e., there is not large agreement across states that one particular set of ideological principles is clearly superior to others), and states (either one's own or others) are vulnerable to regime change or war occurs that makes such domestic change more likely.

The vulnerability of regimes during periods of high ideological polarization is the key factor that magnifies the incentives for states to try to export their ideological principles. If state X that is dedicated to ideology A is susceptible to revolution to ideology B, adherents to A and B in other countries will have a strong security interest in seeing their co-ideologues emerge victorious in X. Proponents of ideology A in other states will fear that a revolution to ideology B in state X will result in a reduction of their international influence (including the loss of a likely ally), as well as a probable gain in influence (including the creation of a likely ally) for proponents of ideology B in other countries. The same calculations will create incentives for supporters of ideology B abroad to aid revolutionary forces in state X. The fluidity of internal politics in domestically vulnerable states, in sum, will tend to push leaders in other countries to view outcomes as a security gain or a loss for either themselves or their ideological rivals. Spain's revolutionary domestic situation from 1936 to 1938, for example, pushed both fascist Germany and Italy and communist Russia to spend considerable resources on ideological exportation in these years. Both sets of powers believed that the ideological outcome of the Spanish Civil War would have major international effects, most notably on Spain's choices of allies and enemies.

To put the preceding analysis another way, when states are vulnerable to revolution, representatives of rival ideological beliefs in other countries are caught in an "ideological security dilemma."[14] Successful regime change from ideology A to ideology B in state X will tend to make proponents of B in other countries more secure. The more B's ideological principles spread, the fewer the ideological enemies in the system. B's increase in security, though, will make proponents of ideology A less secure. The greater the number of governments that are dedicated to ideology B, the more proponents of A will feel surrounded by ideological enemies. Given these anticipated outcomes resulting from the ideological contest in state X, proponents of ideology A will confront powerful incentives to interfere in X to maintain the ideological—and thus security—status quo, while B will be inclined to interfere to take advantage of a newly created opportunity to increase international influence and security at A's expense.

It is worth highlighting that the preceding incentives that push states to try to promote their principles in ideologically contested regimes will exist even if the former are not themselves particularly vulnerable to regime change (this is the case for Turkey during the Arab Spring era). Others' ideological vulnerability increases the likelihood of states gaining or losing an ally or enemy depending on the ideological outcomes in each of these domestic contests. The incentives for ideological exportation, though, will become even more powerful if the exporting state is plagued by internal ideological divisions. When governments are themselves vulnerable to regime change, they will fear that revolution abroad will increase the likelihood of revolution at home. These states, as a result, will confront powerful domestic-based incentives (in addition to the security-based ones discussed above) to try to boost the power of co-ideologues in other countries.

TURKEY'S INTEREST IN IDEOLOGICAL PROMOTION DURING THE ARAB SPRING

Although the focus of this chapter is on Turkish leaders' interest in regime exportation during the Arab Spring, it is worth noting that Turkey's policy-makers pushed for the spread of democracy in neighboring countries based on the Turkish "model" well before the revolutionary developments of 2011 and 2012. President Turgut Özal of the Motherland Party, for example, asserted in 1991 that Turkey's regime type is "a good example for the rest of the Islamic world. . . . Our experience with economic reform in the past 10 to 11 years . . . and also our experience in the past 45 of democracy" will allow Turkey to become an ideological inspiration for others.[15] A year later Prime Minister Süleyman Demirel of the True Path Party declared that "Turkey is commit-ted to being a model [for former Soviet Republics] of democracy, rule of law, tolerance, respect for human rights and economic liberties." In 1993, Demirel stated that "in Central Asia we are the emissaries of Europe. We are the Eu-ropeans who are taking European values to Central Asia."[16] Tansu Çiller (also of the True Path Party) made similar statements after she became prime min-ister in 1993.[17] Çiller often told U.S. and other Western politicians that there were "essentially two models in the Islamic world: Turkey and Iran," and that it was a major interest for Western states to support Turkey in this ideological struggle.[18] The policies of ideological exportation in reaction to the Arab Spring were thus not new; they were a continuation of long-standing prefer-ences, spanning numerous Turkish political parties, in existence since at least the end of the cold war. This fact is important because it demonstrates the systematic effects that ideologies tend to have on states' security policies. An-alyzing Turkish leaders' reactions to the Arab Spring both confirms and helps us understand these enduring tendencies of international politics.

Turkey during the era of the Arab Spring was governed by the Justice and Development Party (JDP), which first came to power in 2002. JDP leaders were some of the most forceful advocates of political liberalization in Turkey's history. JDP policymakers, for example, adopted the UN Charter of Human Rights and the European Charter for the Protection of Human Rights and

Basic Liberties as core ideological references for the party.[19] These politicians also passed major liberalizing reforms in a number of areas, including freedoms of expression, association, assembly, and religion; the prevention of torture; minority rights; and civil-military relations.[20] Much of this legislation was designed to alter Turkish domestic politics in order to meet the criteria necessary for Turkey to join the European Union (EU).

As with their predecessors, JDP leaders in the 2000s also called for liberalization in neighboring regions, especially the Middle East, as a key means of improving Turkey's security. Indeed, from virtually the time of their ascension to power in 2002, JDP politicians, as Philip Robins summarizes, committed themselves to be "proselytizers of democratization among the membership of the [Organization of the Islamic Conference]."[21] These policymakers, according to scholar Aysegul Sever, believed that "an improvement in democracy, economy, and human rights in the Middle East [would result in] . . . improvements in the regional security situation. The [JDP] government agreed that a democratic Middle East with a well-functioning socio-economic system would serve Turkish security interests."[22]

Although JDP leaders before the Arab Spring repeatedly both declared an interest in the spread of democracy as a means of advancing Turkey's interests and dedicated important resources toward realizing this objective, there were significant limits to these policies.[23] Two factors were particularly important in reducing these politicians' push for liberalization in the Middle East. The first resulted from a combination of relatively high levels of trust and a norm against threatening fellow Muslim-majority countries, even if these countries were illiberal in terms of their domestic politics.

The JDP was established largely by reformers who were members of Islamist parties (Welfare and Virtue) that had been banned from political activity by Turkey's Constitutional Court in 1998 and 2001, respectively. Although JDP leaders were much more liberal politically than their Islamist predecessors, the advancement of Islamic identity and interests remained more central to these individuals' worldview than that possessed by almost all other governing parties in Turkey's history. As scholar M. Hakan Yavuz explains, "Most ministers, advisors and parliamentarians of the AKP [JDP] stress Islam as their core identity and define national interests within an Islamic framework. . . . The leadership of the AKP believes that Turkey in general and the AKP in particular represent Islamic civilization."[24] Consistent with these views, JDP leaders claimed that Islam should be a key unifying social force in

Turkey, regardless of other cultural or ethnic differences.[25] The same beliefs created an interest in the protection of Islamic rights in other countries, as well as feelings of solidarity and trust with other Muslim-majority countries. As an expression of these feelings, JDP leaders often referred to their counterparts in fellow Muslim-majority countries as "siblings," "brothers," or part of a collective "we."[26]

JDP leaders' commitment to Islamic solidarity affected both the incentives to export liberalism to other countries and the policies that were acceptable to achieve this end. Because feelings of trust toward other Muslim-majority countries applied even to states, like Iran and Syria, that were dedicated to highly illiberal ideological principles, the perceived need to try to spread liberal ideological principles abroad as a means of alleviating threats to Turkey's security was lowered.[27] If, in other words, illiberal Muslim-majority states were not viewed as particularly high threats due to JDP leaders' beliefs in Islamic solidarity, the security-based imperative to convert ideological rivals was reduced. Reinforcing this trend was the fact that JDP politicians' commitment to Islamic solidarity created a normative stigma against threatening fellow Muslim-majority countries. This position limited the means available to Turkey in efforts to promote liberalism abroad.

A second factor that reduced JDP leaders' interest in liberalism promotion was a growing belief in the accuracy of the core predictions of economic liberal theory, namely, that increasing trade among states is a powerful force for peaceful relations.[28] Because the positive relationship between trade and peace exists largely independently of regime type, cooperative relations and thus improvements in security can obtain independently of political liberalization in other countries.

The importance to JDP leaders of Islamic solidarity and the rise of the "trading state" mentality formed the foundation of what became known as the "zero problems" doctrine of Turkish foreign policies. The doctrine refers to Turkey's commitment to maintain peaceful, nonthreatening relations with all neighboring countries (especially Muslim-majority ones), as long as these states do the same toward Turkey.

The objective of zero problems was in fundamental tension with the goal of promoting liberalism in illiberal countries. Because pushing for liberalization would have invariably created significant "problems" with illiberal regimes (assuming the latter had little interest in reform), the pursuit of one of these objectives necessarily meant downplaying the other. Zero problems was thus in key ways a status quo doctrine that worked for cooperative relations with existing (even authoritarian) governments in Middle Eastern countries, but not necessarily their peoples.

Understanding both the incentives pushing Turkey to support liberalization in the Middle East that had frequently been in play since the end of the cold war and the barriers to the adoption of such policies that existed for JDP politicians is critical to explaining Turkey's inconsistent reactions to the early major developments of the Arab Spring that I described above. The doctrine of zero problems was not very salient to Turkey's relations with Egypt. Turkey had little investments in this country (thus the economic liberal foundations of zero problems were not in play), and relations between Mubarak and Erdoğan were cool, if not competitive.[29] Supporting the Egyptian uprisings thus did not necessitate the sacrifice of a "problem-free," cooperative relationship. Existing frictions and little economic interactions with Egypt, in other words, meant that there was not a major conflict between Turkish leaders' zero problems doctrine and their commitment to support the spread of democracy. This reality made the latter choice much easier to make in the Egyptian case.

Similar dynamics did not, however, exist for Turkey in relation to Libya and Syria. Turkey at the beginning of the Arab Spring had $15 billion worth of investments in Libya and 25,000 citizens living and working there.[30] Personal relations between Gadafi and Erdoğan were also good. In December 2010, for example, the Turkish prime minister had received the Gadafi International Prize for Human Rights. Turkish leaders' early refusal to offer support for the Libyan rebels against Gadafi's dictatorship is an example of economic interests and dedication to problem-free relations trumping goals of liberalism promotion.

Similar calculations that dominated in the Libyan case were on display during the early months of the uprisings in Syria. Turkey's relations with Syria were the crowning jewel of the zero problems strategy. Syria was a highly illiberal state with which Turkey had had very hostile relations in the recent past. The two states had even come close to war in the late 1990s due to the latter's continued support of the militant Kurdistan Workers Party, or PKK (a terrorist organization dedicated to Kurdish independence).[31]

Under JDP leadership, however, relations with Syria steadily improved. By 2011, Turkey was Syria's largest trading partner, and Syrians and Turks no longer required visas to visit each other's country. In 2010, the two countries formally agreed to significantly enhance their cooperation against Kurdish terrorists.[32] These economic and strategic considerations no doubt played a central role in Turkey's initially tepid response to the Syrian uprisings that I highlighted at the beginning of this chapter. Turkey's early reaction to the demonstrations in Syria seemed to be another example of commitment to zero problems superseding dedication to democracy promotion and material interests trumping ideological ones.

By the fall of 2011, however, Turkey had become a forceful supporter of the overthrow of the Assad regime. By this time Prime Minister Erdoğan even likened Assad to "Hitler, Mussolini, and Ceausescu of Romania."[33] The JDP government moved to the forefront of supporting the protesters in Syria, including forcefully condemning the Syrian regime's brutality, cutting off dialogue with it, supporting punishing international sanctions (including helping to freeze the Syrian government's financial assets, stopping financial transactions with Syrian banks, imposing a travel ban on senior Syrian leaders, and working to stop weapons sales to Syria), and hosting an armed opposition group dedicated to the overthrow of the Assad government. Turkey even allowed this group to initiate attacks across the border in Syria from inside a camp that was guarded by the Turkish military.[34] The Turks also pushed the United States to open by force "humanitarian corridors" into Syria that would allow aid to be sent to besieged cities in Syria's interior.[35]

Turkey's policies that worked for regime change in Syria had major costs, both immediate and potential, which make these actions all the more noteworthy. In terms of doctrinal and normative costs, Turkey's Syria policies after the summer of 2011 both violated the taboo against threatening fellow Muslims and demonstrated the failure of the zero problems strategy. Turkey's leaders by the fall of 2011 concluded that it was not possible to have problem-free relations with some illiberal regimes.

Likely more important to Turkish policymakers were the potential material costs created by pushing for regime change in Syria. This policy meant enmity not only with Syria, but also with Iran.[36] Syria and Iran are longtime allies, and Tehran has remained committed to helping the Assad regime stay in power despite the popular uprisings and their brutal suppression.[37] Iranian officials warned Turkey of "adverse consequences" if they continued to work for Assad's downfall, and instead advised that Turkey "draw lessons from the bitter historical experiences of other countries" that opposed Iran.[38] Although extensive direct military hostilities between Turkey and either Syria or Iran are unlikely, they are not completely improbable. Syrian forces in April 2012, for example, shelled Syrian refugee camps located inside Turkey, and Syrian leaders have stated that Turkey's level of support for the demonstrators was "considered to be declaring war" on Syria.[39] Relations between the two countries became particularly tense in June 2012 after Syria shot down a Turkish military jet that had briefly flown into Syrian airspace.[40] A more likely scenario than war, however, is that both Iran and Syria could retaliate for Turkey's interference in Syrian politics by once again arming Kurdish rebels in Turkey, thereby fueling Turkey's most threatening domestic problem. These security dangers stand in addition to significant potential economic costs, since the trade levels between Turkey and Syria and Iran are substantial.[41] Spurring the rebellion will also most likely result in massive refugee flows into Turkey. By June 2012, more than 32,000 Syrian refugees were sheltered in Turkey.[42] This number will only grow as the efforts to topple the Assad regime intensify.

Turkey's leaders moved to the forefront of the push for regime change in Syria despite the major risks associated with this policy because these costs were more than offset by the anticipated benefits associated with this pursuit. The key reason that the benefits of democracy promotion were believed to be so high was due to the ideological polarization of the Middle East and North Africa that resulted from the Arab Spring uprisings and the subsequent domestic vulnerability revealed in numerous countries. As the Arab Spring and the consequent ideological polarization of the Middle East and North Africa progressed, the security benefits created by regime promotion intensified to the point where they became more powerful for Turkish leaders than countervailing incentives (e.g., adherence to the zero problems doctrine).

There is little doubt that Turkey's key decisionmakers, at least by the summer of 2011, viewed the Middle East and North Africa as an ideologically polarized system in which Turkey's interests were intertwined with the ideological outcomes in other countries. Prime Minister Erdoğan referred to this interconnectedness of interests in his parliamentary victory speech in June 2011 (which was the first of such speeches by Erdoğan that focused on foreign policies): "I greet with affection the peoples of Baghdad, Damascus, Beirut, Amman, Cairo, Tunis, Sarajevo, Skopje, Baku, Nicosia and all other friends and brother peoples who are following the news out of Turkey with great excitement. . . . Today, the Middle East, the Caucasus and the Balkans have won as much as Turkey."[43] Erdoğan in this last statement was clearly referring to the power of demonstration effects, namely, that the success in Turkey of a party dedicated to democracy, human rights, and Islamic identity would inspire similar ideological groups throughout the Islamic world.

Turkey's support of kindred ideological parties would not be merely inspirational, however. Instead, Erdoğan promised in his June 2011 parliamentary victory speech that Turkey would "become much more active in regional and global affairs. . . . We will take on a more effective role. We will call, as we have, for rights in our region, for justice, for the rule of law, for freedom and democracy."[44] This speech marked the beginning of the reassertion of democracy promotion at the expense of the zero problems doctrine. By August, President Gül proclaimed that "today in the world there is no place for authoritarian administrations, one-party rule, closed regimes."[45]

Kardaş summarizes Turkey's policies pushing for democracy promotion as follows (writing in October 2011):

> Over time, Turkey moved to claim ownership of the democratic wave and tried to lead the regional transformation, which basically took two forms. In the countries undergoing regime change in a relatively peaceful fashion, Turkey accelerated contacts with the groups that stood to gain in the new political structures. In the countries where the regimes have resorted to violence, Turkey increasingly supported the popular opposition, as well as calling on the regimes to heed people's demands for political reforms. . . . Turkish leaders, officials, academics, or representatives from NGOs [nongovernmental organizations] or think tanks have [also] been frequently touring [these] countries, and at the same time, many delegations have been visiting Turkey. President Abdullah Gül's visit soon after Mubarak's fall and Erdoğan's Arab Spring tour [i.e., state visits to Egypt, Tunisia, and Libya], on one hand, and Turkey's hosting of the leaders of the Egyptian youth movement, on the other, are illustrative examples of this multi-level interaction.[46]

Turkey's leaders became increasingly interested in democracy promotion as the Arab Spring intensified because the vulnerability of regimes throughout the Middle East and North Africa created an opportunity for Turkey to increase its influence in these regions. Numerous public opinion polls and related data have documented that Turkey—especially in states like Tunisia, Egypt, and Libya that are trying to create new political systems after ousting authoritarian governments—is the most popular country in the Islamic world. One 2012 pubic option poll found that 80 percent of respondents had a favorable view of Turkey, and 60 percent considered Turkey's political system under the JDP a model for their country.[47] Leading political parties in Tunisia and Egypt have explicitly modeled themselves on the JDP in Turkey.[48] The sources of this popularity and emulation are clearly ideologically based. The success of the JDP in creating a dynamic economy and advancing political rights while also protecting religious identities is a source of tremendous appeal throughout the Islamic world. To put this analysis another way, Turkey under the JDP's leadership—due to this party's ideological principles—possesses large amounts of "soft power" (which is the ability to influence other countries through persuasion and attraction of beliefs) in relation to Muslim-majority countries.[49]

Turkey's leaders, however, can maximize their soft-power influence only if groups dedicated to similar ideological principles govern. The domestic vulnerability created by the Arab Spring uprisings significantly increased the likelihood of such developments coming to pass. As this probability increased, so, too, did Turkey's incentives to support democracy promotion. As one senior Turkish official stated in the fall of 2011, "What's happening in the Middle East is a big opportunity, a golden opportunity" for Turkey. Suat Kiniklioğlu, the JDP's deputy chairman of external affairs, similarly asserted that his government's reactions to the Arab Spring were designed "to make the most of the influence we have in a region that is embracing our leadership."[50] Foreign Minister Davutoğlu even suggested that Turkey could provide a force for liberalization and cooperation in the Middle East analogous to that played by the EU in Europe. [51]

If Turkish policymakers refused to support co-ideologues in other countries (i.e., if Turkey's leaders maintained their commitment to zero problems with authoritarian regimes), Turkey was likely to squander its potential influence based on ideological affinity. This apparently was already starting to happen. According to one analyst writing in April 2011, "Erdoğan's reticence in addressing the violent crackdowns on civilians in Libya and Syria has also sparked criticism that he has double-standards when he picks fights," which was leading to Turkey's increasing isolation.[52] Or to another observer writing in November 2011, "After initially adopting a neutral stance [toward the Arab Spring demonstrations], Turkey soon recognized that its indecisiveness was damaging its image" in the Islamic world.[53] For example, after Turkey's government originally refused to support a NATO-enforced no-fly zone in Libya, anti-Turkish demonstrators in a number of Libyan cities burned Turkey's flag and attempted to overrun Turkey's consulate.[54] There were thus important costs to Turkey created by *not* adopting ideology-based policies in an ideolog-ically polarized era. Turkey's leaders, as a consequence, confronted increasingly powerful incentives to support democracy promotion in neighboring regions as a key means of enhancing its reputation and influence.

It is worth noting that prominent countries recognized the opportunity that Turkey had to advance its interests if it engaged in regime promotion in an ideological polarized era. Iranian leaders, for example, derided Prime Minister Erdoğan's calls for Egypt and Tunisia to adopt secularism in their new consti-tutions. The Iranians no doubt hoped to see these countries adopt more hard-line Islamist governments. Ayatollah Mahmoud Hashemi Shahroudi, the former chief of Iran's judiciary, scornfully dismissed Turkey's efforts to spread democracy in the Middle East as an example of "liberal Islam" that was de-signed to try to counter Iran's regional influence.[55] Ali-Akbar Velayati, senior adviser to Supreme Leader Ali Khamenei, made similar statements, as did Yahya Safavi, the former commander of the Revolutionary Guards.[56] These assertions indicate that the Iranians believed that they were caught with Turkey in an ideological security dilemma, which I discussed earlier. The more that Turkey is able to spread its ideological principles in those states made vulnerable by the Arab Spring, the more Iran's regional influence will be cur-tailed. Ali Nader, an Iranian analyst at the RAND Corporation, summarizes the relationship between Turkey's support of regime promotion and threats to Iran's interests as follows: "Iranian conservatives . . . worry that Turkey is presenting an alternate model to the Islamic Republic in the region. . . . The Iranian government claimed that the Arab Spring has been inspired by the Iranian Revolution of 1979. . . . Turkey [is] basically offering itself as [an al-ternative] model for the Arab population in the region. This contradicts with Iranian interests."[57]

American policymakers have recognized similar dynamics. U.S. leaders in the wake of the Arab Spring have pushed for Turkey to assert itself as an ide-ological model throughout the Islamic world.[58] The Americans clearly believe that the spread of Turkey's "liberal Islamic" system is an effective way of pro-tecting U.S. interests given the political realities of the era. If Turkey does not provide the ideological inspiration in domestically vulnerable regimes, more radical, and more anti-American, Islamist groups might.

Ideological allies are most likely to increase cooperation during ideologi-cally polarized eras because it is precisely in these times that leaders' ideo-logical identities are most salient to their perceptions and policies. The Arab

Spring is no exception to this trend, as indicated by the fact that American-Turkish relations have become even closer since 2011. Ömer Taşpinar aptly describes these dynamics as follows: "The Arab Spring . . . dramatically changed the Western discourse about Turkey. Instead of asking 'who lost Turkey' or complaining about the Islamization of Turkish foreign policy, analysts began discussing whether the new regimes in the Arab world would follow the 'Turkish model.'"[59] Erdoğan in September 2011 described Turkey's alliance with America as a "model partnership."[60] Closer ties with the United States based on similar ideological principles is another major benefit for Turkey resulting from policies of regime promotion in an ideologically polarized system.

CONCLUSION

This chapter had two primary objectives. The first was to document Turkish leaders' dominant reactions to the Arab Spring. The second was to demonstrate how a key dimension of these policies—an increasing interest in ideological promotion—was part of an important pattern in international relations. Because ideological relationships often have major effects on leaders' threat perceptions, policymakers frequently confront powerful incentives to try to export their ideological principles as a means of increasing the number of allies in the system and reducing the number of enemies. These incentives tend to be especially strong during periods of ideological polarization. Ideologically polarized eras are created when states—as was the case during the Arab Spring—are vulnerable domestically to revolution. At these times, ideological rivals will be particularly sensitive to ideology-based opportunities and threats based on the domestic outcomes in other countries.

Turkish leaders' behavior as the Arab Spring progressed supports this pattern. JDP politicians were originally highly inconsistent in advocating democracy promotion when the Arab Spring began. They supported demonstrators in countries with which Turkey had little economic interests and strategic cooperation (e.g., Egypt), and stood by regimes with which Turkey shared important material interest (Libya, Syria). Over time, however, the Turkish government became much more assertive for regime change, even in countries that shared major interests with Turkey. The key reason for this shift was the realization that nonideological foreign policies were hurting Turkey's interests by squandering its large reserve of soft power throughout the Islamic world. Turkey is extremely popular because of its commitment to democracy and Islamic identity. Not supporting popular protests for basic rights during the Arab Spring would have been a major blow to this popularity by demonstrating Turkey's hypocrisy and selfishness. Supporting democracy movements, in contrast, offered the opportunity of helping groups in other countries come to power that were highly sympathetic to Turkey, while simultaneously tightening its ties with established liberal allies led by the United States. Helping to spread democracy based on the Turkish model also inhibited proponents of rival ideological beliefs—such as Islamist Iran—from increasing their regional influence. Democracy promotion, in short, offered Turkey major opportunities to increase its security. In the case of Turkey and the Arab Spring, ideology and "interests" were thus not fundamentally opposed—as is often asserted in the international relations literature—but inextricably interconnected.

NOTES

1. I want to thank the Earhart Foundation and the Richard Paluse Mission-Related Research Award from Duquesne for providing generous financial support of the research that contributed to this chapter.

2. Quoted in Anthony Shadid, "Turkey Predicts Alliance with Egypt as Regional Anchors," *New York Times*, September 18, 2011; Nathalie Tocci, Ömer Taşpınar, and Henri J. Barkey, *Turkey and the Arab Spring: Implications for Turkish Foreign Policy from a Transatlantic Perspective* (Washington, DC: German Marshall Fund, 2011), 3.

3. Quoted in Steven A. Cook, "Arab Spring, Turkish Fall," foreignpolicy .com, May 5, 2011, http://www.foreignpolicy.com/articles/2011/05/05/arab _spring_turkish_fall?.

4. Ibid.

5. Şaban Kardaş, "Turkey's Syria Policy: The Challenge of Coalition Building," *On Turkey* (German Marshall Fund of the United States), February 17, 2012, 1; Tarik Oğuzlu, "The 'Arab Spring' and the Rise of the 2.0 Version of Turkey's 'Zero Problems with Neighbors' Policy," Center for Strategic Research Papers (Ankara, Turkey: Center for Strategic Research, February 2012), 6.

6. Cook, "Arab Spring, Turkish Fall"; Tocci, Taşpınar, and Barkey, *Turkey and the Arab Spring*, 3.

7. Both quotes are from Oğuzlu, "The 'Arab Spring,'" 7, 10.

8. Şaban Kardaş, "Turkey and the Arab Spring: Coming to Terms with Democracy Promotion?," Policy Brief (Washington, DC: German Marshall Fund of the United States, October 2011), 1.

9. For others who define ideology in this way, see John M. Owen, *The Clash of Ideas in World Politics: Transnational Networks, States, and Regime Change, 1510–2010* (Princeton, NJ: Princeton University Press, 2010); Stephen M. Walt, *Revolution and War* (Ithaca, NY: Cornell University Press, 1996); Mark L. Haas, *The Ideological Origins of Great Power Politics, 1789–1989* (Ithaca, NY: Cornell University Press, 2005); Mark L. Haas, *The Clash of Ideologies: Middle Eastern Politics and American Security* (New York: Oxford University Press, 2012); Mark L. Haas, "Missed Ideological Opportunities and George W. Bush's Middle Eastern Policies," *Security Studies* 21, 3 (July–September 2012): 416–454. Parts of this chapter's argument and evidence are derived from these last three sources.

10. See Haas, *Ideological Origins*, 5–18; Haas, *Clash of Ideologies*, 7–15; Owen, *Clash of Ideas*, 32–52; and Walt, *Revolution and War*, 32–45.

11. For case study analyses demonstrating how ideological convergence, or increasing ideological similarities among states, is often an important source of international conflict resolution, see Owen, *Clash of Ideas*, 54–55, 68–70, 77, 115–119, 154–157, 196–199, 267–269; and Benjamin Miller, *When Opponents Cooperate: Great Power Conflict and Collaboration in World Politics* (Ann Arbor: University of Michigan Press, 1995), 39–42, 53–55, 241.

12. For extensive analysis of regime promotion by multiple ideological groups over the last five hundred years, see Owen, *Clash of Ideas*. Owen finds that since 1510 states have used force on more than two hundred separate occasions to alter or preserve the ideological principles and institutions of another country. Instances of engagement policies designed to support specific ideological groups in other countries are much greater in number.

13. Ibid., 40.

14. The traditional security dilemma is a realist international relations concept that asserts that it is very difficult for one state to make itself feel safe without making a neighboring country feel less safe. When one state increases its military spending to enhance its security, others will feel more endangered.

15. Quoted in David Aikman, "Hoping Saddam Hussein Would Just Go Away," *Time*, May 13, 1991.

16. Both Demirel quotations are from Idris Bal, *Turkey's Relations with the West and the Turkic Republics: The Rise and Fall of the "Turkish Model"* (Aldershot, UK: Ashgate, 2000), 81, 52, respectively.

17. Ibid., 59.

18. Quoted in Yalim Eralp, "An Insider's View of Turkey's Foreign Policy and Its American Connection," in *The United States and Turkey: Allies in Need*, ed. Morton Abramowitz (New York: Century Foundation Press, 2003), 116. Turkish leaders' interest in regime promotion in the 1990s was more than just talk. For details on the significant resources dedicated to these policies, see Haas, *Clash of Ideologies*, 212–213.

19. Metin Heper and Şule Toktaş, "Islam, Modernity, and Democracy in Contemporary Turkey: The Case of Recep Tayyip Erdoğan," *The Muslim World* 93, 2 (April 2003): 176.

20. For details, see William Hale and Ergun Özbudun, *Islamism, Democracy, and Liberalism in Turkey: The Case of the AKP* (London: Routledge, 2010), 57–62.

21. Philip Robins, "Turkish Foreign Policy Since 2002: Between a 'Post-Islamist' Government and a Kemalist State," *International Affairs* 83, 1 (2007): 302. According to Foreign Minister Gül in a 2003 statement, "Now that Europe has finally overcome the divisions on the continent and virtually 'ended European history' [by the near universal spread of liberalism], time has come for another major project that would end the recent history in the Middle East. . . . The call for reform in the Middle East is louder than ever" (Abdullah Gül, "Turkey's Vision for the Transatlantic Partnership," *The National Interest*, June 18, 2003). The foreign minister asserted at the 2003 Organization of the Islamic Conference Thirtieth Term Foreign Ministers Meeting in Tehran that Muslim-majority countries "have to act with a fresh and new vision. This should be a vision where better management and transparency prevail, basic rights, freedom and gender equality are regarded as superior values and rude and rhetoric slogans don't have place." Implementing these liberalizing domestic policies, Gül believed, would help avoid "destructive wars" in the region (quoted in "Turkish Foreign Minister: Islamic Countries Should Act with Fresh, New Vision," BBC Monitoring Europe, May 28, 2003).

22. Aysegul Sever, "Turkey's Constraining Position on Western Reform Initiatives in the Middle East," *Mediterranean Quarterly* 18, 4 (Fall 2007): 133.

23. For details on the resources dedicated to democracy promotion, see Haas, *Clash of Ideologies*, 221–222.

24. M. Hakan Yavuz, *Secularism and Muslim Democracy in Turkey* (Cambridge: Cambridge University Press, 2009), 209.

25. Ibid., 264–265.

26. For details on these points, see Haas, *Clash of Ideologies*, 192.

27. Probably the best example of JDP leaders' trusting relations toward other Muslim-majority countries was relations with Iran for most of the 2000s. Although Iranian capabilities were growing substantially in this decade, JDP politicians' threat perceptions toward Iran were much lower compared to those possessed by preceding Turkish leaders. For details, see Haas, *Clash of Ideologies*, 187–192.

28. Oğuzlu, "The 'Arab Spring,'" 4; Greg Sheridan, "World's a Stage for Turkey," *Weekend Australian*, January 21, 2012.

29. Tocci, Taşpınar, and Barkey, *Turkey and the Arab Spring*, 3.

30. Ibid.

31. For details, see Robert Olson, *Turkey's Relations with Iran, Syria, Israel, and Russia, 1991–2000: The Kurdish and Islamist Questions* (Costa Mesa, CA: Mazda, 2001).

32. Cook, "Arab Spring, Turkish Fall"; Richard Weitz, "Global Insights: Turkey Turns on Syria's Asad," *World Policy Review*, December 6, 2011.

33. Quoted in Sebnem Arsu, "Turkish Premier Urges Assad to Quit in Syria," *New York Times*, November 22, 2011.

34. Liam Stack, "In Slap at Syria, Turkey Shelters Anti-Assad Fighters," *New York Times*, October 27, 2011; Judy Dempsey, "The Hazards in Turkey's New Strategy," *New York Times*, October 24, 2011.

35. "Turkey Expected to Pressure US on Syria, Iran," BBC Monitoring Europe, February 13, 2012.

36. Tensions between Turkey and China and Russia also increased after the latter two powers vetoed in February 2012 a UN resolution that would have backed an Arab plan that urged Assad to give up power and start a transition to democracy. Turkish Foreign Minister Davutoğlu expressed his frustration with the two great powers: "Unfortunately, yesterday in the UN, the Cold War logic continues. Russia and China did not vote based on the existing realities but more a reflexive attitude against the West" (quoted in Joseph Logan and Patrick Worsnip, "Russia, China Veto of Syria UN Resolution Sparks Outrage," Reuters, February 5, 2012).

37. Iran, according to both American and European officials, has provided Syria not only advice on how to crush the democracy movement, but also coercive supplies such as teargas and equipment to help disrupt protesters' communications, as well as billions of dollars in assistance to aid the Syrian government (Anthony Shadid, "Syria Broadens Deadly Crackdown on Protestors," *New York Times*, May 8, 2011).

38. Quoted in "Paper Looks into Regional Competition Between Turkey, Iran," BBC Monitoring Europe, October 18, 2011.

39. Quoted in Harvey Morris, "Time to Dial the Turkey-Syria Hotline," *New York Times*, April 10, 2012. See also Neil MacFarquhar, Sebnem Arsu, and Alan Cowell, "Tensions Mount as Syria Truce Seems Elusive," *New York Times*, April 10, 2012.

40. Eric Schmitt and Sebnem Arsu, "Backed by NATO, Turkey Steps Up Warning to Syria," *New York Times*, June 26, 2012.

41. For details, see United Nations Commodity Trade Statistics Database, http://comtrade.un.org/db/.

42. Liam Stack, "Turkey Vows Action After Downing of Jet by Syria," *New York Times*, June 23, 2012.

43. Quoted in Susanne Güsten, "Mandate for a New Turkish Era; Erdogan Boldly Changes Tack with Broad Outreach to a Region in Turmoil," *International Herald Tribune*, June 16, 2011.

44. Quoted in ibid.

45. Quoted in Morris, "Time to Dial."

46. Kardaş, "Turkey and the Arab Spring," 2, 3.

47. "Some See Turkey as a Useful Model for New Arab Regimes," Agence France-Presse, February 5, 2012. For similar polling data, see "Erdogan Most Popular Leader by Far Among Arabs," Inter Press Service, November 21, 2011.

48. "Emerging Arab Islamists Look to 'Turkish Model,'" *Daily News Egypt*, December 4, 2011; Asef Bayat, "Arab Revolts: Islamists Aren't Coming!," *Insight Turkey* 13, 2 (2011): 12–13.

49. It is worth highlighting that Turkey is not the only state that possesses substantial soft power in relation to liberalizing groups in the Middle East. Most notably, the United States does as well, even with groups that are hostile to many of America's policies in the region. According, for example, to Shadi Hamid, who has interviewed numerous leaders of the Muslim Brotherhood, "The Brotherhood actually feels more comfortable with America than it does with America's adversaries: 'The U.S. is a superpower that is there and will be there, and it is not to anyone's benefit to have this superpower going down, but we want it to go up with its values and not with its dark side,' one senior Brotherhood official told me. 'What are the values driving China across the globe? . . . It's just pure profit. The Russians and the Chinese, I don't know their values! Western European and American core values of human rights and pluralism—we practiced this when we were living there.'" Quoted in Shadi Hamid, "Brother Number One," *Foreign Policy* online, June 7, 2012, http://www.foreignpolicy.com/articles/2012/06/07/brother_number_one?page=full.

50. Both quotations are from Anthony Shadid, "In Riddle of Mideast Upheaval, Turkey Offers Itself as an Answer," *New York Times*, September 26, 2011.

51. Ibid.

52. Pelin Turgut, "How Syria and Libya Got to Be Turkey's Headaches," *Time*, April 30, 2011.

53. Sinan Ulgen, "Turkey's 'No Problems' Policy Is Problematic," *Daily Star* (Lebanon), November 28, 2011.

54. Sarah Akram, "Turkey and the Arab Spring," *Strategic Studies* 31, 3 (September 2011): 23–31.

55. Quoted in Mustafa Akyol, "The Problem with 'Zero Problems,'" *New York Times*, November 15, 2011; and in Gonul Tol, "Ankara Is Trying to Have It Both Ways," *New York Times*, November 15, 2011.

56. "Senior Adviser to Iran's Supreme Leader Says Turkey's Secularism Not Suitable for Arab States," AlArabiya.net, December 13, 2011; "Paper Looks into Regional Competition."

57. Ali Nader et al., "Arab Spring and Its Effect on Turkey's Regional Policy," *SETA Policy Debate*, October 2011, 7. See also Robert F. Worth, "Effort to Rebrand Arab Spring Backfires in Iran," *New York Times*, February 2, 2012.

58. Mark Landler, "New Challenges for Obama and Turkey's Premier," *New York Times*, September 19, 2011.

59. Tocci, Taşpınar, and Barkey, *Turkey and the Arab Spring*, 9.

60. Quoted in "Interview with Recep Tayyip Erdogan," *Charlie Rose Show*, September 21, 2011.

9

Israel and the Arab Spring: The Victory of Anxiety

ILAN PELEG

W HAT IS KNOWN TODAY as the Arab Spring has been interpreted by most Israeli politicians and commentators, and even by many in the Israeli public at large, in extremely negative, sometimes even apocalyptic terms.[1] Pessimism in regard to this series of uprisings, demonstrations, and violent conflicts has also dominated the historical analogies invoked by many Israeli analysts. Most Israelis have tended to view this political earthquake as inviting long-term regional instability, facilitating the rise of radical sociopolitical forces in their already "rough neighborhood," and producing increased hostility toward Israel and its allies. Even though one commentator interpreted the Israeli reaction to the Arab Spring as merely "a frosty response," in reality the reaction of most Israelis has been much more negative.[2]

Although many of those reactions are understandable and even justified, the outbreak of the Arab Spring for the most part had nothing to do with Israel or its long-term hostile relationships with the Arab world. Starting in Tunisia, a country relatively detached from the Israeli-Palestinian conflict, the central gravitational point of the uprising has been the call of the Arab masses for democratization, liberty, and representation, demands aimed at the traditional authoritarian Arab regimes and protesting their corruption. The absence of "an Israeli agenda" for the Arab protesters, especially in the beginning of the uprising, has been noted by many commentators. And yet with the passage of time, Israelis and others have tended to look at the Arab Spring as dramatically impacting Israel's position in a negative way.[3] This chapter, in contrast, will offer a more balanced approach to understanding the essence of the Arab Spring approach, its fundamental causes, and its likely long-term results—even though predicting the future of the Middle East in such a fluid situation is exceedingly difficult.

First, this chapter will *describe* the Israeli reaction to the Arab Spring by focusing on the "majority opinion" among Israelis, as well as on some alternative voices among politicians, commentators, and the general Israeli public. Second, the chapter will *explain* why most Israelis have reacted the way they have, attempting to contextualize the Israeli reaction by examining historical, ideological, and political factors. Third, the chapter will *highlight* some of the policies adopted by Israel in regard to the Palestinians, the Arabs, and the world at large under the impact of these dramatic regional events. Fourth, the chapter will *dwell* on the sensitive and overwhelmingly important relations between Israel and the United States in the wake of the Arab Spring, emphasizing both similarities and differences in the American and Israeli responses to these Middle Eastern events. And finally, the chapter will try to *assess* the longer-term impact of the Arab Spring on Israeli politics and on Israel's relationships with other nations in the region and beyond.

DESCRIBING THE ISRAELI REACTION

The reactions of many Israelis to the Arab Spring contain elements of collective, large-scale groupthink. Although Irving Janis introduced the term "groupthink" into the lexicon of political analysis to describe small-group propensities for irrational response to foreign policy challenges,[4] some of the Israeli reactions to the Arab Spring fit his concept rather well. Politicians, commentators, and analysts have tended to reinforce each other in an almost endless chorus, ushering in a competition of negative superlatives rarely seen in responses to other events.

Government spokespersons sometimes encouraged the Israeli public in its strong threat perception of the Arab Spring.[5] The most authoritative among those voices was Benjamin Netanyahu's. In a major November 2011 Knesset address, the prime minister said that he believed the Arab Spring had taken the Arabs "not forward, but backward." In his view, Israel was now surrounded by a potentially hostile sea of "illiberal, anti-Western, anti-Israeli and anti-democratic" fundamentalism.[6] While his pessimistic reading of the regional map was understandable, it did nothing to soothe the apocalyptic national mood already promoted by other commentators.

The Israeli reaction to the Arab Spring has had several prominent elements, emphasizing in particular a few specific threats:

1. Domestic political instability in the Arab countries, especially those neighboring Israel. Analysts have noticed, correctly, that the quietest Israeli borders over the last several decades have been with non-democracies such as Egypt, Jordan, and Syria, while the borders with more democratic political entities, such as Lebanon, the Palestinian Authority on the West Bank, or Hamas-ruled Gaza, have been significantly less stable.

2. Regional instability leading eventually to the possible renewal of Arab-Israeli wars in which all or most Arab states would align against Israel under some kind of renewed Nasserite pan-Arabism or even, more frighteningly, pan-Islam. Several Israelis raised specifically the possibility of a two-front war. An even more nightmarish scenario would be an important country such as Egypt getting closer to Iran, Israel's archenemy in the Middle East.[7]

3. The danger that moderate countries, particularly Egypt and Jordan, would break diplomatic relations with Israel as a result of internal pressures and that this would further isolate Israel in the region and in the world. Many in Israel have expressed fears that the 1979 peace treaty with Egypt might be abrogated or vacated from its content. At the same time, in a November 2011 public opinion poll, 50.6 percent of Israeli Jews thought that the treaty would not be officially cancelled, but that relations with Egypt would be harmed.[8] To date, this seems to be a fairly realistic assessment.

4. The rise of Islamists of all stripes, but especially radical Islamic movements in the Arab countries. Thus, for example, Barry Rubin wrote an article under the title "Egypt Gets Its Khomeini: Qaradawi Returns in Triumph," comparing the leader of Egyptian Muslims to the Iranian Muslim revolutionary.[9] The fear of many Israelis has been that Islamists will come to power either through democratic elections or through violent means during the revolutionary period. The argument has been that once they get power, the Islamists will either abrogate the peace their country has signed with Israel altogether (e.g., in the case of Egypt) or

will adopt a more hostile position toward the Jewish state than did their predecessors (e.g., in the case of Syria).[10] More specifically, Israelis have often expressed the fear that certain Islamists, particularly Egypt's Muslim Brotherhood, will have a negative influence over Hamas in Gaza, thus complicating Israel's relations with the Palestinians.[11]

5. The possibility or even likelihood of a rise in Palestinian radicalism. Many Israelis read the marches of Palestinians toward the Syrian-Israeli cease-fire line on the Golan Heights in May and June 2011 as a danger sign for the future, linking the Arab Spring and the Palestinian issue. The Israeli public was split on the likely radicalization of the Palestinians in the territories: 57.6 percent of Jews thought that the likelihood of radicalization was low, and only 37.8 percent thought it was high (the Israeli Arab public was even less worried about the chances for such radicalization). As for the impact of the Arab Spring on Israeli Arab citizens, almost 66 percent of the Jews and more than 75 percent of the Arabs thought that the likelihood of an Arab revolt in Israel was low. Regarding the overall impact of the Arab Spring on Israeli-Palestinian peace, Israeli Jews were split almost equally (with a slight majority viewing it as negative); Israeli Arabs were more positive.[12] One consequence of the Arab Spring was a Hamas-PLO agreement to unite, but the Netanyahu government quickly dismissed it as a negative move.

6. An increase in anti-Israeli terrorism if neighboring Arab regimes lose control over areas adjacent to Israel or if those regimes support and even cooperate with terrorist groups. Many Israelis have been particularly worried about the lack of effective Egyptian control over the Sinai.[13]

7. A lack of strong or decisive reactions to the events of the Arab Spring and their consequences by outside powers, especially the United States. Many Israeli commentators accused the United States of not truly understanding the Middle East and not reacting forcefully enough to the events; the U.S. reaction to the Egyptian demonstrations was particularly criticized. As early as February 2011, most Israeli Jews (unlike most Israeli Arabs) thought that the United States was wrong "when it supported anti-Mubarak demonstrators in Egypt."[14]

8. Increased political pressure on Israel from outside powers, especially the United States, in order to preempt or restrain political radicalization in the Arab world, counter Iran, and achieve other allegedly

American goals.[15] Many commentators thought that Israel would eventually have to pay a political price for the Arab Spring.

9. The possibility that "popular regimes [in the Arab world] may prove less tolerant of a Jewish state in their midst than the Washington-dependent dictatorships they displaced."[16] The fundamental idea here has been that the Arab populace is inherently and inalterably anti-Israel and that therefore popular regimes would be more inclined toward anti-Israel policies than elite-based regimes.

10. The possibility of a revolt in Israel. Only a relatively small minority of Israeli Jews (7.3 percent) thought there was such a possibility, although more Arabs in Israel (21.1 percent) thought it was possible. In rejecting the possibility of an internal uprising, most Israelis reasoned that their country was a democracy and that the public could change the government through elections.

Combining all or most of those factors into a seemingly coherent whole, most Israelis have adopted a rather pessimistic view of the events in the Middle East since December 2010. A few specific assaults have been connected to this overall sense of vulnerability, including repeated attacks on the Sinai gas pipeline from Egypt, an assault on the Israeli Embassy in Cairo, and an August 18, 2011, terrorist attack near Eilat.

Analytically speaking, the overwhelmingly negative reactions of many Israelis to the Arab Spring were based on problematic reasoning. First, they reflected a tendency to overgeneralize; events such as the fall of Husni Mubarak generated a huge echo chamber of endless negativity among those who already tended to see the Arab Spring as a threat to Israel. Second, and most importantly, the thinking process of many Israelis has been dominated by a false dichotomy between democracy and Islam. Israelis often assume that any strengthening of the Islamic factor in Arab countries will come necessarily at the expense of democracy (even though Islamists were the target of authoritarian secular Arab regimes and fought, in fact, for more democracy) and that any Islamist participation in governance will be disastrous for Israel, the United States, and the West in general.

These types of interpretations failed to look at the Arab Spring in broader terms, ignoring popular desires for democratic institutions, broad-based political freedoms, effective and corruption-free governance, and so forth. The dichotomy of democracy versus Islam, superimposed on the Arab Spring, has been clouding assessment of the event, not clarifying it. Interpreting the Arab Spring "Islamically" has encouraged some Israelis to become overly defensive.

In a very general way, the developments in the Arab world have shaken the self-confidence of Israelis. Writing in the *Washington Post* during the outset of the Egyptian demonstrations, Aaron David Miller, who had served as an adviser to several American presidents, observed, "It is impossible to overstate the angst, even hysteria, that Israelis are feeling about their neighborhood as they watch what is unfolding in the streets of Cairo."[17]

Side by side with the negative views held by most Israelis, an alternative, more optimistic perspective emerged. It had a few elements:

1. An argument that more democratic regimes in the neighboring countries might create more stability in those countries. Yossi Beilin, a former Israeli minister of justice, described the Arab Spring positively as the "empowerment of the Arab society."[18] He speculated that this would mean more involvement in efforts to bring peace to the region. Moreover, in a Brookings Institution poll conducted between November 10 and November 20, 2011, 46 percent of Israelis expressed sympathy toward the Arab Spring, agreeing that it was about "ordinary people seeking dignity, freedom and better life"; 44 percent thought that if the Arab Spring led to more democracy in the Arab world, that would be better for Israel.[19]

2. A possibility of a regional pro-Western camp in the Middle East committed to democracy. While most politicians on the right of the political spectrum in Israel, headed by Prime Minister Netanyahu, sounded the alarm about the Arab Spring, former Defense Minister Moshe Arens stated that the Arab Spring could benefit democracy in the region as a whole.[20]

3. An argument that Israel's peace treaties with Egypt and Jordan were highly stable, reflective not merely of Israel's interests but also of the long-term interests of those countries and that therefore those treaties were not seriously endangered by the Arab Spring. Analysts adopting this position argued that a new political elite in Egypt would quickly realize the enormous benefits from the peace treaty with Israel and would act to maintain it.

4. An assertion that not all Islamists were radicals and that, in fact, some of them (including the Muslim Brotherhood in Egypt and other countries)

were moderate and democratically inclined (having been the main vic-
tim of totalitarianism). Some commentators emphasized the possibility
of Israeli-Sunni cooperation against the Shia-led Iranians.

5. Attention to the fact that the Palestinian territories remained calm
   throughout the Arab Spring and that the West Bank was being led
   by moderates. Some commentators think that the new Egyptian government may actually fulfill an important role as mediating between
   Israelis and Palestinians and that such mediation would eventually
   produce a peace settlement between the parties. Moreover, as has been
   noted, Hamas has emerged in opposition to the Syrian regime.

6. Recognition by some analysts that whatever the public sentiment in
   the Arab countries resulting from the Arab Spring, some of them
   will not be able to dramatically change their foreign policy, including
   that on Israel. For example, the post-Mubarak regime in Egypt will
   have huge internal challenges and will need international and especially American assistance, which will prevent it from severing relations with Israel.

It is worth noting that the analysis offered by Israeli commentators has been
dominated by what might be called "the prophets of doom," whereas the general public seems to be somewhat more balanced in its opinions. Thus, in
March 2011, Israeli Jews and Arabs were asked separately to assess whether
the antiregime struggles in the various Arab states were positive or negative
from an Israeli perspective. Among Jews, a full 46.7 percent saw the events as
positive and 29.7 percent considered them as negative; among Arabs, the numbers were 55.5 percent and 34.4 percent, respectively.[21] When asked to assess
the demonstrations from the perspective of the Arab people, 53.1 percent of
the Jews thought they were positive and merely 29.3 percent thought they were
negative; 65.5 percent and 28.9 percent of Arabs held the corresponding opinions. So at least at the beginning of the uprising, the Israeli Jewish public was
not sold on the idea that these developments were negative. Opinions seem to
have shifted in a negative direction with the passage of time.

In May 2011, the Peace Index reported that in assessing the impact of the
Arab Spring on Israel, 38.9 percent of Israeli Jews thought that Israel's situation
had worsened, while less than 11 percent thought it had improved.[22] This
change might have reflected the impact of the numerous negative interpretations
of experts, public commentators, and politicians. Even more negative results

were reported in November 2011: this time the assessment of the situation as "worsening" had reached 68.5 percent of the Israeli Jewish public.[23]

EXPLAINING THE ISRAELI RESPONSE

In order to explain comprehensively the overwhelmingly negative Israeli response to the Arab Spring, we need to adopt three different, albeit related, forms of analysis: historical, ideological, and political. Historically, this reaction ought to be understood as part of the long-term hostility between Arabs and Israelis, hostility that has created and has sustained an understandable nervousness and a proclivity for negative reactions on both sides of the generally hostile border between Israel and its Arab neighbors. So it is no wonder that the region-wide instability associated with the Arab Spring has generated deep anxiety among most Israelis. Furthermore, many Israelis have looked at the events of the Arab Spring against the background of the last two decades or so, appreciating the fact that recent Arab-Israeli relations have been more positive than in the past, especially in terms of Israel's relations with Egypt and Jordan, as well as less-formal relations with other moderate, pro-Western Arab countries. From an Israeli perspective, the Arab Spring has put in jeopardy the development of better Arab-Israeli relations in years to come.

But beyond this historical perspective, Israel's negative reaction to the Arab Spring has an ideological dimension. Many Israelis tend to view the Arab world as fundamentally hostile to their national goals and even their independent national existence as a sovereign, independent Jewish state in the Middle East. This is particularly the case for those who belong to the nationalist right, including the current government and its leader, Prime Minister Netanyahu. Viewing the Arab world as hostile is at the center of the right's belief system.

Netanyahu's ideology is fundamentally nationalist. He is a believer in the maximal territorial expansion of Israel and views the Arab world, including the Palestinians, as inalterably hostile to Israel.[24] Within this ideological framework, any change in the Arab world that might have negative implications for Israel's security, including events that are part of the Arab Spring, is likely to be magnified. This is precisely what has happened in reaction to the Arab Spring. Netanyahu himself became the leader of the "negativist" camp, interpreting the events in the most apocalyptic terms possible.

Israeli reaction to the Arab Spring has a political component. The political reality in Jerusalem since 2009 has been that of a nationalist, right-wing government with an ideological tendency to prevent the repartition of the land despite enormous worldwide expectations that a two-state solution has to be implemented. In that light, the reaction of the Netanyahu government, and of the Israeli public led by it, could have been expected. It is a government with no trust whatsoever in the Arab "street" and minimal trust in Arab elites, with the exception of Western-sustained autocrats such as Mubarak.

The Israeli reaction to the Arab Spring became part and parcel of an overall, ongoing debate in Israel on the nature of the Middle East and Israel's relations with it. The "hawks," under the active leadership of the government, tended to adopt a completely negative attitude toward the Arab Spring, while the "doves," more liberal circles in the opposition to the current government, allowed for a more cautious and sometime moderately positive attitude. Thus, for example, some commentators on the right found that the Arab Spring "proves once again that the Arab-Israeli conflict is not the central problem in this region [the Middle East]" and therefore that "this is not the time for Israel to be taking territorial or other risks."[25] Other hawks argued that there was no reason to believe that democracy would result from any of the Arab revolutions, as if Arabs were constitutionally unable to democratize. More "dovish" elements saw the potential for democracy in the demonstrations of the Arab masses.

HIGHLIGHTING OLD-NEW ISRAELI POLICIES

Although it has been commonly argued—even assumed—that the Arab Spring "changed everything" in terms of Israel's position in the Middle East, it could be conversely argued that Israel's position in the region has not changed a great deal.[26] Israel continues to be a regional power, easily the strongest military power in the area, although it is unpopular with the vast majority of the countries in the region and even less popular with the Arab masses. The pessimists' stance has been that as the influence of the masses in the region grows, Israel's position will markedly deteriorate; equally, to the extent to which new political elites adopt the policies of old political elites, continuity in terms of Israel's position will prevail. To date, we have seen little evidence that the new elites have adopted new policy positions, particularly in foreign policy.

One of the most interesting questions is whether, and in what ways, the Arab Spring has led to actual, observable changes in Israeli policy. While the fundamental approach, attitudes, and goals of Israel's foreign policy seem to have remained constant, in some tactical areas changes have been introduced:

1. The Arab Spring has strengthened the reluctance of the current Israeli government to move forward toward a negotiated agreement of the Israeli-Palestinian conflict and take action to facilitate such an agreement (by stopping settlement activity on the West Bank, for example). The overall, sometimes unverbalized argument has been that in a time of regional instability, Israel could not and should not transfer territories to the Arabs, including the Palestinians. While Netanyahu did not have a reputation for pushing aggressively the peace process before the beginning of the Arab Spring in late 2010, the onset of regional instability made it significantly easier for him to promote his hawkish line even further, especially within Israel. Thus, the Arab Spring, a series of events that were initially unlinked to Arab-Israeli relations, became the last nail in the "peace process coffin."

2. The Arab Spring has had a budgetary impact on Israel. Pressures to cut the defense budget, particularly as a result of social protests in Israel during the summer of 2011, have been resisted with the argument that Israel may have to soon face again the Arab armies, possibly in an all-out war. In general, the powerful defense lobby has been successful.

3. The Arab Spring has caused some changes in the relationships between Israel and the neighboring Arab states, although it is too early to fully assess those changes. The relationships between Israel and Egypt, cold but stable under Mubarak, have become even more distant, although in the "crunch" the Egyptian government responded positively to Israeli needs (e.g., rescuing Israeli personnel from the besieged Israeli Embassy). The equally crucial relations with Jordan were also maintained. Thus, for example, Foreign Minister Avigdor Lieberman gave a speech in which he openly endorsed the territorial integrity of the Hashemite Kingdom, a very important posture in view of possible Palestinian pressures to the contrary.[27] Even in the case of Syria, a declared enemy, the Israeli government remained rather detached from international efforts to unseat Bashar al-Assad. Interestingly, despite the hostility of many Israelis toward Syria and the Assad regime, the Israeli public has been split over the benefit of a possible collapse of that regime, and an overwhelming number of Israeli Jews (84.1 percent) supported the idea that "Israel should sit quietly on the sidelines" while the Syrian conflict goes on.[28] At the same time, the Israeli Jewish public was more sympathetic (49.8 percent) to the idea of Western

countries providing aid to the opposition forces.[29] Israelis remained extremely ambivalent in regard to the Syrian revolt. Their government remained uninvolved, thus strengthening the perception that it preferred the Middle East status quo to the evolution of a more participatory new order. Needless to say, the instability in Syria makes an Israeli-Syrian peace treaty more remote than ever.

4. As a result of the Arab Spring, Israel seems to be pursuing new relationships with a number of countries in the eastern Mediterranean, Africa, and even the Arab world. There has been somewhat of a return to David Ben-Gurion's so-called periphery strategy, in which Israel tried to compensate for the hostility of its immediate Arab neighbors by developing strong geostrategic relations with countries such as Iran and Turkey, Christian elements in Lebanon, the Kurds, etc. Among Israel's recent "diplomatic targets" have been several European countries, including Greece, Italy, Bulgaria, and Romania, but also Cyprus in the Eastern Mediterranean.[30]

5. One real consequence of the Arab Spring was the agreement reached between the PLO and Hamas to create a united Palestinian front. It is interesting to note, however, that most Israelis, and most particularly the Netanyahu government, dismissed this agreement as unpromising and negative. The prime minister found in this agreement yet another reason for Israel's inability to negotiate with the Palestinians.

All in all, the Arab Spring has strengthened the "wait-and-see" policy of the Netanyahu government.[31] The division in the Israeli public has enabled Netanyahu to stay on the sideline on most issues. Given its ideology and structure, there is little reason to think that the Netanyahu government would have moved toward a final resolution of the question of Palestine had the Arab Spring never sprung. The Arab Spring gave Netanyahu and the Israeli right new arguments against the establishment of a Palestinian state, but it did not create those arguments. Netanyahu's traditionally grim view of the region was fortified by the recent developments but did not fundamentally change as a result of them.

In asking the Israeli public (in March 2011) what ought to be done in view of the Arab Spring, the Peace Index reported that the vast majority of Israeli Jews—70. 2 percent—agreed with the claim that Israel should remain passive "at this stage," while only 40 percent of Israeli Arabs agreed with this position.[32]

It is hard to know whether the Israeli Jewish public simply accepted the position of the Netanyahu government or dictated it. What is clear, however, is that there was no concentrated effort by the government to convince the public to see any positive element in the Arab Spring.

In the quiet competition between the pessimists and the optimists, the former have clearly prevailed. Their position has become even more dominant than before. A more diverse picture of the Arab Spring emphasizing the fall of the autocrats and the possibility of democracy was ignored in favor of an exclusive emphasis on the dangers of instability and Islamism. This position justified and legitimized Netanyahu's do-nothing approach, particularly on the Palestinian front. Rather than pushing for a Palestinian settlement as a way to promote stability, the government adopted a passive position, using the Arab Spring as a pretext for paralysis.

No other country has become more important for the pessimist/optimist battle than Egypt. The debate has been focused on the nature of Egyptian Islamist movements, especially the Muslim Brotherhood. While the pessimists interpreted it as a radical movement, the optimists have emphasized its pragmatic and even moderate character. They thought that with the Brotherhood's influence over Hamas in Gaza, Egypt could fulfill an important role in negotiating a deal between Israelis and Palestinians.

DWELLING ON THE AMERICAN FACTOR
AND THE EMERGING DIVERGENCE

The Arab Spring caught both Israel and the United States by surprise. Intelligence services, foreign ministries, academics, and politicians were completely unprepared for these events. As close allies and essentially pro-status-quo states, the United States and Israel could have been expected to have similar reactions. Yet they didn't, and this divergence of opinions may very well increase in years to come. In many ways, the Arab Spring complicated American-Israeli relations, already characterized by different views on a variety of issues.

From an Israeli perspective, the deepening rift between Israel and the United States occasioned by the Arab Spring has been worrisome. When the Arab Spring began, Israelis hoped and expected that America would automatically express its strong, unwavering support for its friends in the Middle East, mostly also Israel's friends, whatever their domestic stance with their publics or chance of survival in the face of popular uprising. The United States took a different position. While the Israeli position toward the unrest was extremely negative (especially in the case of Egypt), supportive of the existing regimes (e.g., in the case of Jordan), or ambivalent (e.g., in the case of Syria), the American position was verbally sympathetic to what Washington perceived as a democratic wave against authoritarian tradition. At the same time, Washington was careful not to get directly involved in yet another "shooting war" in the Middle East.[33] While the Israeli policy looked decisive, the American position looked waffling, and while Israel emerged as clearly supporting the old regimes, the United States was much more nuanced. Moreover, Washington showed sympathy to the rebels in the different Arab countries.

Israeli strategic thinkers noted the dramatic change. Efraim Inbar, a prominent Israeli analyst, wrote about the United States that "its friendship with Israel is no longer self-evident,"[34] a position incompatible with the statements of practically all American political figures, including President Barack Obama. Inbar speculated that "Israeli use of force as a preventive or preemptive move could exacerbate the strained Jerusalem-Washington relationship,"[35] a far-reaching conclusion in view of the centrality of such a move on Israel's part.

The most important "test case" in terms of Israeli-American divergence has been Egypt. When the American administration decided not to support President Mubarak against the demonstrators, Israelis of all stripes saw that as a sign of U.S. unreliability and even untrustworthiness. The American argument that Mubarak lost the confidence of the Egyptian people after more than three decades of authoritarian and abusive rule, manifested so clearly in his attempt to pass on the presidency to his son, failed to convince most Israeli commentators, let alone government officials. The Egyptian uprising, and the American reaction to it, heightened the tension between Washington and Jerusalem, tensions that have dominated their relations since Obama's inauguration and Netanyahu's resumption of the Israeli prime ministership.

Interestingly, Israelis saw a direct link between the situation in Egypt and the issue of whether a resolution on the Palestinian issue was even possible. This was reflective of the tendency among Israelis to look at everything systemically, as if all parts of the complicated Middle East were connected and as if all were aligned against them. As a result of the unrest in Egypt, many Israelis concluded that "the only border Israel can fully control today is the one with the West Bank,"[36] thus leading them away from a two-state settlement with the Palestinian Authority. This Israeli position further antagonized Washington. Obama put the resolution of the Israeli-Palestinian issue at the top of his Middle East agenda upon assuming office in January 2009.

Dov Waxman has argued persuasively that "at the root of today's tensions [between Israel and the United States] are increasingly differing strategic perspectives."[37] Haim Malka has expressed this idea somewhat differently when he states, "Increasingly U.S. and Israeli responses to their common challenges and threats differ significantly."[38] While Waxman talks about "strategic perspectives" and Malka about "responses to common challenges," both emphasize divergence of opinion and policies, as well as a negative trajectory in U.S.-Israeli relations in years to come. I agree with this reading of the situation but wish to emphasize its multiple roots—a disagreement about the resolution of the Israeli-Palestinian conflict, the use of force in the Middle East, the appropriate response to the Iranian challenge, and, indeed, the overall response to the Arab Spring.

In looking into United States and Israeli responses to the Arab Spring, we must note the negativity on both sides. Israelis tended to look at the Obama administration's reaction to the Arab Spring as naïve, timid, shortsighted, and unsophisticated, guaranteeing the emergence of foes to Western power. Americans saw Israel, particularly the one led by Netanyahu, as "stuck somewhere between denial and defiance."[39] But this divergence of views was not merely about calling names or gaining points in an endless debate between a superpower and its regional ally. It was also about supporting different "teams." While many Israelis stood on the side of the autocrats (notably Mubarak and Abdullah II) or, at most, showed "neutrality" (Syria), the American administration expressed support for the democratic forces challenging those autocrats. While Israel feared the ascendance of democracy in the Arab world, assuming that it would reflect the hostility of Arab public opinion toward Israel, the United States seemed to have concluded that the uprising could not and should not be stopped. While the public debate was ostensibly about being on the "right side of history," it was actually about being politically on the victorious side.

The Israeli-American "debate" has been particularly sharp in terms of the appropriate response to the Islamists in the new constellation of political power in the Middle East. In the Israeli belief system, Islamists are not to be trusted under any and all circumstances. They are implacable enemies of the Jewish state. For the United States, the picture is more complicated and more nuanced. There are some radical Muslims and some moderate Muslims, and the United States needs to find a way to talk to the latter, especially if and when they come to power. Israelis tend to argue that Islamists should not be allowed to come to power; Americans do not believe that can be done—and certainly not through the use of force.

In general, American-Israeli disagreement about the Arab Spring has to be understood structurally; it reflects the difference between the narrower view of a local power and the broader perspective of a superpower. Most Israelis expect the United States to show unshakable commitment to Israel, its overall interests, and, especially, its security. Americans look at their commitment to Israel as only one component of their multifaceted regional and even global policy. Other components include U.S. relations with Arab states, as well as America's "desire to advance democratization in the region and gain the goodwill of the new Arab leaders."[40] For the United States, strong ties with Arab countries are vital. Moreover, for the United States, the resolution of the Palestinian problem through a two-state solution is a key component for establishing a stable Middle East. For many Israelis, including major elements within the current government, this American design is problematical. For many Americans, the Palestinian issue is a source of instability and therefore a source of the Arab Spring, a position that many Israelis do not accept.

In many ways, Israeli commentators are caught on the horns of a dilemma. On the one hand, they view Israel as continuing to be dependent on American support. On the other, they see the American position in the Middle East and in the world in general as declining. Their interpretation of the U.S. regional standing is that it is on the retreat. Inbar, in a comprehensive analysis of the overall post–Arab Spring, entitles his section on the United States "The Decline of American Clout."[41] Rather harshly, he views the U.S. response to recent Middle East events as "confused, contradictory, and inconsistent."

ASSESSING THE LONG-TERM IMPACT: EXPLORING THE UNPREDICTABLE

Since we are still in the midst of the Arab Spring, we cannot know what will be the final results of this series of momentous events. Yet some trends are already identifiable, although only tentatively.

In general, there has been a tendency by most analysts to exaggerate the impact of the Arab Spring on Israel's position in the Middle East, its policies, and its politics. A more balanced view is called for. At the same time, it could be argued that the Arab Spring has further intensified Israel's isolated position in the region and possibly beyond. The Palestinian issue also indicates Israel's increasing isolation. Given that post-Spring Israel is even more reluctant than pre-Spring Israel to reach a territorial settlement with the Palestinians, it seems that post–Arab Spring Israel will continue to be highly isolated. This isolation will be marked by continuing divergence of interests, perceptions, and policies with Israel's "natural friends," the United States and the western Europeans.

In realpolitik terms, the single most important geostrategic result of the Arab Spring has been the fall of the Mubarak regime. Nevertheless, pessimistic and almost apocalyptic predictions in regard to Egyptian-Israeli relations have not come to pass. Speculation about the abrogation of the Egyptian-Israeli peace treaty (1979), the return of Egypt to pan-Arab policies à la Nasser, and the future chaotic nature of the Sinai Peninsula, among other things, have not yet materialized.

Much of the negativity in analyzing Egyptian-Israeli relations has focused on the Sinai. On August 18, 2011, there was a terrorist attack from the Egyptian-held Sinai across the border into Israel. Several civilians were killed, and Israeli politicians at least partially blamed Egypt. Four Egyptian border police officers were killed in the incident as well, leading to an attack on the Israeli Embassy in Cairo, the recalling of the Egyptian ambassador from Tel Aviv, and mutual accusations between the two countries. Nevertheless, despite this serious public crisis and cross-border violence, both countries worked toward a peaceful settlement of the dispute, assisted actively by the United States. While the Arab street exploded, the generals acted to calm passions.

The issue of the Sinai, like other Israeli-Arab issues, has deeper roots than cross-border tensions. But despite the pessimism of the Israeli press, there are mutual interests in solving such issues by peaceful means. When it comes to the Sinai, an area characterized by lawlessness for decades, Israel and Egypt share deep concern about the chaotic nature of the situation. Therefore, there is a reason to believe that they can find a way for dealing with future incidents.

This sense of realism ought to be applied to other areas as well. The Israelis are naturally worried about the "isolating processes" that they believe have come to dominate the Middle East as a result of the Arab Spring. But just as the Sinai was unstable long before the Arab Spring, Israel's isolation in the area, indeed in the world, was evident long before the Arab Spring erupted. While many Israeli commentators note the aggressive attitude of Iran and the unfriendly attitude of Turkey toward Israel, those are not really new phenomena.

All in all, when we look at the actual policies of most Arab governments, they seem to want to continue past policies. In Egypt, for example, the Supreme Council of the Armed Forces is generally committed to the status quo. Similarly, the Muslim Brotherhood, the strongest force to have emerged as a result of the uprising, has indicated that it will honor Egypt's international obligations. The peace treaty between Israel and Egypt is among the most important obligations that Egypt has taken upon itself over the last thirty-five years. It is linked to a whole gamut of Egyptian relations with the outside world, including, most importantly, Egypt's relations with the United States.

Beyond the specific issues related to the Arab Spring, the danger is that the overall interpretation of it might continue to be radically negative and completely controlled by the old Israeli narrative. Thus, there has been a strong tendency in Israel to link any change in the Arab world with "Islamism" and therefore to relate any Islamism with nondemocratic, anti-Israeli, and anti-Western attitudes. The asserted dichotomy between Islamism and democracy is simplistic and wrong. The tendency in Israel has been to think that democratization will lead to Islamism as an anti-Israel threat. A more balanced, and therefore more positive, perspective ought to be considered, giving a chance for improvement in regional relations.

Columnist Rami Khouri has described the Arab Spring as "the birth of Arab politics."[42] If Khouri is right, then Israel must find a way of reaching out to the new forces active in this new politics. Not to do so is dangerous. Israel needs to find a way of combining a realist foreign policy with a progressive bent. A realist perspective on the conflictual relations of Israel and its neighbors indicates that Israel's quietest borders have been with autocratic states, not with democratic or semidemocratic ones. Does this mean that if neighboring Arab countries adopt democracy, Israel's security would be threatened? It might. Yet it is doubtful that Israel, or for that matter the United States, can really control the development toward democracy.

Some Israeli commentators have conflated the Arab Spring with the overall decline of the Arab Middle East, a conclusion that emphasizes the instability generated by the upheavals and the rise of non-Arab powers.[43] It is, however, somewhat premature to reach such a conclusion, because the Arab Spring may energize the Arab world, especially if new forces emerge. Moreover, some of the non-Arab forces that have allegedly emerged at the expense of the Arab states—notably Iran and Turkey—are increasingly anti-Israeli. Arab states that suffer from internal instability, such as Egypt, Syria, Lebanon, and Jordan, may become a source of constant regional volatility and therefore of threats on Israel's borders. A rapprochement between some of the weakened Arab states and a non-Arab foe of Israel—for example, an Egyptian-Iranian alliance— could be truly threatening for Israel.

Another potentially long-term development resulting from the Arab Spring is the rise of Saudi Arabia to a leadership position in the region, possibly heading a broad anti-Iranian coalition. In fact, despite the overwhelming Israeli pessimism in regard to the Arab Spring, such a long-term result could work in Israel's favor, particularly regarding Iran. The active role of Saudi Arabia not merely in its close neighborhood (Bahrain, Yemen) but also in other parts of the Middle East (Syria) indicates that such a scenario is not far-fetched.

Above all, the Arab Spring has made peace in the Middle East between Israelis and Arabs more remote than ever before. While some of this assessment is based on cold realistic calculation—how can Israel conclude peace with anyone in such an unstable region?—much of it is about a psychological state of mind. It is about the triumph of anxiety. The Arab Spring strengthened the fear factor in Israel and especially the political forces associated with that fear factor, the traditional right. Although some commentators have argued that the Arab Spring might result in tougher Israeli security demands if and when negotiations start (e.g., presence on the Jordan River, demilitarization of the Palestinian state), the deeper meaning of the Arab Spring is that negotiations are simply unlikely to start at all.

The assumption of many Israeli analysts has been that the Arab world has been unwaveringly hostile to Israel and that no matter what Israel does, this hostility will remain constant. Moreover, they further assume that the new forces in the region, especially the Islamists, are even more hostile to Israel and that Israel cannot change that hostility through its actions. It seems to me that such fatalistic assumptions could lead inevitably to one and only one result— no change in Israeli policy. Such a result would be tragic, a classic case of self-fulfilling prophecy.

NOTES

1. See, for example, the Peace Index of the Israel Democracy Institute, which has collected large amounts of information on the attitudes of Israelis. In assessing the response of the Israeli public to the Arab Spring, I will rely heavily on the Peace Index; whenever possible, I will use other sources as well. In this essay, I will use "Arab Spring" as shorthand for the Middle East demonstrations, protest, and violent acts (including the wars in Libya and Syria) since December 2010. Concepts such as "awakening," "uprising," or even "revolution" will be used interchangeably.

2. Daniel L. Byman, "Israel: A Frosty Response to the Arab Spring," in *The Arab Awakening: America and the Transformation of the Middle East*, ed. Kenneth M. Pollack (Washington, DC: Brookings Institution Press, 2011), 250–257.

3. Maybe the most comprehensive assessment of the impact of the Arab Spring on Israel's overall situation has been offered by Efraim Inbar, "The 2011 Arab Uprisings and Israel's National Security," *Mideast Security and Policy Studies* No. 95 (Ramat-Gan, Israel: The Begin-Sadat Center for Strategic Studies, Bar-Ilan University, February 2011).

4. Irving L. Janis, *Victims of Groupthink: A Psychological Study of Foreign-Policy Decisions and Fiascoes* (Boston: Houghton Mifflin, 1972).

5. Byman calls this perception, alternatively, the "fear factors," in "Israel," 250.

6. Quoted in Leslie Susser, "Seize the Spring," *Jerusalem Report*, February 27, 2012, 20.

7. When Egypt allowed two Iranian ships to go through the Suez Canal, Israelis took notice. Yet to date, an Egyptian-Iranian alliance has not materialized. There is plenty of evidence that the major Sunni Arab countries, such as Egypt and Saudi Arabia, fear the growing Iranian influence in the region.

8. Israel Democracy Institute (IDI), "Peace Index," November 2011, http://www.peaceindex.org/files/The%20Peace%20Index%20Data%20 0-%20November%202011.pdf.

9. Quoted in Eric Rozenman, "The 'Arab Spring': Democratic Promise or Threat?," *Midstream*, Spring 2011, 9.

10. Much of the "analysis" on what the Islamist may or may not do in regard to Israel tends to be rather speculative, often not based on any hard evidence.

11. Hamas has its origins in the Egyptian Muslim Brotherhood. Yet if the Brotherhood comes to power in Egypt, it may decide to try moderating Hamas in Gaza.

12. IDI, Peace Index, March 2011, http://www.peaceindex.org/files/The%20 %Peace%20Index%20Data%20-%20November%202011.pdf.

13. Inbar calls it the "Somalization" of the Sinai. See Inbar, "The 2011 Arab Uprisings," 15.

14. IDI, Peace Index, February 2011, http://www.peaceindex.org/files/The %20%Peace%20Index%20Data%20-%20November%202011.pdf.

15. For speculation about such a scenario, see Aaron David Miller, "2011: The Year of the (Bad) Initiative," *New York Times*, March 11, 2011.

16. Rozenman, "The 'Arab Spring,'" 8–11.

17. Aaron David Miller, "Why Israel Fears a Free Egypt," *Washington Post*, February 4, 2011.

18. Yossi Beilin, "The Empowerment of the Arab Society," www.bitterlemons .org/inside.php?id=96, June 13, 2011.

19. Shibley Telhami, "Jewish Citizens of Israel," in *2011 Public Opinion Polls of Jewish and Arab Citizens of Israel*, Brookings Institution, 3–5, http://www .brookings.edu/~/media/research/files/reports/2011/12/01%20israel%20poll %20telhami/1201_israel_poll_telhami_presentation.

On the other hand, the majority Israelis thought that the impact of the Arab Spring on Israel was "mostly for the worse" (51 percent) rather than "mostly for the better." Those contradictions reflect the fact that the Israeli public has been torn in regard to the Arab Spring.

20. Moshe Arens, "Growing Mideast Democracy Could Benefit Israel," *Haaretz*, April 5, 2011. While Arens mentioned the concern about Islamist takeover, his tone was less alarmist than that of many other right-leaning commentators.

21. IDI, Peace Index, March 2011.

22. IDI, Peace Index, May 2011, http://www.peaceindex.org/files/The%20 %Peace%20Index%20Data%20-%20November%202011.pdf.

23. IDI, Peace Index, November 2011.

24. See, for example, Ilan Peleg, "The Israeli Right," in *Contemporary Israel: Domestic Politics, Foreign Policy, and Security Challenges*, ed. Robert O. Freedman (Boulder, CO: Westview Press, 2009), 21–44.

25. Comments by General Uzi Dayan, reported by the Begin-Sadat Center for Strategic Studies, "What Arab Spring?," Bulletin no. 28 (Spring 2012).

26. I share in this respect the opinion expressed by Brent E. Sasley, "Israel and the Arab Spring: But the Season Doesn't Matter," Huffington Post, December 28, 2011.

27. For a pessimistic view on Jordan, see Herb Keinon, "Anti-normalization Forces Gaining Strength in Jordan," *Jerusalem Post*, August 10, 2011; and Eli

Lake, "Muslim Brotherhood Seeks End to Israel Treaty," *Washington Times*, February 3, 2011.

28. IDI, Peace Index, February 2012, http://www.peaceindex.org/files/The%20%Peace%20Index%20Data%20-%20November%202011.pdf.

29. Ibid.

30. Inbar, "The 2011 Arab Uprisings," 25.

31. Yossi Klein Halevi, "Israel's Neighborhood Watch: Egypt's Upheaval Means That Palestine Must Wait," *Foreign Affairs*, February 1, 2011.

32. IDI, Peace Index, March 2011.

33. For example, the United States reacted very differently to the Syrian revolt than to the Libyan revolt.

34. Inbar, "The 2011 Arab Uprisings," 10.

35. Ibid.

36. Halevi, "Israel's Neighborhood Watch."

37. Dov Waxman, "The Real Problem in U.S.-Israeli Relations," *Washington Quarterly*, Spring 2012, 71–87.

38. Haim Malka, *Crossroads: The Future of the U.S.-Israel Strategic Partnership* (Washington, DC: Center for International and Strategic Studies, 2011), 56.

39. Waxman, "The Real Problem," 75.

40. Byman, "Israel," 256.

41. Inbar, "The 2011 Arab Uprisings," 5–7.

42. Quoted in Salman Shaikh, "A Failure to Communicate," *Foreign Policy*, February 9, 2012, http://www.foreignpolicy.com/articles/2012/02/09/a_failure_to_communicate?page=0,1.

43. See, for example, Inbar, "The 2011 Arab Uprisings," 4.

10

Russia and the Arab Spring: A Preliminary Appraisal

ROBERT O. FREEDMAN

INTRODUCTION

I think that these processes [of the Arab Spring] have no direct impact on us. Although one should recognize that there are certain financial costs as we had to stop our involvement in some economic projects and military and technical cooperation in some cases. I am sure that the ongoing events cannot break the huge, mutually fruitful potential of cooperation that has been stockpiling for years. . . . [However, i]f the region's countries turn out to be under weak control of the central authorities, this would be fertile soil for international terrorism's efforts, illicit drug trafficking, trans-border crime, and illegal migration.

Russian Deputy Foreign Minister Mikhail Bogdanov,
Interfax, July 5, 2011

WHEN THE "ARAB SPRING" erupted on the world scene in January 2011, Russia, like the rest of the world, was caught by surprise.[1] Before going into the Russian reaction to the developments in the Arab world, however, I want to first evaluate the position of Russia in the Middle East at the time of the uprisings. Thus, we will examine Russia's goals in the region under Russian leader Vladimir Putin, although, as will be noted in the chapter, several elements of Russian policy in the Middle East, particularly Russian policy in Iran and Libya, have also been shaped by Russian President Dmitry Medvedev. Next, an assessment will be made of the success Putin had achieved in attaining his goals on the eve of the Arab Spring. The final section of the chapter will discuss the Russian reaction to the Arab Spring, with particular attention to Libya and Syria, countries where Russian policy has diverged most strongly from that of NATO.

PUTIN'S GOALS FOR THE MIDDLE EAST

As they have developed in the more than ten years since he became Russia's leader, Putin's goals in the Middle East are basically fourfold. First, he has sought to restore Russia's status as a great power, thereby ending U.S. dominance of the post–cold war world. The United States had become vulnerable in the Middle East because of its ongoing wars in Iraq and Afghanistan as well as the failure of its leadership in the Arab-Israeli peace process. Both developments had angered and alienated many Middle Eastern states. Second, he has sought to develop the Russian economy, particularly in the high-tech area. He has sought to sell not only sophisticated armaments but also nuclear reactors to Middle Eastern states while at the same time trying to get them to invest in the Russian economy. Third, as Russian oil and natural gas reserves become more expensive to exploit, Putin has sought to establish partnerships with Middle Eastern oil and natural gas producers. Fourth, he has sought to minimize Middle Eastern aid to Chechen and other Islamist insurgents in Russia's North Caucasus region.[2]

THE RUSSIAN POSITION IN THE MIDDLE EAST IN DECEMBER 2010

First, there is no question but that after Boris Yeltsin's decade of relative ab-sence from the Middle East (1991–2000)—except for Iran and Turkey—and Putin's own first term in which his posture toward the Middle East was basically defensive, the Russian leader has succeeded in restoring Russia's presence in the region. Second, while Russia certainly has a renewed pres-ence, there is a question as to the degree to which Moscow has been able to exercise real influence in the Middle East. Third, as Moscow increased its presence in the Middle East, this has also presented a dilemma in terms of which side to back in the numerous conflicts that pervaded the region. Fi-nally, the Middle East has become of increasing economic importance to Moscow, and Putin has pursued economic relationships with almost all the countries in the region.

One of Putin's goals as he began to pursue a more assertive role in the Middle East beginning in late 2004 was to demonstrate Russia's renewed visibility in the region, as Putin sought to compensate for setbacks in Beslan and Ukraine. He accomplished this through personal visits to Turkey, Egypt, Israel, and the Palestinian territories in the December 2004–April 2005 period; to Saudi Arabia, Jordan, Qatar, the United Arab Emirates, and Iran in 2007; to Libya in 2008; and to Turkey in 2009. Major arms sales to Iran and Syria took place in 2005. Moscow gave diplomatic support to rogue states and organizations such as Syria and Iran in 2005 and Hamas and Hizbullah in 2006. And Russia gained observer status at the Islamic Conference in 2005.

There is a question, however, as to how much this renewed presence had led to renewed influence for Russia in the Middle East. As Moscow deepened its relations with many of the countries of the Middle East, it began to run into serious problems of choice. Not only was it stuck on the horns of the Israeli-Palestinian conflict, as Moscow endeavored to maintain good ties with both Israel and Mahmoud Abbas's Palestinian Authority, but also, after the Hamas seizure of power in Gaza in June 2007, to try to maintain good ties with both Hamas and the Palestinian Authority. Another difficult problem of choice for Moscow lay in the rapidly escalating political conflict between Iran and the Sunni states of the Middle East, especially Saudi Arabia, Egypt, and Jordan. Russia's agreement to minor UN Security Council sanctions against Iran both before and after Putin's visit to Saudi Arabia, Jordan, and Qatar in 2007; a delay in completing the Bushehr reactor; and Russia's vote in the International Atomic Energy Agency in late 2009 to condemn Iran for building a secret nuclear facility near Qomall seem to have been aimed, in part, at assuaging Sunni Arab anger at the role Moscow had played in developing Iran's nuclear program and military capability. Indeed, in 2007–2008 Moscow sought to balance the ties it had developed with rogue states and organizations, such as Iran, Syria, Hamas, and Hizbullah, with ties to major Sunni Arab states, such as Saudi Arabia, the United Arab Emirates, Qatar, and Jordan. This, plus improved ties with the United States (the START agreement had just been signed), appears to explain Moscow's willingness to agree to a somewhat tougher sanctions resolution against Iran in June 2010, as well as to its canceling its SAM-300 deal with Iran. However this angered Iran and put the worst chill in Russian-Iranian relations since Putin became Russia's president in 2000. Nonetheless, it was still a very open question as to whether Russia, given the expanding Islamic insurgency in the North Caucasus and its own expanding economic interests in Iran, especially in Iran's oil and natural gas sectors, would actually vote to endorse serious sanctions against Iran that would include a ban on trade with and investments in the Islamic Republic, in particular in the energy sector.

Finally, economic gain was also a goal of Putin's increased activity in the Middle East, and in this area his efforts met with a modicum of success. Turkey became a major trade partner for Russia, especially as a market for Russian natural gas exports, and it could also become a major hub for Russian oil and natural gas exports to Europe and the Middle East. Russia and Turkey also signed an agreement in 2010 under which Russia would sell nuclear reactors to Turkey. Arms sales, as in the case of the Soviet Union, were also a component of Russian foreign economic policy, and Iran was a major market for such Russian weapons systems as combat aircraft and submarines, until the June 2010 sanctions resolution, which barred certain classes of arms from sale to Iran. Moscow also began to penetrate the arms markets of Saudi Arabia and the United Arab Emirates. Economic relations also played a role in Russian-Israeli relations, as Putin's desire to wean Russia off its dependence on energy exports made Israel's small, but high-tech economy very attractive, particularly in the area of nanotechnology, which Russia was trying to develop. Israel also signed an agreement to provide military drones to Russia and agreed to build a drone factory in Russia. In addition, by the latter part of the decade Russia was beginning to run into problems producing oil and natural gas, which had become more difficult and more expensive to extract. Consequently, Gasprom, Lukoil, and Rosneft, among other Russian energy companies, sought deals with Iran, Iraq, Saudi Arabia, Qatar, Algeria, and other Middle Eastern states where the cost of production was considerably below that of Russia.

Thus, by December 2010, Russia under Putin had reemerged in the Middle East as a diplomatic, economic, and military supply actor. Yet its political influence remained limited, and it appears that Putin's primary achievement in the region was to demonstrate that Russia was again a factor in the Middle East, even if its influence in the region continued to be limited. The Arab Spring, however, was to challenge all of Putin's goals, and it is not yet clear, despite the optimistic tone of Deputy Foreign Minister Bogdanov's comments, whether Russia has yet come to grips with the implications of the Middle East revolutions.

RUSSIA'S INITIAL ENCOUNTER WITH THE ARAB SPRING

The Arab Spring caught Russia, as it did the United States and indeed the rulers of the countries affected, unaware.[3] In a dynamic somewhat reminiscent of the events in Eastern Europe in 1989, the revolutions quickly spread from Tunisia to Egypt and then to Yemen, Libya, Bahrain, Syria, and Jordan.

As far as the Russian leadership was concerned, there appeared to be some initial concern that the revolutions in the Arab world could spread to Russia as well. Russia itself was marked by an autocratic government, widespread corruption—something President Medvedev had openly complained about—and rising prices, with inflation reaching nearly 10 percent in 2010.[4] Indeed, Russia's prodemocracy opposition cheered the events in Tunisia and Egypt, with comments such as "The [revolutionary] train stopped at the station in Cairo. Next stop: Moscow" and "Start packing your bags, Vladimir."[5] Medvedev took a tough line on such attitudes, and in an almost cold war–era response, asserted that the revolts in the Arab world were instigated by "outside forces" also trying to topple the Russian government. In Medvedev's words, "Let's face the truth. They have been preparing such a scenario for us, and now they will try even harder to implement it."[6]

However, Medvedev's concern initially appeared very much exaggerated. First, Russia had gone through a chaotic period only a decade before under Yeltsin, and with the exception of a relatively small group of reformers, Russians at first showed little inclination to oust the ruling duo of Medvedev and Putin by street protests. Second, unlike the case in Egypt, the Russian religious authorities in the Orthodox Church had closely aligned themselves with the regime (a situation somewhat reminiscent of Czarist Russia). As far as Western instigation of the Arab Spring was concerned, Russia's leading Middle East expert (and former prime minister and foreign minister) Yevgeny Primakov, no friend of the United States, publicly ruled out the idea that the United States had orchestrated the revolts, asserting that he was convinced, after visiting the United States, that the developments in Egypt "provided a true shock for the Americans."[7]

Nonetheless, following the announcement in the fall of 2011 that Putin would again run for president—an action that would allow him to stay in power until 2024—coupled with the fraudulent Duma (parliamentary) elections of December 4, 2011, it suddenly appeared that the Arab Spring had indeed come to Russia as tens of thousands of Russians took to the streets to protest. As will be shown below, the mass protests were to affect Russian policy toward the Arab Spring in general and to the situation in Syria in particular.

In weighing the rapidly changing situation in the Middle East caused by the Arab Spring, Moscow could note some short-term gains to its Middle East position, as well as the possibility of some long-term losses. By early March 2011, the price of Brent oil had risen 24 percent since the beginning of January, reaching more than $110 per barrel. This enabled Russia to meet its projected budget deficit from the increased oil revenues and even rebuild its sovereign wealth fund, which had been depleted by the 2008 world economic crisis, even though Russia remained plagued by capital flight.[8] In addition, with the possibility of natural gas supplies to Europe being cut off due to the turmoil in the Middle East and North Africa—the Europeans had been trying to diversify their sources of natural gas by buying LNG (liquefied natural gas) from the Middle East so as to lessen their dependence on Moscow— Russia saw the possibility of increasing its natural gas sales to Europe. Indeed, in a visit to Brussels in late February, Putin took pride in pointing to Russia as a reliable natural gas supplier.[9]

On the downside, however, Moscow had to worry about its own oil and gas investments in the Middle East, which were at risk if the turmoil got worse, as well as the possible loss of arms and industrial deals it had signed with countries such as Libya and Syria. Another problem for Moscow lay in the possibility that conservative Islamist forces, both of the Salafi and Muslim Brotherhood type, could be the big winners of the Arab Spring, particularly if free and fair elections were held in countries such as Tunisia, Egypt, and Syria. Given that Russia's North Caucasus continued to simmer with Islamic unrest, with continuing Islamist attacks in Dagestan, Chechnya, northern Ossetia, and Ingushetia and an Islamist terror attack on Moscow's Domodedovo airport in January 2011, Moscow had cause for concern. Islamist victories in Egypt, Tunisia, and Syria, and possibly in Libya as well, could give added impetus to the Islamic uprising in the North Caucasus—something Putin had tried to prevent by having Russia admitted to the Islamic Conference as an observer and by courting Saudi Arabia.[10] Indeed in Brussels Putin had stated, "Regardless of the calming theories that radical groups coming to power in North Africa is unlikely, if it happens it can not but spread to other areas of the world, including the Northern Caucasus."[11]

On the other hand, in countries like Tunisia and Egypt, the ouster of leaders closely linked to the United States and the West held some potential benefits for Moscow. Especially in Egypt, the close link between the Mubarak regime and Washington made the United States highly unpopular, despite U.S. President Barak Obama's speech in Cairo in June 2009. Whether or not Moscow could benefit from the situation was, however, an open question. Egypt's Supreme Council of the Armed Forces, which was essentially running the country into June 2012 and appeared to be doing so even after the Egyptian presidential elections, had close ties with the U.S. military, and there was a good bit of suspicion that the Egyptian army would be highly influential in the new government. In addition, because of a serious drought in Russia in 2010, Putin had declared a ban on wheat exports in August 2010, thereby considerably complicating Egypt's efforts to import the grain because Russia had accounted for more than half of Egypt's wheat imports before the embargo. The end result was that when Russia again began to export wheat in 2011, the Egyptians excluded Russia from a June 2011 tender, with the vice chairman of Egypt's State Wheat Purchasing Agency stating, "Last year the Russians failed to ship some quantities that were agreed upon, even before the ban came into effect, and that is why I am wary of the Russian side. When we are sure that the Russian side is stable, we will re-include it."[12] While Egypt subsequently did buy Russian wheat, it was at a sizable discount.

RUSSIA AND LIBYA

If Russia hoped to make gains in Tunisia and Egypt, it sought to avoid losses in Libya and Syria, whose regimes were seriously challenged by the Arab Spring. Indeed, the Russian leadership may have remembered the "Death to Russia" signs carried by antiregime demonstrators in Iran in 2009. In the case of Libya, Russia appeared to be following what might be termed a zigzag policy, first opposing sanctions on Libya and then agreeing to them; first opposing a no-fly zone over Libya and then agreeing to it; and then, while criticizing NATO for using excessive force in Libya, agreeing to serve as a mediator between the Libyan rebels and the Gadafi regime, even as it urged Muammar al-Gadafi himself to step down.

What explains these apparent contradictions in Russian policy? In part, they were caused by disagreements between Medvedev and Putin that broke out into the open over the no-fly zone. In part, they were caused by Moscow's disinclination to oppose the Arab consensus, which supported both sanctions and the no-fly zone. By offering to mediate the conflict, Russia was able to demonstrate its importance in the Middle East. And by maintaining ties with both the Gadafi regime and the rebels, who with NATO support had been able to consolidate their position in the city of Benghazi by May 2011, Moscow evidently hoped to preserve both its investments and its markets in Libya no matter which side eventually won the civil war.

Unlike the situation in Tunisia and Egypt, Russia had major economic interests in Libya. According to a Russian arms supply specialist, Russia had signed $2 billion in arms contracts with Libya and had another $1.8 billion in contracts under negotiation.[13] Thus, Russia could lose almost $4 billion in arms sales should Gadafi fall. In addition, during his 2008 trip to Libya, Putin had signed a number of major industrial agreements, which were now also in jeopardy. Consequently, when the United States and its NATO allies began to call for sanctions against the Gadafi regime because of its brutal crackdown on dissidents, the Russian Foreign Ministry claimed that the proposed sanctions would not be effective and rejected them, although Russian Foreign Minister Sergei Lavrov, in a joint statement with foreign policy chief Catherine Ashton of the European Union (EU), did say, "We condemn and consider unacceptable the use of military force to break up peaceful demonstrations."[14]

Several days later, however, Medvedev reversed the Foreign Ministry's position and agreed to the sanctions, which included an arms embargo, joining in a unanimous Security Council Resolution (No.1970) that also called for Gadafi's actions to be referred to the International Criminal Court. As Medvedev stated, "We strongly call on the current Libyan authorities to show restraint and not allow a worsening of the situation and the killing of civilians. If they do not, such actions will qualify as crimes, carrying all the consequences of international law."[15]

Gadafi, however, rejected Medvedev's threat, and as Libyan government forces bore down on Benghazi, there were increasing calls for a no-fly zone to protect the inhabitants of that city. These calls came not only from the United States and the EU, but also from the Arab League, an organization that Moscow, as it was seeking to increase its influence in the Middle East, was loathe to oppose. Although Lavrov initially denounced the proposed military intervention as "unacceptable,"[16] Medvedev overruled him, and the end result was that Russia chose to abstain on the UN Security Council Resolution (No. 1973) authorizing the no-fly zone, thus allowing it to be adopted. Russia's abstention, however, brought to the surface a major dispute in the Russian leadership over Libya policy. Medvedev had already fired the Russian ambassador to Libya for opposing the sanctions,[17] but Putin, speaking at a missile factory in Votkinsk, publicly denounced the resolution, calling it "defective and flawed" and asserting, "It allows everything. It resembles 'Medieval calls for Crusades.'"[18] Medvedev, in turn, publicly contradicted Putin several hours later, stating, "In no way is it acceptable to use expressions that ensure the clash of civilizations, such as crusades and so forth. This is unacceptable. Otherwise everything may wind up far worse."[19] The Putin-controlled Duma, perhaps trying to prevent the dispute from escalating, adopted a compromise position, voting 350–32 to call on NATO to stop all military action against Libya, but also stating that the Russian abstention on Resolution No. 1973 was "appropriate."[20]

Over the next several months, as NATO airstrikes increased in intensity, Russian criticism of NATO military action grew, but Moscow proved unable to stop the NATO attacks. By the latter part of May, therefore, Moscow adopted a new policy, one of mediation between the rebels and the Gadafi regime. It invited representatives of both the Gadafi regime and the rebels to Moscow, and at the G-8 Summit in late May, Medvedev, after meeting with President Obama, offered to try to persuade Gadafi to step down from power. As might be expected, Gadafi was less than enthusiastic about the Russian mediation offer, and Libyan Deputy Foreign Minister Khalid Kaim stated at a news conference that Libya had expected solidarity from Russia after forty years of close commercial and political links, not a deal made in France that aligned Moscow with the West in an attempt to oust Gadafi. Kaim also stated that Libya would not accept any mediation efforts from Moscow unless Russia worked through the African Union—long an ally of Gadafi's.[21]

It appears that Moscow got Gadafi's message because after appointing Mikhail Margelov, chairman of the Russian Federation Council's International Affairs Committee, as special envoy to Libya, Medvedev sent him to meet the Libyan rebels in Benghazi. And then Margelov was dispatched to the African Union summit in Equatorial Guinea in late June, where, after meeting with a number of African leaders, he stated that Russia would step up its contacts with the African Union in seeking a settlement on Libya.[22] Moscow appeared now to back the African Union's road map for settling the Libyan conflict, which, in calling for "broad dialogue" between the sides, was unacceptable both to the Libyan rebels and to NATO. However, the African Union's offer to mediate the talks seemed to eclipse the month-long Russian effort. Medvedev, who personally met with President Jacob Zuma of South Africa when he was on a visit to Moscow in early July, nevertheless sought to highlight Russia's close cooperation with the African Union in its peacemaking efforts.[23]

Unfortunately for Moscow, however, by September the Gadafi regime had fallen to a Western-backed Transitional Council and Russia turned out to be the major loser, diplomatically, economically, and militarily. The lesson Moscow took from this development was not to allow another UN Security Council resolution to be passed that could, as in the case of Libya, lead to regime change. This concern was to dominate Russian policy toward Syria after the fall of Gadafi.

RUSSIA AND SYRIA

Unlike the situation in Libya, Russian policy toward the Syrian uprising has been much more consistent. Although the crackdown by the Bashar al-Assad regime on its citizens has been every bit as brutal as that by Gadafi, not only has Moscow opposed Libya-type military intervention in Syria, it has also opposed sanctions against the Assad regime. This has been the case because Syria has long been a major ally of Moscow in the Middle East and, unlike the mercurial regime of Muammar al-Gadafi, the Assad regime has real, if diminishing, influence in the Arab world. The regime has ties to Hizbullah, which since February 2011 has been the dominant power in Lebanon, and, to a lesser degree, to Hamas, which controls Gaza and had its headquarters in Damascus until the intensification of the Assad regime's crackdown on protesters in 2011. In addition, Syria has close ties to Iran, and Moscow, whose relations with Iran had deteriorated after the Security Council sanctions resolution against Iran in 2010, appears to have little interest in further alienating Tehran with pressure on the Islamic Republic's primary Arab ally, Syria. Syria also was a major market for Russian arms, most recently the Bastion antiship missile, the Pantsir air defense system, and the Yakhont cruise missile system,[24] and unlike the case in Libya, Moscow had been given the use of naval facilities in Tartus by the Syrian government. Finally, unlike the case in Libya, there was no Arab consensus on dealing with Syria.

Consequently, when the uprising in Syria began, Moscow steadfastly opposed foreign intervention, especially intervention legitimized, as it had been in Libya, by a UN Security Council resolution. In late April, as the uprising against Assad intensified, Alexander Pankin, Russia's deputy permanent representative to the United Nations, stated, "The current situation in Syria, despite the increase in tension, does not represent a threat to international peace and security." Intervention would be "an invitation to civil war."[25] While constantly opposing UN resolutions on Syria, not only those condemning the Assad regime for its crackdown on peaceful protesters but also those dealing with its secret nuclear program (first revealed by an Israeli raid in September 2007), Russia was also willing to call on the Syrian government to bring to justice those responsible for the deaths of demonstrators and to make reforms.[26] Consequently, when Assad did make some halfhearted reforms, they were praised by Moscow, with Lavrov urging the Syrian protesters to engage in a dialogue with the Syrian regime. After meeting with the French foreign minister in early July 2011, Lavrov stated that what was needed to calm the situation in Syria was to "transfer the Syrian situation onto a political track as expeditiously as possible. It requires good will on both sides, the authorities need to continue reforms, to pursue them more intensively—this is what we say to our partners in Damascus. . . . On the other hand, the opposition must give up its absolutely uncompromising stance as well as ignoring any suggestions from the Syrian authorities, and begin a dialogue. After all, what has been done and promised is no small thing."[27]

As in the case of Libya, however, Moscow sought to keep ties not only with the Syrian government, but also with the Syrian opposition. Thus, the Russian Afro-Asian Solidarity and Cooperation Society invited a delegation of the opposition to visit Moscow. This was a low-level invitation reminiscent of the Soviet Afro-Asian Peoples Solidarity Association making similar invitations during the Soviet era to maintain contact with opposition groups.[28] Interestingly enough, however, the Syrian group also met with Margelov—possibly as a means of generating additional pressure on the Assad regime to commit itself to serious, regime-preserving reforms. But as Margelov pointedly noted, "Leaders come and go, politicians come and go, but for Russia there remains a single reliable and trusted friend, the Syrian people."[29] In any case, as far as both Syria and Libya were concerned, Moscow was trying to salvage its position no matter who came out on top in the struggle for power. Indeed, a leader of a Syrian opposition delegation visiting Moscow, Radwan Ziadeh, dutifully stated, "We would like the warm relations between Syria and Russia to be preserved even after the President Assad regime is replaced in Syria."[30] However, as the Syrian regime intensified its crackdown on anti-regime protesters, the Syrian opposition and much of the Sunni Arab world, led by Saudi Arabia, became highly critical of Russia, thereby threatening

Russia's current position in the Arab world, which Putin had tried so hard to build.

The fall of Gadafi seemed to inspire the Syrian opposition, and demonstrations against the Assad regime intensified. But Moscow continued to support Assad, as evidenced by its opposition to any anti-Syrian vote in the UN Human Rights Council. Antiregime demonstrators burned Russian flags in protest. Then at a news conference in Moscow on September 9, Syrian opposition leader Ammar Al-Qurabi pointedly noted, "Russia was late in recognizing the new authorities in Libya. This is the second mistake. The first mistake was made in Iraq [with Saddam Hussein]. We wish that Moscow would not repeat a mistake of this kind for the third time—in respect to what is happening in Syria."[31]

But Moscow did not heed al-Qurabi's warning. On October 4, 2011, as civilian casualties mounted in Syria, Russia vetoed a proposed anti-Syrian Security Council resolution that, while containing no sanctions, did warn that sanctions would be forthcoming if the Syrian government continued oppressing its citizens. The resolution also condemned the Syrian regime for "systematic human rights violations and the use of force against civilians."[32]

In vetoing the resolution, Russia's UN representative, Vitaly Churkin, asserted that the resolution was "based on the philosophy of confrontation," that the threat of sanctions was "unacceptable," and that the resolution was a pretext for "regime demise."[33] However, in an apparent attempt to salvage its reputation in the Sunni Arab world following the veto, Russia announced visits of Syrian opposition delegations at the Foreign Ministry level, a major step above the level of the Russian Afro-Asian Solidarity and Cooperation Organization, the previous venue of such visits. In addition, Medvedev made the strongest criticism of Assad to date, issuing a statement asserting, "If the Syrian leadership is incapable of conducting reforms, it will have to go." Medvedev, however, then qualified his statement by adding, "This decision should be taken not by NATO or certain European countries; it should be taken by the Syrian people and the Syrian leadership."[34] Meanwhile, the then Syrian National Council president, Burhan Ghalioun, who represented the leading opposition group to Assad, bemoaned the Russian (and Chinese) veto, stating, "Supporting Bashar al-Assad in his militarist and fascist project will not encourage the Syrian people to stick to peaceful revolution."[35] Ghalioun's remarks were prophetic, because, following the Russian veto, as Assad felt emboldened to step up his military crackdown on the demonstrators, they fought back, which ultimately led to the emergence of a Free Syrian Army rebel force.

As the fighting escalated, the Arab League, meeting in Cairo, called for a "national dialogue" between Syria's government and opposition to help end the violence and avoid "foreign intervention in Syria." This call also warned Syria that it faced expulsion from the Arab League if it did not comply.[36] From Moscow's point of view, the Arab League's resolution, which the Syrian representative at the League repudiated as a "conspiracy,"[37] had a number of positive elements. First, it called for a dialogue between the Syrian regime and its opponents—just what Moscow was trying to achieve by inviting opposition delegations to Moscow. Second, its desire to avoid "foreign intervention" coincided with Moscow's goal, as the Russian leadership clearly wished to avoid a repetition of the Libyan experience.

Given this situation, Russia decided to back the Arab League plan. Lavrov stated, "Moscow has given active support to the plan for the settlement of the crisis in Syria proposed by the League of Arab States [LAS], and has hailed the willingness of the Syrian Government to start implementing it. The implementation of these measures and other points of the LAS initiative would offer an opportunity for a constructive and concrete political dialogue between the Syrian Government and opposition with the aim of taking the path of conciliation without any external interference."[38]

Unfortunately for Moscow, rather than toning down his repression of the domestic opposition, Assad increased it, leading Moscow to deplore the regime's actions in the Syrian city of Homs as "inevitably alarming." However, in an attempt to be "evenhanded," Moscow also blamed "armed extremists who were provoking retaliation from the authorities to derail the League of Arab States initiative."[39] But Moscow soon found that it could not play the evenhanded game in Syria and soon shifted back to fully supporting Assad. Thus, when the Arab League, witnessing Assad's accelerated crackdown, suspended Syria's membership, Lavrov called the suspension "incorrect" and blamed the United States and NATO for it.[40]

The end result of the failed negotiations was a more decisive Russian shift to the side of the Syrian government. In January 2012, a Russian naval flotilla visited the Russian base in Syria at Tartus—an action hailed by the governor of Tartus as evidence of the "honorable position adopted by Russia which stood by the Syrian people."[41] Russian ships also came to Syria to resupply the Assad regime with weapons and ammunition. When confronted over this resupply effort and

Assad's use of Russian weaponry to kill his own people, Moscow replied that there was no UN Security Council resolution prohibiting the supply of weapons to Syria, and that until there was one, Moscow would do as it pleased.[42]

In adopting this position, the Russian leadership was clearly taking a major gamble. By backing Syria, it was alienating most of the Sunni Arab world, especially the Gulf Cooperation Council (GCC), led by Saudi Arabia. In looking for reasons for this policy, besides Russia's major investments in Syria and its desire to prevent the loss of another ally to the West, we need also to consider Russian domestic politics. By December 2011, the Arab Spring, albeit belatedly, had arrived in Moscow and was challenging Putin's leadership. Putin asserted that he saw the same forces at work in Russia as in Syria, which may account for the increased backing for Syria in the early months of 2012 and for the sharp deterioration of U.S.-Russian relations occurring at the same time.

While Putin was confronted by Moscow's deteriorating diplomatic position in the Middle East because of Russia's support for the Assad regime, in December 2011 he was confronted by a version of the Arab Spring at home. Some of the same issues that had motivated Arabs to take to the streets were also at work in Russia: rising prices, leaders who had been in power for too long, and rampant corruption. Two events appear to have precipitated the protests in Russia: Putin's decision to switch places with Medvedev (Putin had been Russia's president from 2001 to 2008 and then became prime minister while Medvedev became president) and run again for president in March 2012 and the Duma election of December 4, 2011, which was widely seen as fraudulent. Fifty thousand people took to the streets of Moscow on December 10 to protest the election results and to call for new elections. As TV cameras rolled, there were shouts from the crowd of "Russia Without Putin." Further demonstrations followed on December 24 of 100,000 people and on February 4, 2012, of 160,000 people despite the bitter cold. Unlike in the case of Egypt, however, the demonstrators succeeded neither in bringing down the Putin regime nor in preventing Putin's reelection on March 4, 2012, although demonstrations continued after the election.

PUTIN'S ATTEMPTS TO SALVAGE THE RUSSIAN POSITION IN THE MIDDLE EAST

Throughout February, as Putin concentrated on the Russian presidential election, the Russian position in the Middle East deteriorated, as Moscow found itself isolated in no fewer than three UN votes concerning Syria. It faced increasingly sharp criticism not only from the United States and such EU states as France and Britain, but also from GCC Arab states. As a result, in March Russia made a few gestures to the Sunni Arab world by offering some measured criticism of the Assad regime, and in the latter part of March, Russia joined a watered down UN Security Council presidential letter calling for a cease-fire in Syria. Nonetheless, despite the criticism, Moscow remained a strong backer of Assad and worked hard to prevent any UN sanctions against his regime.

Moscow's Middle East position had suffered a major blow when, on February 4, 2012, it vetoed a weak UN Security Council resolution that, while criticizing Syria, did not call for an arms embargo or for Assad's resignation, as a recent Arab League peace plan had done. The Soviet veto took place even though Assad was escalating his crackdown on Syrian protesters. Despite a visit by Lavrov to Damascus after the veto, the crackdown continued unabated, which made matters worse for Moscow. Opposition leader Ghalioun strongly criticized the veto, stating that Russian credibility had been lost amid the continuous shelling of the Syrian people. Ghalioun called Lavrov's visit to Damascus "an interference in Syrian affairs" that was "targeted against the Syrian people."[43] Saudi Arabia also criticized Moscow, saying it should have coordinated with the Arab League before the veto.[44] Prominent Sunni Islamic scholar Yusuf al-Qaradawi carried the criticism further, calling on Muslims to boycott the products of Russia and China (which also vetoed the resolution) because the money that Muslims spend on their products "turns into a weapon that kills Syrians."[45] Arab League Secretary General Nabil al-Arabi remarked that Russia and China had lost diplomatic credibility in the Arab world after the veto.[46] In addition to a desire to preserve Russia's political, economic, and diplomatic positions in Syria, Moscow's decision to veto may have also been influenced by two other factors. The first was continuing disunity within the Syrian opposition, with the Syrian National Council, by February 2012, being unable to unite the fractious Syrian opposition groups. The second was the apparent unwillingness of the United States, the EU, and Turkey, despite their strong rhetoric on the Syrian crisis, to take any military action. President Obama was preoccupied with his reelection campaign, the European Union was bogged down in a severe economic crisis and, in any case, did not have the military capacity to act without the United States, and Turkey appeared hesitant to act alone.

Following the veto, the opponents of the Assad regime introduced a resolution in the UN General Assembly strongly condemning the Syrian crackdown and calling on Assad to relinquish power to his vice president (this had been part of the Arab League plan, which also called for the formation of a national unity government and free elections in Syria). The resolution also called on UN Secretary General Ban Ki Moon to appoint a special envoy for Syria. The resolution, which Moscow could not veto, passed overwhelmingly, with 137 in favor, 12 (Russia was one of the 12) opposed, and 17 abstaining.[47] The negative Russian vote led Saudi Foreign Minister Saud al-Faisal to step up Saudi criticism of Moscow: "The stand of those countries that thwarted the UNSC Resolution and voted against the Resolution in the General Assembly on Syria, gave the Syrian regime a license to extend its brutal practices against the Syrian people."[48]

Russia, however, did not appear moved by the criticism. Indeed, it awarded the prestigious Pushkin Medal to a proregime Syrian writer, Ali Ursan, who had publicly applauded the 9/11 attacks.[49] Russia also announced that it would not participate in a "Friends of Syria" meeting that Moscow claimed was being organized to help the opponents of Assad. In addition, Putin, in a preelection speech on February 27 where he sought to rally anti-American support behind his nationalist position, warned against a U.S.-led Libyan scenario in Syria.[50] Several days later came a vote in the UN Human Rights Council on a resolution, drafted by Turkey and Qatar, that condemned Syria for human rights violations and put the blame for the violence squarely on the Syrian security forces. Russia, voting against the resolution, again found itself in the minority, losing 37–3, with 3 abstentions. Nonetheless, Russia denounced the resolution, calling it "one-sided and politicized" because it did not equally criticize the Syrian opposition for the violence.[51] Meanwhile, the situation for Russians working in Syria was deteriorating, something unhappily noted by Russian Orthodox Archbishop Alexander Yelisov, who bemoaned the exodus of his Russian-speaking parishioners from Syria.[52] In addition, the Russian Embassy in Damascus closed its secondary school for safety reasons.[53]

As the criticism of Russian policy toward Syria mounted, Lavrov contended that Russia was not losing support in the Arab world.[54] However, a number of Russian commentators, witnessing the Arab criticism of Russian policy, publicly disagreed with the Russian foreign minister.[55] In any case, once the Russian presidential elections were completed on March 4, with Putin proclaimed the winner, there was some hope that Moscow would moderate its position on Syria. The Russian Foreign Ministry, however, issued a statement on March 5, 2012, stating, "Russia's position on a Syrian settlement was never subject to political considerations and is not formed under the influence of electoral cycles, unlike those of our Western colleagues."[56]

Nonetheless, by early March it must have appeared to Russian leaders that they had to back off from their close embrace of the Assad regime—at least orally—if Moscow was to salvage even a part of its position in the Middle East. Foreign Ministry spokesman Alexander Lukashevich stated on March 2 that Moscow was not treaty-bound to help Syria if it was invaded,[57] and Lavrov, later in the month, asserted, "We believe the Syrian leadership reacted wrongly to the first appearance of peaceful protests and . . . is making very many mistakes." Lavrov added that "the question of who will lead Syria in a transition period can only be decided in a dialogue between the government and its opponents." Lavrov maintained, however, that demanding Assad resign as a condition for such a dialogue—as the Syrian opposition was doing—was "unrealistic."[58]

In addition to somewhat distancing itself from the Assad regime—if only in words—Moscow sought to rebuild its relationship with the Arab League throughout March. This was no easy task, however, as both Qatar and Saudi Arabia clashed with Lavrov at the March 2012 meeting in Cairo. Saudi Arabia had been incensed by a statement issued by the Russian Foreign Ministry on March 4 that Saudi Arabia was supporting terrorism by aiding the Syrian opposition. The Saudis called the statement "dangerous and irresponsible."[59] For its part, Qatar remained incensed at a comment made by Churkin, who reportedly had threatened to "wipe Qatar off the map" at a UN meeting in February.[60] By mid-March, Moscow's strategy was to build on one element of a February 17 UN General Assembly resolution—a call for a special UN envoy to Syria—and to shape it to protect the Assad regime from serious pressure. The end result on March 22 was the watered down, nonbinding UN presidential letter calling for a cease-fire by both sides to be monitored by UN officials, a withdrawal of the Syrian army from populated areas, freedom of movement for journalists, and facilitation of a Syrian-led political transition to a democratic, plural political system. The letter also, very vaguely, warned of "further steps as appropriate."[61] The whole process was to be under the supervision of UN Special Envoy Kofi Annan, a former UN secretary general. Whether or not the Annan mission would work, however, was a very open question, given the opposition's unwillingness to negotiate with Assad, whom they considered a murderer, and Assad's hesitancy throughout the month of April to remove the Syrian army from populated areas, end his crackdown on protesters, or allow foreign journalists—as well as UN monitors—free passage throughout Syria. Nonetheless, Russia's agreement to the UN presidential letter, however weak it was, is a useful point of departure to draw some preliminary conclusions about Russian policy toward the Arab Spring.

CONCLUSIONS

The Arab Spring caught the Russians, like everyone else, by surprise. After exhibiting an initial concern that the popular uprisings in the Arab world would spread to Moscow—something that would happen in the late fall of 2011—the Russian leadership sought to formulate a policy to deal with the new situation. While Moscow hoped to take advantage of the ouster of pro-Western leaders in Tunisia and Egypt, it also was genuinely worried that Islamist regimes might come to power in these countries, with a negative impact on Russia's restive North Caucasus region. In addition, while it certainly profited from the rise in oil prices caused by the Arab Spring, Moscow had to be concerned about the possible toppling of regimes in Libya and Syria—regimes with which it had major economic, political, and military ties. In the case of Libya, open disagreement between Prime Minister Putin and President Medvedev appeared to account for the zigzag nature of Russian policy, which first opposed and then endorsed UN sanctions and first opposed and then acquiesced in a UN Security Council resolution establishing a no-fly zone over Libya. In the case of Syria, Russian policy was much more straightforward: Moscow came out strongly both against sanctions and against Libya-like foreign military intervention. However, in both cases the Russians sought to hedge their bets by establishing ties with rebel groups, albeit initially at a lower level in Syria than in Libya, where Medvedev tried—and failed—to serve as a mediator. In Libya and in Syria, Moscow called for the regimes to stop attacks on peaceful protesters, in this area, at least, acting in solidarity with the United States and the European Union. As the events unfolded, Moscow also sought to closely coordinate its actions with key regional organizations such as the Arab League and the African Union in the case of Libya, first siding with the Arab League in its call for sanctions and a no-fly zone over Libya, and then with the African Union in its attempts to generate dialogue between the Gadafi regime and its opponents.

Unfortunately for Moscow, however, its attempt to sit on the fence on Libya, and even lean a bit toward Gadafi by backing the pro-Gadafi African Union as the primary mediator in the Libyan conflict, proved to be a major failure. When the Gadafi regime fell in September 2011, and later in October Gadafi himself was killed, Moscow suffered a major blow diplomatically, as well as economically and militarily as billions of dollars of contracts were lost, including almost $4 billion in arms sales. The outcome in Libya reinforced Putin's desire not to have the Libyan experience replicated in Syria. Consequently, Moscow vetoed two UN Security Council resolutions on Syria, one in October 2011 and another in February 2012, and also voted against a UN General Assembly resolution condemning the Assad regime, as well as a UN Human Rights Council resolution that criticized Syria. These Russian actions led to a sharp increase in both Western and Arab criticism of Russia, with the Arab criticism led by Saudi Arabia and Qatar. In the face of these developments, Moscow sought to rehabilitate its position in the Arab world, first by criticizing Syria, albeit relatively mildly, and then by trying to work with the Arab League in shaping a UN Security Council presidential letter establishing a UN special envoy for Syria (Kofi Annan) to negotiate a cease-fire monitored by the United Nations. The fact that the presidential letter was nonbinding, however, demonstrated that this was more of a public relations effort on the part of Moscow to try to rebuild its position in the Middle East than a serious effort to end the bloodshed in Syria.

What then accounts for Moscow's stubborn support for the Assad regime? In part, it reflects an effort to keep from losing the multibillion-dollar military contracts it has in Syria and the naval facility in Tartus. In part, it stems from Russian domestic politics, where in the face of public protests during the Russian presidential campaign, Putin played the Russian nationalist card, blaming the United States not only for instigating the Arab Spring–like demonstrations in Russia but also for backing the Syrian opposition against the Assad regime. In taking this position, Putin, who has a quasi-zero-sum-game view of world politics, was demonstrating to his public and to the rest of the world that he could stand up to the United States, particularly after Russian losses in Libya. Putin may also be calculating that Assad will win the battle with the opposition, given its deep divisions, the continuing support Assad is getting from Syrian Alawites and Christians, and the unwillingness, at least so far, of the United States, the European Union, and Turkey to use their military power to set up a "liberated zone" in Syria, like the one that existed in Benghazi, Libya.

Yet there are serious costs involved for Moscow in taking its pro-Assad stance. First, it alienates key Sunni Arab states, such as Saudi Arabia and Qatar, countries Putin had been trying to win over since 2007. Indeed, in many ways, as a result of his backing of Syria (and his resistance to further sanctions against Iran), Putin is back to his Middle East position of 2005–2006 when Russia's primary support in the Middle East came from the rogue regimes of Syria and Iran, as well as from Hizbullah and Hamas (although Hamas's move away from Syria has weakened this "rogue coalition"). Second, backing the Assad regime increases Russia's negative image throughout the Sunni Arab world, as the burning of Russian flags has shown. Third, it angers the United States and puts the U.S.-Russian "reset" button, created by President Obama, in jeopardy, particularly if Republican candidate Mitt Romney wins the U.S. presidential election in November 2012. Unless there is a major change in the Russian position on Syria—and no such change appears on the horizon at the time of this writing—then Russia will seem to have made its choice on Syria, despite the costs involved. Whether this is the right choice remains to be seen.

In sum, the Arab Spring, which also paid a visit to Russia, has posed serious problems for Moscow. In its response to the first sixteen months of the Arab Spring, Russian policy, while highly visible, has also been highly reactive and, in the case of Libya, not well coordinated. Even though the Arab Spring has proven to be diplomatically costly for the United States, especially in Egypt, the Arab Spring may prove far more costly to Putin's regime, both at home and in the Middle East, if it continues to support the Assad regime in Syria.

NOTES

1. I want to thank my student Alex Shtarkman for his research help on this chapter.

2. For an analysis of Putin's goals in the Middle East, see Robert O. Freedman, "Can Russia Be a Partner for NATO in the Middle East?," in *NATO-Russia Relations in the Twenty-First Century*, ed. Aurel Braun (New York: Routledge, 2008), 110–135. For an analysis of Russia's standing in the Middle East in December 2010 on the eve of the Arab Spring, see Robert O. Freedman, "Russia Returns to the Middle East: 2005–2011," *Maghreb Review* 36, 2 (2011): 127–161.

3. For a perceptive analysis of the early Russian reaction to the Arab Spring, see Stephen Blank and Carol Saivetz, "Russia Watches the Arab Spring," Radio

Free Europe/Radio Liberty, June 24, 2011. For a Russian view, see Sergei Filatov, "The Middle East: A Perfect Storm," *International Affairs* (Moscow) 57, 3 (2011): 55–74.

4. Cited in Charles Clover, "Inflation Severs Russians' Fragile Grip on Material Comforts," *Financial Times*, July 5, 2011.

5. Cited in Viktor Davidoff, "Egypt's Lessons for Moscow," *Moscow Times*, February 14, 2011.

6. Cited in Nabi Abdullaev, "Kremlin Sees Peril in Arab Unrest," *Moscow Times*, February 24, 2011.

7. Ibid.

8. See Andrew E. Kramer "Russia Cashes in on Anxiety over Supply of Middle East Oil," *New York Times*, March 7, 2011.

9. See Stephen Castle, "Putin Questions Europe's Foreign and Energy Policies," *New York Times*, February 24, 2011. Of course, Ukrainians, who twice had their gas cut off by Moscow, might question Russia's reliability.

10. See Freedman, "Russia Returns."

11. Cited in Reuters, "Russia Tells West Not to Meddle in North Africa," *Moscow Times*, February 25, 2011.

12. Cited in Bloomberg, "Egypt Rejects Russian Wheat," *Moscow Times*, June 22, 2011. See also Bloomberg, "Russia Targets Asia with the Largest Discount on Wheat," *Moscow Times*, August 3, 2011.

13. "UN Sanctions on Libya May Cost Russia $4 Billion," *Moscow Times*, February 28, 2011.

14. Cited in Nikolaus Von Twickel, "Moscow Opposes Sanctions for Libya," *Moscow Times*, February 25, 2011.

15. See "UN Sanctions on Libya."

16. Reuters, "Russia—Outside Meddling in Libya 'Unacceptable,'" *New York Times*, March 10, 2011.

17. Ellen Barry, "Leaders' Spat Tests Skills of Survival in the Kremlin," *New York Times*, March 25, 2011.

18. Reuters, "Putin Rips 'Medieval Crusade' in Libya," *Moscow Times*, March 22, 2011.

19. Ibid.

20. "Russian Duma Calls on West to Stop All Military Operations in Libya," Interfax, March 23, 2012 (World News Connection [hereafter WNC], March 23, 2011).

21. Ellen Barry, "In Diplomatic Reversal Russia Offers to Try to Persuade Qaddafi to Leave Power," *New York Times*, May 28, 2011.

22. "Margelov Discusses Libya with African Leaders," Interfax, June 29, 2011 (WNC, June 29, 2011).

23. Göskel Bozkurt, "Medvedev—Pressure NATO on Libya," *Turkish Daily News*, July 4, 2011.

24. Cited in Konstantin Pakhalyuk, "Between Assad and the Opposition," politikom.ru, July 5, 2011 (WNC, July 6, 2011).

25. Cited in Neil MacFarquhar, "Push in UN for Criticism of Syria Is Rejected," *New York Times*, April 27, 2011.

26. See Reuters, "Russia Calls for Justice as UN Dithers on Condemnation," *Haaretz*, April 25, 2011.

27. Cited in "US Denies Support for Syrian Road Map," *Turkish Daily News*, July 1, 2011.

28. See Robert O. Freedman, *Moscow and the Middle East: Soviet Policy Since the Invasion of Afghanistan* (New York: Cambridge University Press, 1991).

29. Cited in "Kremlin Envoy Calls for End to Syrian Violence," *Moscow Times*, June 29, 2011.

30. Cited in "Syrian Government Wants to Preserve Friendly Relations with Russia—Opposition Leader," Interfax, June 29, 2011 (WNC, June 29, 2011).

31. Cited in "Syrian Opposition Warns Russia That Its Unclear Stance May Damage Its Image," Interfax, September 9, 2011 (WNC, September 9, 2011).

32. Cited in Colum Lynch, "Russia and China Block Syria Resolution at UN," *Washington Post*, October 5, 2011.

33. Cited in Agence France-Presse (hereafter AFP), "Russia, China Veto Sanctions on Syria," *Turkish Daily News*, October 5, 2011.

34. Cited in "Russia's Medvedev Tells Assad to Reform or Else," NOW (Lebanon), October 7, 2011 (WNC, October 7, 2011).

35. Cited in "Russia, China Vetoes Slammed," *Turkish Daily News*, October 5, 2011.

36. Cited in "Syria Slams Arab League for Acting as Tool of the West," *Turkish Daily News*, October 20, 2011.

37. Ibid.

38. Ibid.

39. "Russia Backs Arab League Initiative for Syria," Rossiya TV, November 10, 2011 (WNC, November 10, 2011).

40. Cited in AFP, "Russia Condemns Syria's Suspension from the Arab League," *Turkish Daily News*, November 15, 2011.

41. AFP, "Russian Naval Flotilla to Leave Syrian Waters," *Turkish Daily News*, January 8, 2012.

42. Jay Solomon, "New Bid to Stifle Iran Aid to Syria," *Wall Street Journal*, February 19, 2012.

43. Cited in "Ghalioun: Credibility of Russian Foreign Policy 'Gone,'" NOW (Lebanon), February 8, 2012 (WNC, February 8, 2012).

44. Cited in "Saudi Arabia Urges Russia to 'Advise' Syria to End Bloodshed," *Jordan Times*, March 5, 2012.

45. "Sunni Scholar Sheikh Yousuf Al-Qaradawi Calls to Boycott Russian and Chinese Products, States They Are the Enemies of the Arab Nation," Al Jazeera, February 5, 2012 (cited in Middle East Media Research Institute Report, February 6, 2012).

46. Cited in Reuters, "Russia, China Lose Credit in Arab World—Arab League Chief," *Jordan Times*, February 7, 2012.

47. Rick Gladstone, "General Assembly Votes to Condemn Syrian Leader," *New York Times*, February 17, 2012.

48. Cited in "Arabs, Russians Discuss Syria Amid Splits," NOW (Lebanon), March 10, 2012 (WNC, March 10, 2012).

49. David M. Herszenhorn, "Russian Cultural Honor for a Controversial Syrian," *New York Times*, February 23, 2012.

50. Charles Clover, "Putin Launches Tirade Against US," *Financial Times*, February 28, 2012. See also Vladimir Isachenkov, "No 'Reset' for Putin's Campaign," *Washington Times*, February 27, 2012; and Artur Blinov, "Putin Article Sets Out Views on Arab Spring, Foreign Intervention," *Nezavisimaya Gazeta Online*, March 1, 2012 (WNC, March 1, 2012).

51. Cited in "Russia Calls UN Human Rights Council Resolution on Syria One-Sided, Politicized," Interfax, March 1, 2012 (WNC, March 1, 2012).

52. Cited in "Russian Orthodox Church Losing Flock in Syria," Interfax, February 29, 2012 (WNC, February 29, 2012).

53. "Russian Embassy School in Syria to Be Closed for Safety Reasons—Russian Foreign Ministry," Interfax, February 13, 2012 (WNC, February 13, 2012).

54. "Moscow's Position on Mideast Will Not Put Arab Partners OFF—Lavrov," Interfax, March 1, 2012 (WNC, March 1, 2012).

55. "Pundits Look at Implications of Russian Stance on Syria," Channel One TV (Moscow), February 12, 2012 (WNC, March 12, 2012). One commentator,

Mikhail Zygar, stated that Russia had made a terrible mistake because "it had set itself against [the] Syrian people as well as the whole Arab world where it allegedly was struggling for influence."

56. Cited in "Russia Dampens Hopes of Post-Poll Shift on Syrian Stance," NOW (Lebanon), March 6, 2012 (WNC, March 6, 2012).

57. "Russia Not Bound to Aid Syria in Case of Invasion—Spokesperson," RIA Novosti, March 2, 2012 (WNC, March 2, 2012).

58. Cited in Reuters, "Russia: Syria's Assad Regime Has Made Many Mistakes," Haaretz, March 21, 2012.

59. Cited in "Saudi Daily: Riyadh Hits Out at Russia's Falsehoods," Arab News Online, March 8, 2012 (WNC, March 8, 2012).

60. Cited in "The Moscow-Riyadh War of Words: A Conversation with Dr. Theodore Karasik," Saudi-U.S. Relations Information Service Report, April 9, 2012, 6, www.susris.com.

61. Cited in Rick Gladstone, "UN Council Unites over Plan for Syria," International Herald Tribune, March 23, 2012. See also Geoff Dyer and Charles Clover, "UN Backs Annan Peace Plan," Financial Times, March 23, 2012.

11

Same Old Story? Obama and the Arab Uprisings

JEREMY PRESSMAN

WITH THE ARAB UPRISINGS, the Obama administration was forced to address many of the same foreign policy issues as previous U.S. administrations, especially that of George W. Bush.[1] In terms of the wording of lofty presidential democracy rhetoric, the conflict between national security and democracy promotion interests, and small programs to support economic and political development, Barack Obama's policies were what we could have imagined from Bush had he been president during this period. They were consistent with long-standing U.S. practice. But on two other issues the Obama administration arguably carved a different pathway: the nature of U.S. military intervention and the decision to engage with political Islam in Egypt and elsewhere.

Obama's democracy rhetoric in prominent speeches both before and after the Arab uprisings matched that of Bush as Obama extolled the glory and universality of democracy. Yet despite his words, the primacy of security and economic needs was apparent under Obama and consistent with past administrations. Where political reform might threaten short-term security interests—for example, energy, U.S. basing, or military alliances—the short-term security interests have won out with the brief, noteworthy exception of U.S. policy during Husni Mubarak's fall. Only when the U.S. position was already hostility or regime change was the push for leadership change and reform especially strong.

Meanwhile, small-scale programs aimed at economic and political development continued under Obama. The administration provided additional funding to support civil society, economic development, and political reform as organizations such as the International Republican Institute (IRI), the National Democratic Institute (NDI), the Overseas Private Investment Corporation (OPIC), and the U.S. Agency for International Development (USAID) worked to fund, train, and educate budding entrepreneurs and reformists.

Yet on other matters the Obama administration did not simply follow past U.S. tendencies. It was much more cautious about military intervention, with only aerial intervention in Libya and an unwillingness for more than a year to attack Bashar al-Assad's regime in Syria. The U.S. military effort was far less than Bush interventions like Afghanistan (2001) or Iraq (2003) and was consistent more generally with Obama's greater reliance on small operations and multilateral action. The intervention in Libya had a large NATO role and the Arab League and UN stamp of approval; the United States was leading from behind. Given the U.S. track record on intervention and the inherent uncertainty of its likely impact, I see Obama's caution as a positive development and a necessary correction of the Bush years.

The other area of Obama innovation has been in choosing to deal directly with Egypt's Muslim Brotherhood. Given both the Bush experience with Hamas (especially 2006–2007) and how well Islamists have done in elections across the Arab world since the early 2000s, including in Tunisia and Egypt after the Arab Spring uprisings, the Obama move is probably recognition of the reality of dealing with Islamist-led governments in an increasing number of states in the Middle East in the near future.

This chapter will address the Middle Eastern policies of the Bush and Obama administrations, noting the democracy rhetoric as well as the recurring pattern of democracy promotion competing with, and often losing out to, other U.S. national interests. To demonstrate the conflict between democracy promotion and U.S. national interests, the discussion will include a brief review of multiple countries. Following that, the analysis will look at programs for the economic and political development of Mideast countries. The chapter will then deal with issues in which Obama policy appears different from Bush policy—namely, military intervention and engagement with Egypt's Islamists. The chapter will conclude with a reminder that the United States does not control events on the ground in the Arab uprisings; its influence is limited.

DEMOCRACY RHETORIC AND CONFLICT OF INTERESTS

The gap between Obama administration rhetoric and actual policy is consistent with gaps in past administrations, such as George W. Bush's. It is nothing new, and it is not specific to one political party, whether Democratic or Republican. Bush's second term in particular began with sweeping claims about the centrality of spreading freedom and democracy in the world. As events played out, other interests often competed with the promotion of democracy and human rights.

When President Bush pushed for greater freedom in his second inaugural address on January 20, 2005, he did not make exceptions in terms of which countries would be expected to embrace freedom. He said, "All who live in tyranny and hopelessness can know: the United States will not ignore your oppression, or excuse your oppressors." He said all, not most or some. While he did have one brief paragraph that spoke directly to U.S. allies, the message seemed to include only allies who were "free nations."[2] Bush did not set out any argument that suggested nonallies would be treated differently from allies as the U.S. government called for the expansion of democracy and freedom.

Yet in practice, the Bush administration treated allies differently—more lightly—on the question of democracy and democratization. Allies helped protect U.S. national interests on access to energy resources, counterterrorism, and the security of Israel. Adversaries undermined those same interests. In implementing his push for freedom, Bush pressured Iraq, Iran, Lebanon, and the Palestinian Authority, but Egypt and Saudi Arabia much less so.[3] Saddam Hussein's Iraq was a U.S. adversary and international pariah, and Iranian-U.S. relations were (and continue to be) confrontational, to greater and lesser degrees, since 1979. Egypt and Saudi Arabia were considered strong partners, and thus the democracy issue was much more muted. In short, strategic interests drove U.S. policy.[4] Tamara Cofman Wittes has highlighted the "conflicts-of-interests problem" whereby U.S. officials see short-term security needs as more pressing than the prospect of democratization and democracy.[5]

With nonallied or enemy states, however, the U.S. calculation is different since the goal is often regime change. Rather than conflicting with other vital interests, as is the case with allies, pushing for human rights and democracy against enemy authoritarian regimes dovetails nicely with a policy of regime change. Obama himself offered an example with regard to Iran. He noted, "The Arab Spring, as bumpy as it has been, represents a strategic defeat for Iran."[6]

By that he meant that the spread of political rights in the Middle East is anathema to Iran's dictatorship and that Iran was facing the potential loss of its major regional ally, Syria's Assad. Should political reform around the region invigorate Iran's reformers, the U.S. government would be pleased. In this and similar cases, domestic liberalization would benefit U.S. security interests.

Another way to think about the tension between rights and other strategic interests is the U.S. government's relative discomfort with two possible outcomes: nondemocratic regimes and anti-U.S. regimes. During the cold war as well as since its end, the United States has often been more concerned about anti-U.S. platforms and policies than it has about the absence of democracy and human rights. Free and fair elections are challenging because they could bring to power a government that is hostile toward U.S. national interests in the Middle East.

For the Bush administration, one early test of this conflict of interests was the Palestinian parliamentary elections of January 2006. Those elections became the exception to the general rule that the United States is fearful of anti-U.S. organizations getting elected. Candidates from Hamas, a Palestinian Islamist movement, defeated Fatah, the major Palestinian secular nationalist movement, winning 74 of the 132 seats. As part of President Bush's campaign for greater democracy, the United States had pressed for the elections and Hamas's inclusion in the elections despite concerns in the Israeli government.

After the election, Condoleezza Rice, U.S. secretary of state, said, "I've asked why nobody saw it coming." If the United States assumed Hamas would lose, the push for the Palestinian elections was not an exception to the general rule; the U.S. government thought it could get democracy (Palestinian elections) and a pro-U.S. winner (Fatah). Rice also asked a telling question: "You ask yourself, Are you going to support a policy of denying the Palestinians elections that had been promised to them at a certain point in time because people were fearful of the outcome?"[7] While the Bush administration answered the question in the negative in this particular case, the usual U.S. answer is the opposite: a willingness to avoid or stymie ballots that will lead to the election of unfriendly governments.

Moreover, the outcome of the election reinforced the conventional wisdom in Washington. The United States, along with Israel and the European Union, quickly moved to isolate the Hamas-led government, and, ultimately, the Bush administration unsuccessfully pushed for the overthrow of the Hamas government.[8] The electoral results also dampened Bush administration enthusiasm for pushing President Bush's freedom agenda.[9] In short, Hamas's election served as a reminder of why the United States had sometimes been reticent to support democratization.

Turning to the Obama administration, we see the same pattern. Despite sweeping presidential rhetoric in June 2009 and May 2011, U.S. policy was limited and more accommodating in Bahrain, Yemen, and Egypt where key security interests might be undermined by regime change. In contrast, with Libya and then Syria, the United States used much stronger rhetoric, calling for regime change and military means in the case of Libya. The United States was happy to see Iran's close ally in Syria, the Assad regime, in danger of collapse.

In June 2009, before the Arab uprisings, President Obama spoke in Cairo, Egypt. While democracy was not the organizing theme of Obama's speech, it was one of a handful of issues that Obama said the United States and the Islamic world must confront together. Obama expressed a strong commitment to basic political rights: "the ability to speak your mind and have a say in how you are governed; confidence in the rule of law and the equal administration of justice; government that is transparent and doesn't steal from the people; the freedom to live as you choose."[10] There was not a single, American institutional model, Obama made clear, but there were these certain rights that all democracies had to respect. Obama made no distinction in terms of whether a country was a U.S. ally or not.

In Obama's major address after the Arab uprisings had started, on May 19, 2011, he also suggested the U.S. government might adjust its policy motives. On the one hand, the president noted that, "we will keep our commitments to friends and partners." But on the other hand, several times during the same address he suggested the opposite: "So we face a historic opportunity. We have the chance to show that America values the dignity of the street vendor in Tunisia more than the raw power of the dictator. There must be no doubt that the United States of America welcomes change that advances self-determination and opportunity. Yes, there will be perils that accompany this moment of promise. But after decades of accepting the world as it is in the region, we have a chance to pursue the world as it should be."[11]

Obama's phrasing makes clear that he was explicitly addressing the very dilemma that pits values against economic and security interests. He seemed willing to risk the "perils." His language was unambiguous, seemingly leaving no room for exceptions: "And now we cannot hesitate to stand squarely on the side of those who are reaching for their rights."

But when we turn to what the United States did in 2011, security interests, as seen through commitments to allies, generally outweighed rights promotion. The United States frequently hesitated to support democracy movements in these cases. In Bahrain, the United States called generally for restraint but did not object to the Saudi-led military repression of the Bahraini opposition movement. The Obama administration passed up the opportunity to castigate or sanction either of two close allies, Bahrain and Saudi Arabia, when the reform movement was forcibly suppressed on March 14, 2011, and thereafter. The U.S. president suggested the way forward was a government-opposition dialogue, exactly the concept the United States rejected and Russia advanced in the Syrian case.[12]

An interesting, related question about Bahrain concerns the factor that most influenced U.S. policy. What U.S. interest mitigated against active support for Bahrain's political opposition? While it would be easy to point to Bahrain's support for basing the U.S. Navy, a stronger reason for the U.S. position was the Saudi-U.S. alliance and Saudi outrage when the Obama administration publicly turned against Egypt's Mubarak just weeks earlier (and I discuss more fully below).[13]

In Yemen, the Obama administration settled for a middling resolution whereby President Ali Abdullah Saleh was, relative to Mubarak, for example, gently moved aside and replaced by his vice president, Abdrabbuh Mansour Hadi. The United States did not denounce the political deal that gave Saleh immunity and had Hadi elected in a one-candidate election. Had Yemen been an adversary where the United States sought to topple the regime, it is hard to imagine that Washington would have liked an agreement that simply shifted the presidency to the longtime vice president. (Note this from Twitter Screenshot, February 27, 2012, 9:32 pm EST: Ali Abunimah @Ali Abunimah, "Sole candidate in Yemen presidential vote won 99.8%. Hillary @StateDept praised "democratic" election. Syria referendum only passed with 89%.) But fighting counterterror operations against al-Qaida in the Arabian Peninsula took precedence.

U.S. policy toward Egypt does not symbolize the *total* domination of U.S. national security interests as the determining factor, but U.S. support for the protest movement was nonetheless more limited than it could have been as 2011 unfolded and the military continued to run Egypt. After first working behind the scenes, the Obama administration did come out quickly against Mubarak in February 2011. It also used military-to-military contacts to encourage the armed forces not to fire on the protesters and to reinforce the message about Mubarak.[14]

But in the ensuing months, the Obama administration almost always chose not to use U.S. aid as leverage, despite public calls to do so, with the Egyptian military and the power behind the throne after Mubarak's fall, the Supreme Council of the Armed Forces (SCAF).[15] Congress disagreed, adding provisions that became law in late December 2011 that require the U.S. secretary of state to certify that Egypt "is meeting its obligations" under its peace treaty with Israel and "is supporting the transition to civilian government including holding free and fair elections; implementing policies to protect freedom of expression, association, and religion, and due process of law." As is often the case, the section includes a waiver for national security reasons.[16]

The most heated U.S.-Egyptian interaction was over Egyptian charges against a number of workers at nongovernmental organizations, including a number of U.S. citizens. While the potential crisis ebbed when Egypt allowed those U.S. citizens charged to leave the country, the question lingers as to whether the U.S. government told Egypt it would lose U.S. military aid if those charged were not allowed to depart.[17]

One example of a moment when the Obama administration could have sided more with Egypt's reformists against the military regime was in December 2011. Protests erupted and violence flared, to different degrees, in both Egypt and Syria. In the aftermath of a widely seen video of an Egyptian woman being beaten and dragged in the street, Secretary of State Hillary Rodham Clinton strongly criticized what had happened in Egypt but did not attach a specific consequence: "This systematic degradation of Egyptian women dishonors the revolution, disgraces the state and its uniform, and is not worthy of a great people."[18] Clinton did not call for specific changes to the political structure. She criticized what had happened without criticizing the military generally or SCAF. A month later, the White House released a very positive sounding summary of a call between Obama and Field Marshal Hussein Tantawi, head of the SCAF. There were few hints of Egyptian-U.S. differences.[19]

In contrast, two days after Secretary Clinton's comments about Egypt, the White House called for Assad "to leave power" in the face of widespread violence and the Syrian government's disregard for the Arab League plan. Assad had lost his legitimacy and had to go.[20] It was a direct rejection of the regime itself, not limited to a condemnation of the behavior.

The difference between Egypt and Syria is that Syrian-U.S. relations are troubled and Syria is a country closely allied with a major U.S. adversary, Iran. So U.S. officials frequently denounced the Assad regime and called for President

Assad to step aside. Early on in the Syrian uprising, President Obama left open the possibility that Assad could lead the reform effort, saying on May 19, 2011, that Assad "can lead that transition, or get out of the way." But as the Syrian government repression continued, the United States switched gears: it no longer saw Assad continuing to lead as an acceptable outcome to the crisis. On January 10, 2012, U.S. Ambassador to the United Nations Susan Rice (@AmbassadorRice) tweeted, "Long past time for Asad to yield to his people's wishes and step aside." President Obama stated that Assad "has demonstrated a similar disdain for human life and dignity" as his father and "must step aside and allow a democratic transition to proceed immediately."[21]

The United States also supported action by the United Nations against Syria. In early October 2011, Russia and China vetoed a Security Council resolution that threatened sanctions against Syria. After China and Russia vetoed another resolution on Syria on February 4, 2012, Rice was "disgusted."[22] Clinton called the veto "despicable."[23] On February 16, the United States voted to support a General Assembly resolution condemning the Assad regime. The vote on that nonbinding resolution was lopsided, 137–12, with 17 abstentions.[24] The United States was also a key player in organizing economic sanctions against Syria.

In Libya, the United States fully sided with the opposition and pursued regime change. In the years prior to the uprising, Muammar al-Gadafi's Libya had taken significant steps on terrorism and nonconventional weapons to end Western opposition to Gadafi's rule. But the United States had no crucial security ties with Libya and did not see Gadafi as a pillar of stable energy markets (as could be said of Saudi Arabia).

Thus, for Obama, the conflict of national security interests and democracy interests has played out in a similar fashion to Bush. Obama still used lofty democratic rhetoric, but security and energy interests almost always took precedence. That makes it easy to push adversaries on political reform but is less likely to occur with allies protecting U.S. interests.

This begs a further question: Why bother with the broad prodemocracy rhetoric if it will be disregarded in many cases of actual policy? Perhaps the lofty rhetoric relates to the deeply held and enduring American belief in American exceptionalism—that the American way of organizing society and politics is best and worthy of emulation. That in turn meant there was popular excitement in the United States with the revolutions and the toppling of dictators. Political leaders, therefore, feel the need to couch U.S. actions in that belief so that the domestic audience appreciates such phrasings and public opinion is supportive. This rhetoric sells the policy. Given the inevitable domestic political and bureaucratic competing pressures, maybe expansive words help universal beliefs about the value of democracy retain at least some impact on the ultimate policy outcome.

Or perhaps such phrasing is simply standard operating procedure or habit. The clash of interests is nothing new; it has existed since the rise of the United States as a global power more than one hundred years ago. Lastly, given these constraints, an astute U.S. politician might use the rhetoric to set out metrics to help shape aspirations even if that U.S. president knows he or she cannot align U.S. policy with said rhetoric. Clinton offered a suggestive comment along those lines: "It's the aspirations that we help instill in people. It's the dreams that people have about what America means to them no matter where they are."[25] Moreover, these aspirations could be instilled not only in people in other countries but also in policymakers inside the U.S. government. For example, the president's Cairo speech in 2009 probably laid some of the conceptual and bureaucratic ground- work for the U.S. reaction in Egypt in January–February 2011.

ECONOMIC AND POLITICAL DEVELOPMENT

Smaller U.S. policy efforts have played an important part in the U.S. response to the Arab uprisings as well. Obama, like Bush, has used funding and training programs to try to help with reform, economics, and the growth of civil society. An alphabet soup of U.S. or U.S.-sponsored agencies has played a part, in- cluding the IRI, NDI, OPIC, and USAID.

Bush's best-known program was the Middle East Partnership Initiative, which channeled money into economic and political advancement. It was founded in 2002 with the aim of empowering citizens and further aiding civil society in the Middle East.

In the fall of 2011, the U.S. Department of State set up a new, small office to address aspects of the Arab uprisings, the Middle East Transitions (MET) office. The office was initially headed by William Taylor, with Tamara Cofman Wittes, then deputy assistant secretary of state for Near Eastern Affairs, also serving as his deputy. Wittes was already supervising the Middle East Partnership Initia- tive. In 1991, the George H. W. Bush administration had set up a similar office, the Freedom Support Act office, to help with political transitions after the end of the cold war and the collapse of the Soviet Union. How was the MET office intended to work? Here is one account: "Taylor's first job will be to lead an effort to develop support strategies for Egypt, Libya, and Tunisia. Then, his office will go about trying to implement those strategies by working within State, around the interagency process, and then with international financial institutions, non-governmental organizations, and stakeholders on the ground. Taylor said he will attend National Security Council meetings on issues related to his brief."[26]

In other words, MET's most important role is coordinating a variety of actors, particularly on economic issues, in a way that supports Arab countries in transitional stages. Meanwhile, USAID continues to be active in the Middle East, and MET and USAID work closely together.[27] In addition, according to OPIC's CEO at the end of 2011, OPIC committed $700 million focused on "tourism, franchising, information communications technology, and renewable energy."[28] On top of that, the United States retains significant voting clout at the International Monetary Fund and World Bank. That gives the United States leverage with countries such as Egypt that rely upon financial support from the IMF and World Bank. Wittes summarized the economic angle: "We can use our foreign assistance—along with other economic tools of statecraft—to ensure that as these nations build their democracies, we help create an environment in which they can deliver broad-based opportunity and real results for their citizens."[29]

For fiscal year 2013, the Obama administration asked Congress for $770 million for the "Middle East and North Africa Incentive Fund." According to Secretary Clinton, the aim of the fund is to support programs "that make a meaningful commitment to democratic change, effective institution building, and broad-based economic growth."[30]

With the uprisings in 2011, the largest financial beneficiary was Egypt, where the United States offered to forgive up to $1 billion in Egyptian debt and guarantee another $1 billion for job creation.[31] Meanwhile, Syria was the target of negative economic policy: international sanctions. In summary, the United States used economic measures and small-scale support for liberalizing political and economic change. Here, U.S. policy was consistent both before and after the uprisings.

MILITARY INTERVENTION

On military intervention, the Obama administration has taken a much more cautious and limited approach than the Bush administration did, for which the signature event was the 2003 invasion of Iraq. The Obama administration did intervene in Libya, but the character of that intervention was wholly different than that seen under Bush. Because Bush's intervention in Iraq in 2003 has been widely covered, this section will jump directly to a comparison with the Obama administration and military intervention.

Thus far, Libya is the only country where an Arab uprising was met with U.S. military intervention. The United States, and then NATO, bombed Libya's government forces extensively, helping the Libyan opposition forces to defeat Gadafi's regime. In the United States, the major justification for the intervention was to stop the murder of Libyans by Gadafi's forces.[32] The size of such killings, real or potential, remains hotly disputed. Britain, France, and the United States did not just want to prevent a humanitarian emergency in Libya; they also wanted to get rid of Gadafi. Warren Bass, director of speechwriting and senior policy adviser to Ambassador Rice from 2009 to 2011, later noted "Qaddafi's determination to hunt his people down like rats as he put it rather than let them have the universal rights that they were standing up for." Bass summarized the Libya outcome this way: "The entire country of Libya was being menaced by one of the world's longest serving dictators and now he's gone."[33] Both his phrasings serve to highlight the humanitarian rationale. So does this February 24, 2011, retweet of Anne-Marie Slaughter (@SlaughterAM), former head of policy planning at the State Department under Obama (she was already outside the administration when this debate took place): "The international community cannot stand by and watch the massacre of Libyan protesters. In Rwanda we watched. In Kosovo we acted."

The Libyan intervention looked very different from Iraq in 2003, much more along the lines of the United States leading from behind. It was a multilateral intervention with Arab League and UN Security Council approval and multiple coalition partners. The U.S. military quickly turned over the operation to NATO. Unlike Iraq, the United States was not involved in any ground component.

On Syria, the Obama administration, as of June 1, 2012, had resisted many calls for U.S. military intervention. The calls came from Congress and pundits, including Republicans, neoconservatives and liberal humanitarians/hawks, the very groups that had vociferously argued for the need to invade Iraq in 2003.[34] In other words, the debate over intervening in Syria re-created many of the same camps as the debate on Iraq, except with Syria the administration was on the noninterventionist side.

In opposing military intervention in Syria, Obama argued that it was different from Libya: "Syria is a much bigger, more sophisticated, and more

complicated country than Libya, for example—the opposition is hugely splintered." He added that unlike in Libya, Russia has blocked UN action on
Syria.[35] Still, it did not prevent the United States from planning for the possibility of intervention in Syria in terms of protecting a safe zone, sending
arms, or attacking Syria's air defense system.[36] Bush had been willing to cir-
cumvent opposition on Iraq; Obama was not willing to do so with Syria.

Greater U.S. hesitance to intervene is a positive change. Finding local partners who can rebuild a society after the United States intervenes is difficult,
and the task itself, whether nation-building, major political reform, or both, is
not an easy one. Military intervention can be messy, with great loss of human
life and disruption of lives for years.

In Syria, maybe the United States keeping its distance militarily might lead
to a better outcome for the Syrian people. Jacob D. Kathman and Reed M.
Wood have found that international military intervention in a situation like
Syria might worsen the violence in the short term, even if such impartial intervention would help end mass killing in the long run.[37] And what some pundits
in the United States have called for is not *impartial* U.S. military intervention
but rather action that sides with the opposition. Patrick M. Regan and Aysegul
Aydin's research on external interventions suggests diplomatic intervention—
mediation—is most effective at ending violence and saving human lives.[38]

The political and operational feasibility of military intervention might be
an additional factor worth considering.[39] The bar for military success in Syria
is higher than Libya given that Syria has a larger military and multiple allies
(Iran, Lebanon, Russia).

TALKING WITH ISLAMISTS

Having U.S. officials talk with Egypt's Muslim Brotherhood demonstrated
that Obama did not simply adopt a cautious line on all fronts regarding Egypt.
Furthermore, the fact that high-level U.S. officials met with leaders of the Muslim Brotherhood is one example of a U.S. government not simply continuing
the same old tendencies, especially given that some U.S. pundits regularly and
loudly denounced the Muslim Brotherhood.[40] U.S. officials followed a similar
path in Tunisia.

We could make the case that past hostility toward Islamist movements
such as Hamas and Lebanon's Hizbullah would suggest a U.S. unwillingness
to relate to a movement whose stance on the United States and Israel, its close

regional ally, ranges from ambiguous to openly hostile. Although the Bush administration pushed for Hamas to be part of the 2006 Palestinian elections, it later supported the isolation of Hamas. As noted above, it refused to deal with the winner of free and fair elections. The United States considers Hamas to be a terrorist organization.

In contrast, the Obama administration recognized the full meaning of the results of the Egyptian parliamentary elections, in which the Muslim Brotherhood emerged as the largest party by far, and began political contacts.[41] Even Senator John McCain, the 2008 Republican Party presidential nominee, and the U.S. congressional delegation of which he was a part met with Muslim Brotherhood leaders on a 2012 trip to Egypt.[42]

This was not the first time the United States had talked to someone from the Brotherhood, but the profile of the issue was far higher in 2011. Much more was at stake as the Brotherhood was likely moving into formal positions of power, including likely dominating Egypt's parliament. The 1980s and 1990s included periods in which the two sides met and periods in which there was no dialogue. For the United States, any contact was usually handled by the U.S. Embassy in Cairo. Since Mubarak's fall, the discussions appear to involve more people; they are not a quiet side conversation run by U.S. diplomats.

The 2011–2012 meetings with Egypt's Brotherhood were broadly consistent with another point that Obama made in his May 19, 2011, speech: "Let me be clear, America respects the right of all peaceful and law-abiding voices to be heard, even if we disagree with them. And sometimes we profoundly disagree with them." In tandem, he articulated some conditions that election victors with whom the United States disagreed still had to accept, such as protecting both the democratic process and the rights of minorities. Secretary Clinton made similar points in a November 2011 speech at the National Democracy Institute.[43]

Still, Obama has not shifted policy vis-à-vis Hamas and Hizbullah. Note Obama's use of the word "peaceful" in the May 19 quotation above. Dealing with newly elected Islamists may be different from shifting course with traditional Islamist adversaries.

CONCLUSION: DO NOT OVERSTATE OR OVERPLAY U.S. INFLUENCE

Any extended discussion of U.S. policy toward the Arab uprisings runs the risk of overstating the ability of the United States to influence the outcomes.

On May 19, 2011, Obama himself was pretty clear about this risk: "Of course, as we do, we must proceed with a sense of humility. It's not America that put people into the streets of Tunis or Cairo—it was the people themselves who launched these movements, and it's the people themselves that must ultimately determine their outcome." Noted analyst Fouad Ajami made a similar point: "America should not write itself into every story: There are forces in distant nations that we can neither ride nor extinguish."[44]

The Egyptian case, for example, raised an important question to think about: Is it not better that the United States did not lead the way in trying to topple Mubarak, brush aside the armed forces, and suppress the Islamist political movements? In other words, U.S. allies may be lucky because the United States gives them a freer hand to set their own destiny. They have greater freedom to maneuver. When the United States intervenes too much, it may inhibit the growth of domestic agents of change, generate resentment against the United States, and fail to account for local cultural and historical factors that are vital to successful reform. Should the United States be denounced for meddling and intervening in some countries while also being denounced for not actively and always supporting political reformists? Maybe U.S. caution or an underlying conservatism about direct military meddling is a positive development.

The United States has responded to the Arab uprisings with political, economic, and military policies. On the economic and political fronts, most U.S. policies have been a continuation of past policies and tendencies, despite some Obama rhetoric that suggested the United States might elevate the status of democratic reform and human rights. The reaction to Mubarak's fall was the most important exception. On military intervention, the Obama administration has thus far avoided a new Iraq. There are no U.S. boots on the ground to try to bring about regime change. Still, events in the Middle East remain fluid, giving ample opportunity for U.S. policy to shift more dramatically in the coming years.

NOTES

1. An earlier version of this chapter was presented at the Asia Institute at the University of Melbourne and at the United States Studies Centre at the University of Sydney.

2. "President Sworn-In to Second Term," http://georgewbush-whitehouse .archives.gov/news/releases/2005/01/20050120-1.html.

3. Jeremy Pressman, "Power Without Influence: The Bush Administration's Foreign Policy Failure in the Middle East," *International Security* 33, 4 (Spring 2009): 149–179, at 159–160.

4. For a different perspective that places greater emphasis than I do here on ideological factors, see Mark L. Haas, *The Clash of Ideologies: Middle Eastern Politics and American Security* (New York: Oxford University Press, 2012).

5. Tamara Cofman Wittes, *Freedom's Unsteady March: America's Role in Building Arab Democracy* (Washington, DC: Brookings Institution Press, 2008), 17–18.

6. Barack Obama interviewed by Jeffrey Goldberg, "Obama to Iran and Israel: 'As President of the United States, I Don't Bluff,'" *The Atlantic*, March 2, 2012, http://www.theatlantic.com/international/archive/2012/03/obama-to-iran-and -israel-as-president-of-the-united-states-i-dont-bluff/253875/.

7. Steven R. Weisman, "Rice Admits U.S. Underestimated Hamas Strength," *New York Times*, January 30, 2006, http://www.nytimes.com/2006/01/30/ international/middleeast/30diplo.html?pagewanted=all. See also James M. Lindsay, "George W. Bush, Barack Obama, and the Future of US Global Leadership," *International Affairs* 87, 4 (2011): 765–779, at 770; and Mandy Turner, "Building Democracy in Palestine: Liberal Peace Theory and the Election of Hamas," *Democratization* 13, 5 (2006): 739–755.

8. David Rose, The Gaza Bombshell," *Vanity Fair*, April 2008, http://www .vanityfair.com/politics/features/2008/04/gaza200804.

9. Thomas Carothers, "The Continuing Backlash Against Democracy Promotion," in *New Challenges to Democratization*, ed. Peter Burnell and Richard Youngs (New York: Routledge, 2010), 59–72, at 66.

10. "Remarks by the President on a New Beginning," June 4, 2009, http://www .whitehouse.gov/the-press-office/remarks-president-cairo-university-6-04-09.

11. "Remarks by the President on the Middle East and North Africa," May 19, 2011, Washington, DC, http://www.whitehouse.gov/the-press-office/2011/05 /19/remarks-president-middle-east-and-north-africa.

12. Ibid. See also Charles W. Moore, "Bahrain, a Vital U.S. Ally," *Washington Times*, December 1, 2011. Moore was commander of the U.S. Navy's Fifth Fleet from 1998 to 2002.

13. Adam Shatz, "Whose Egypt?," *London Review of Books* (online), December 20, 2011, http://www.lrb.co.uk/2011/12/20/adam-shatz/whose-egypt. See also Marc Lynch, *The Arab Uprising: The Unfinished Revolution of the New Middle East* (New York: PublicAffairs, 2012), 140, 228.

14. Lynch, *The Arab Uprising*, 92, 94–95.

15. For a call from a body of experts including former U.S. government officials, see Josh Rogin, "Egypt Working Group Calls for Tough Line on SCAF," The Cable at *Foreign Policy*, November 17, 2011, http://thecable.foreignpolicy.com/posts /2011/11/17/egypt_working_group_calls_for_tough_line_on_scaf. One possible explanation is that the United States, with or without aid, has declining leverage. See Lloyd Gardner, "America Can No Longer Rely on Military Aid to Influence the Middle East," *The Guardian*, January 6, 2012, http://www.guardian.co.uk /commentisfree/2012/jan/06/america-military-aid-influence-middle-east?.

16. HR 2055, "Consolidated Appropriations Act, 2012," 112th Cong., 1st sess., http://www.gpo.gov/fdsys/pkg/BILLS-112hr2055enr/pdf/BILLS-112hr 2055enr.pdf, 437–438. On U.S. aid for Egypt, see also "Statement by Senators Lieberman, and Ayotte on the Situation in Egypt," February 7, 2012, http://.senate .gov/public/index.cfm?FuseAction=PressOffice.PressReleases&ContentRecord_id =5a3f0db4-0d3d-f030-8193-5b00c9a75f59&Region_id=&Issue_id=.

17. For the suggestion that the United States did use aid as leverage in this case, see "[Eric] Trager: Egypt's NGO Prosecution Prompts Reassessment," Washington Institute, March 1, 2012, http://www.washingtoninstitute.org/press-room /view/egypts-ngo-prosecution-prompts-reassessment.

18. "Secretary Clinton's Remarks on Women, Peace, and Security," December 19, 2011, Washington, DC, http://www.state.gov/secretary/rm/2011/12 /179173.htm. See also Agence France-Presse, "Clinton: Egypt's Treatment of Women a 'Disgrace,'" *Egypt Independent*, December 20, 2011, http://www .egyptindependent.com/node/559071. Shatz agreed the United States was relatively soft on SCAF. See Shatz, "Whose Egypt?"

19. "Readout of the President's Call with Egyptian Field Marshal Tantawi," January 20, 1012, http://www.whitehouse.gov/the-press-office/2012/01/20 /readout-president-s-call-egyptian-field-marshal-tantawi.

20. "Statement by the Press Secretary on Syria," December 21, 2011, http://www.whitehouse.gov/the-press-office/2011/12/21/statement-press -secretary-syria.

21. "Statement by the President on Syria," February 4, 2012, http://www .whitehouse.gov/the-press-office/2012/02/04/statement-president-syria.

22. Flavia Krause-Jackson and Henry Meyer, "Russia, China Veto UN Security Council Resolution on Syria," *Business Week*, February 4, 2012, http://www .businessweek.com/news/2012-02-04/russia-china-veto-un-security-council -resolution-on-syria.html.

23. Matthew Lee and Paul Schemm, "Clinton Rips Russia, China for U.N.

Veto on Syria," Associated Press, February 24, 2012, http://news.yahoo.com /clinton-rips-russia-china-u-n-veto-syria-230200591.html.

24. "General Assembly Adopts Resolution Strongly Condemning 'Widespread and Systematic' Human Rights Violations by Syrian Authorities," February 16, 2012, http://www.un.org/News/Press/docs//2012/ga11207.doc.htm.

25. "An Interview with Hillary Clinton," *The Economist*, March 22, 2012, http://www.economist.com/blogs/lexington/2012/03/foreign-policy.

26. Josh Rogin, "State Department Opens Middle East Transitions Office," The Cable at *Foreign Policy*, September 12, 2011, http://thecable.foreignpolicy .com/posts/2011/09/12/state_department_opens_middle_east_transitions_office. See also "Special Briefing on U.S. Support for the Democratic Transitions Underway in Tunisia, Egypt, and Libya," November 3, 2011, http://www.state.gov/r/pa /prs/ps/2011/11/176653.htm.

27. See http://transition.usaid.gov/locations/middle_east/; and especially http://transition.usaid.gov/locations/middle_east/sectors/dg/. See also author's e-mail correspondence with an official from USAID, February 2012.

28. Gabriel Silverman, "Business as Usual for the U.S. in Post–Arab Spring Middle East," Medill National Security Zone, December 6, 2011, http:// nationalsecurityzone.org/site/business-as-usual-for-the-u-s-in-post-arab-spring -middle-east/.

29. Tamara C. Wittes, "Can Foreign Assistance Bolster the Arab Spring?," July 21, 2011, http://mepi.state.gov/mfan_tcw.html.

30. Testimony of Hillary R. Clinton, "Opening Remarks Before the Senate Appropriations Subcommittee on State, Foreign Operations, and Related Programs," Washington, DC, February 28, 2012, http://www.state.gov/secretary /rm/2012/02/184821.htm. See also Josh Rogin, "State Department's New Middle East Fund in Trouble on Capitol Hill," The Cable at *Foreign Policy*, May 18, 2012, http://thecable.foreignpolicy.com/posts/2012/05/18/state_department_s_new _middle_east_fund_in_trouble_on_capitol_hill.

31. On these and other economic measures, see "Remarks by the President on the Middle East and North Africa," May 19, 2011.

32. On the debate inside the White House, see Josh Rogin, "How Obama Turned on a Dime Toward War," The Cable at *Foreign Policy*, March 18, 2011, http://thecable.foreignpolicy.com/posts/2011/03/18/how_obama_turned_on _a_dime_toward_war.

33. Warren Bass interviewed by Steven L. Spiegel, "On the International Community and the Middle East," Israel Policy Forum, February 29, 2012 (but

recorded a few days before February 24), http://israelpalestineblogs.com/2012
/02/29/warren-bass-on-the-international-community-and-the-middle-east/.

34. "Statement by Senators McCain, Lieberman, and Graham on Syria," February 24, 2012, http://mccain.senate.gov/public/index.cfm?FuseAction=PressOffice
.PressReleases&ContentRecord_id=b07d9ac2-e278-a629-8236-3a97ee41c95a
&Region_id=&Issue_id=; Oren Kessler, "50 US Experts Implore Obama to
Press Syria Harder," *jpost.com*, December 22, 2011, http://www.jpost.com
/International/Article.aspx?ID=250455; Steven A. Cook, "It's Time to Think
Seriously About Intervening in Syria," *The Atlantic*, January 17, 2012, http://
www.theatlantic.com/international/archive/2012/01/its-time-to-think
-seriously-about-intervening-in-syria/251468/; Anne-Marie Slaughter, "How to
Halt the Butchery in Syria," *New York Times*, February 24, 2012, http://
www.nytimes.com/2012/02/24/opinion/how-to-halt-the-butchery-in-syria
.html.

35. Obama interviewed by Goldberg.

36. Karen DeYoung, "Talk of Military Aid Rises as Hopes Fade for Peaceful
Syria Solution," *Washington Post*, March 10, 2012, http://www.washingtonpost
.com/world/national-security/talk-of-military-aid-rises-as-hopes-fade-for
-peaceful-syria-solution/2012/03/10/gIQAzis83R_story.html.

37. I appreciate Erica Chenoweth pointing out this research. Jacob D. Kathman
and Reed M. Wood, "Managing Threat, Cost, and Incentive to Kill: The Short-
and Long-Term Effects of Intervention in Mass Killings," *Journal of Conflict Resolution* 55, 5 (October 2011): 735–760.

38. Patrick M. Regan and Aysegul Aydin, "Diplomacy and Other Forms of
Intervention in Civil Wars," *Journal of Conflict Resolution* 50, 5 (October 2006):
736–756.

39. See Sarah E. Kreps, *Coalitions of Convenience: United States Military Interventions After the Cold War* (New York: Oxford University Press, 2011).

40. See also Quinn Mecham, "The Rise of Islamist Actors: Formulating a Strategy for Sustained Engagement," Policy Brief (Washington, DC: Project on Middle
East Democracy, April 27, 2012). For an example of observers denouncing U.S.
engagement with the Muslim Brotherhood, see "Obama Administration Recog-
nizes Egypt's Dangerous Muslim Brotherhood," Fox News, June 30, 2011,
http://www.foxnews.com/on-air/hannity/2011/07/01/obama-administration
-recognizes-egypts-dangerous-muslim-brotherhood. In Congress, for example,
Representative Joe Walsh (R-IL) issued a condemnation of Obama's meeting
with the Muslim Brotherhood. "Walsh Calls on President to Distance Himself

from Muslim Brotherhood," April 6, 2012, http://walsh.ho
?sectionid=49&sectiontree=6,49&itemid=514.

41. Agence France-Presse, "Senior U.S. Diplomat to Meet Eg
Brotherhood," Al Arabiya, January 11, 2012, http://english.alarabiya.
/2012/01/11/187686.html; David D. Kirkpatrick and Steven Lee Mye
tures to Egypt's Islamists Reverse Longtime U.S. Policy," *New York Times*
ary 3, 2012, http://www.nytimes.com/2012/01/04/world/middleeast/us-reve
-policy-in-reaching-out-to-muslim-brotherhood.html?.

42. Sarah el Deeb, "McCain Says Egypt Working on US Case," *Boston Globe*,
February 21, 2012, http://www.bostonglobe.com/news/world/2012/02/21
/mccain-says-egypt-working-case/xyYDr6cywtLYYvSQRWQLfJ/story.html.

43. "Keynote Address at the National Democratic Institute's 2011 Democracy
Awards Dinner," November 7, 2011, http://www.state.gov/secretary/rm/2011
/11/176750.htm.

44. Fouad Ajami, "Five Myths About the Arab Spring," *Washington Post*, January 12, 2012, http://www.washingtonpost.com/opinions/five-myths-about-the
-arab-spring/2011/12/21/gIQA32TVuP_story.html.

e Arab World

ction of the

al and Transnational

JAMES L. GELVIN

O N DECEMBER 17, 2010, Muhammad Bouazizi, soon to be the world's most famous street vendor, set himself on fire in front of the local government building in Sidi Bou Zid, a rural town in Tunisia with a 30 percent unemployment rate. Earlier in the day, his wares had been confiscated and he had been humiliated when he went to complain. The self-immolation touched off protests that reached Tunisia's capital ten days later.

Protesters brought a number of issues to the table: unemployment, food inflation, corruption, poor living conditions, lack of freedoms, and lack of government responsiveness. With the support of the Tunisian General Labor Union, the protests gained momentum. At first, President Zine al-Abidine Ben Ali, who had ruled for a quarter century, tried to pacify the protesters. In a pattern that would be repeated time after time in the Arab world, he promised 300,000 new jobs, new parliamentary elections, and a "national dialogue." This did little to mollify the protesters. By January 14, 2011—less than a month after Bouazizi's self-immolation—military and political leaders had had enough, and with the army surrounding the presidential palace Ben Ali resigned and appointed his prime minister to head a caretaker government. Parliamentary elections were held in October 2011, with a 90 percent turnout. The parliament's main order of business was to draft a new constitution.

About a week and a half after Ben Ali fled, young people, many of whom belonged to the April 6 Movement, began their occupation of Tahrir Square in Cairo. (Even though Tahrir Square was but one site of many in Egypt where protests were held that day, it emerged as the symbolic center of the Egyptian uprising.) The April 6 movement got its name from a date in 2008 when young people using Facebook called for a general strike to support striking workers at a state-run textile factory. The general strike never happened, giving lie to the miraculous powers now ascribed to Facebook and other social media. In 2011, however, the security forces and goons-for-hire failed to dislodge the protesters, and the army announced it would not fire on them. Strikes and antigovernment protests spread throughout Egypt. On February 11, 2011, the army took matters into its own hands: it deposed President Husni Mubarak and established a new government under the Supreme Council of the Armed Forces. This phase of the Egyptian uprising—what might be called the first street phase of the Egyptian uprising—was over in a mere eighteen days.

The uprisings in Tunisia and Egypt created the template—a false template, as it were—through which the media and the general public have viewed the success or failure of other uprisings in the region. There are three aspects of this template. First, in the public imagination at least, both uprisings were largely peaceful, with tech-savvy youth playing the lead role in the drama (an exaggeration on both counts). Second, both uprisings brought down autocrats when the "people's army" refused to shoot at protesters. Third, both got rid of autocrats in a matter of weeks.

No matter what inspiration other uprisings that broke out in the Arab world in subsequent weeks derived from the Tunisian and Egyptian models, however, it would be wrong to look at them through the lens of these two countries. It is true that after Egypt, ongoing protests in Algeria and Yemen took a new turn as young people adopted the Egyptian style of protest. In both places, however, protests had very un-Tunisian, un-Egyptian results. In Bahrain, protests modeled on those in Egypt led to an invasion by troops and police from Saudi Arabia and the United Arab Emirates and fierce repression. In Jordan, Saudi Arabia, and Morocco, kings who had presented themselves as "reformers" now faced lists of demands, including expanded representation, an end to corruption, and constitutional checks on monarchic power—but, significantly, they did not face calls for the end of the regime, as had autocrats in Tunisia and Egypt. In Libya, a "Day of Rage" was held after the arrest of a prominent human rights lawyer. He represented families of the 1,200 "disappeared" political prisoners who had been murdered in cold blood in one single incident in 1996. Libya soon descended into a six-month civil war, which ended only after a fierce NATO air campaign. For the second time, outside intervention determined the course of an uprising. Finally, after months of predictions that "it couldn't happen in Syria," it did. In March 2011, Syrian security services arrested ten schoolchildren age fifteen and younger in the provincial city of Daraa. Their crime? Borrowing a slogan from the Egyptian uprising, they wrote as graffiti "Down with the *nizam* [regime]" on walls. When their parents went out on the streets to protest, the security services fired, killing several. The next day, 20,000 residents of Daraa took to the streets. The Syrian bloodbath had begun.

These were the main sites of protest. There were others, less publicized. So what is going on?

METAPHORICALLY SPEAKING

There are two metaphors commonly used to describe what has been happening in the Arab world since December 2010. The first and most commonly used metaphor is "Arab Spring." Despite its popularity and the resulting incentives to use the term for recognition purposes, there are three problems with this title. First, it is calendrically inaccurate: only one of the uprisings—the uprising in Syria—actually broke out in a month that is in spring, although it broke out before the actual arrival of that season. The others began in the dead of winter, a season hardly appropriate for an uplifting title.

The second problem with the title "Arab Spring" is that it is misleading. Spring is commonly associated with joy and renewal. The jury is still out on all the uprisings, and as of this writing a number have turned pretty sour. A year and a half after Bouazizi's self-immolation, the forces of reaction have pushed back the forces of change in most of the states in which uprisings broke out. Time will tell if this remains the case. After eighteen months, only events in Tunisia have given cause for (cautious) optimism—Ben Ali was gone, the army was back in its barracks, elections were held, the next election was scheduled, and work on a new constitution had begun. Libya and Yemen were states in which breakup or total anarchy still remained a possibility, the Egyptian army had yet to abdicate the power it had seized on February 11, 2012, and Syria continued its descent into hell. This is not the sort of scorecard that breeds confidence.

The final problem with the title "Arab Spring" is that it was already taken. Conservative commentators used the phrase in 2005 to refer to events in the Arab world that occurred in the wake of the American invasion of Iraq in 2003 and the announcement of President George W. Bush's "freedom agenda."[1] During that Arab Spring, Iraq held its first post-Saddam elections, the Cedar Revolution broke out in Lebanon, Saudi Arabians voted in municipal elections, Kuwait gave its women suffrage, and Husni Mubarak pledged that the next presidential elections would be the cleanest in Egyptian history.

Unfortunately, the fulfillment of the promise of that Arab Spring proved elusive. In 2006, sectarian violence raged in Iraq, and after a second round of parliamentary elections in March 2010, it took American diplomats eight months to broker a deal that enabled the formation of a government. Although the Syrian army was forced out of Lebanon, Lebanese politics soon reverted to its usual dysfunctional state. While the first municipal elections were held in Saudi Arabia in 2005, the government postponed the next round, originally scheduled for 2009. Unsurprisingly, when those elections were finally held in September 2011, women were excluded from the electorate. And, of course, Mubarak's pledge proved so hollow that in 2010 he could renew it, vowing that the next presidential elections would be the cleanest in Egyptian history. The only success story was women's suffrage in Kuwait. In sum, the first Arab Spring was a nonevent unworthy of emulation.

It should be noted that participants in the uprisings themselves, along with Arab observers, frequently complain about the Arab Spring metaphor (commonly translated, awkwardly, into Arabic as *rabi al-thawrat al-arabiyya*—"the spring of the Arab revolutions") on a number of grounds.[2] Besides the fact that the title discounts the often-sizable contributions made by non-Arab communities, such as the Berber community, to the uprisings, the title Arab Spring obscures the fact that what has been occurring in the Arab world since 2010 should not be viewed as an isolated event. Rather, it is the culmination of a decades-long struggle for human dignity in the region. Over the course of the last three decades, for example, protesters throughout the Arab world have, on numerous occasions, taken to the streets or participated in less dramatic forms of protest, such as petition campaigns, in their quest for human and democratic rights:

+ The so-called Black October riots of 1988 in Algeria, which prompted the first free elections (subsequently overturned) in the Arab world.

+ The Bahraini *intifada* (uprising) of 1994–1999, which began with the circulation of a petition signed by an estimated 10 percent of the island's population demanding the restoration of a constitution that stipulated the election (not appointment) of a majority of parliamentarians and the expansion of the franchise to women.
+ The brief Damascus spring of 2000, a period of intense political ferment that began after the death of Syrian president Hafiz al-Assad with the circulation of a petition signed by ninety-nine intellectuals demanding, among other things, the end of emergency rule, the release of political prisoners, and freedom of speech, assembly, and expression.
+ The formation of *Kefaya* (Enough!) in Egypt in 2004, an amalgam of political currents ranging from nationalist to communist to Islamist that called for the resignation of Mubarak and for electoral reform.
+ The Cedar Revolution of 2005, during which protesters demanded not only the removal of Syrian forces from Lebanon, but also parliamentary elections free from Syrian interference.

And the list goes on.[3]

Lest we forget, agitation for social and economic justice—issues central to many of the current uprisings and protests—also has a venerable history in the region. Beginning with the "IMF riots" of the 1980s, when populations from Morocco to Jordan resisted the introduction of neoliberal policies, this agitation continued through the surge of Egyptian labor activism from 2004 to 2010, during which 2 million Egyptian workers and their families participated in more than 3,000 strikes, sit-ins, and walkouts.[4] The growing militancy of Egyptian labor set the stage for the strike wave that spread throughout the country on February 10, 2011, a development that possibly convinced the military to depose Mubarak the next day.

The second metaphor commonly used to describe what has been happening in the Arab world since Bouazizi's death is "wave." There are pluses and minuses to viewing the various uprisings as part of a wave. On the plus side, there is no denying that later Arab uprisings borrowed techniques of mobilization and symbols from earlier ones. Town squares that became the sites of protest throughout the Arab world were renamed "Tahrir" after the main site of protest in Cairo, and many uprisings began with a scheduled "Day of Rage," also borrowed from the Egyptian model. In addition, slogans first chanted on the streets of Tunisia and Egypt, such as "The People Want the End of the Regime," and "*Irhal!* [Go!]," shouted at Tunisian and Egyptian presidents Ben Ali and Mubarak, went viral. Then there is the highly touted use of social networking sites for the purpose of mobilization, not to mention the common demands for human and democratic rights and social justice.

There are, however, two main objections to the use of the wave metaphor. Most significantly, the metaphor makes it seem that the spread of the uprisings and protests from state to state was inevitable, like a wave washing over a beach. Its use thus obscures the fact that the uprisings and protests spread as a result of tens of thousands of individual decisions made by participants who chose on a daily basis to face the full repressive power of the state. The wave metaphor also obscures the fact that the goals and styles of the uprisings and protests have varied widely from country to country. The goal of some has been the complete overthrow of the regime, while the goal of others has been the reform of the regime. In some places, initial protests came about after meticulous preparation; in others, the spark was spontaneous. And there have been times when uprisings have been predominantly peaceful and other times when they took a violent turn.

Despite its problems, the wave metaphor might be salvaged if we remain aware that what is taking place in the Arab world has both transnational elements and national elements. The transnational elements are found mainly in terms of inputs: over the course of the last half century, all Arab states came to share similar characteristics, and over the course of the last two decades, all Arab states have faced similar shocks that made them vulnerable to popular anger. The national elements are found in terms of the trajectories taken by the uprisings: Variations in local history, state structure, and state capability in the Arab world have opened up possibilities for each and foreclosed options for each. This made it impossible for Libyans and Syrians, for example, to replicate the relative peacefulness and quick resolution that marked the initial phases of the Tunisian and Egyptian uprisings.

TRANSNATIONAL INPUTS

Overall, there are four transnational factors that made all states in the Arab world vulnerable to popular anger. First, beginning in the late 1970s, and accelerating over the course of the last decade, the United States and international banking institutions have persuaded or coerced regimes throughout the region to adopt social and economic policies associated with neoliberalism.

These policies shredded the post–World War II ruling bargain that had connected Arab governments with their populations.

Before the 1980s, states throughout the Arab world had played an uncontested role in their national economies in an effort to force-march economic development. They also provided a wide array of social benefits for their populations, including employment guarantees, health care, and education. In addition, consumer goods such as food and petroleum products were subsidized by the state. In some states—Nasser's Egypt, post-independence Algeria, Gadafi's Libya, post-1958 Iraq, Syria at various times, and others—regimes justified their policies using a populist discourse that extolled anticolonialism and the virtues of the revolutionary masses. In others—Jordan and Saudi Arabia, for example— rulers appealed to tradition or efficiency. Whether "revolutionary" or "reactionary," however, governments came to the same destination, although via different routes. In return for their generosity, Arab states expected obedience. Overall, then, the ruling bargain connecting states with their populations might be summed up in three words: benefits for compliance.[5]

Neoliberal economic policies got their tentative start in the Arab world in December 1976, when Egypt negotiated a $450 million credit line with the International Monetary Fund (IMF). In return, the Egyptian government pledged to cut commodity supports and direct subsidies. Over the course of the next three decades, the IMF negotiated ever-more-expansive agreements with cash-strapped governments in the region. These agreements were fairly consistent across the board: governments agreed to cut and target subsidies, remove price controls, privatize government-owned assets, balance their budgets, liberalize trade, deregulate business, and the like. Neoliberalism thus violated the norms of the ruling bargain.

As mentioned earlier, populations throughout the Arab world confronted the new dispensation by engaging in acts of resistance that ranged from revolt to labor activism. Those populations have found two aspects of neoliberalism particularly repellent. The first is the fraying of the social safety net and threats to middle-class welfare, particularly in the form of cuts to across-the-board subsidies for food and fuel. At the recommendation of the IMF, across-the-board subsidies were replaced by subsidies targeted to those who live in "absolute poverty." The second aspect of neoliberalism populations found repellent was the sell-off of publicly owned enterprises. For many, privatization threatened state-employment guarantees. Furthermore, privatization did not lead, as promised, to free-market capitalism, but rather to crony capitalism, as regime loyalists took advantage of their access to the corridors of power. Privatization also widened the gulf between rich and poor (although it may come as a surprise to all but Occupy Wall Street that that gulf has still not reached American levels).[6] The worst of the crony capitalists—Ahmad Ezz in Egypt, Rami Makhlouf in Syria, anyone named Trabelsi in Tunisia—thus came to symbolize systemic corruption in the buildup to the uprisings.

The second factor that has made regimes in the Arab world vulnerable is demography. Approximately 60 percent of the population of the Arab world is under the age of thirty. Even more telling is the percentage of youth between the ages of fifteen and twenty-nine, the period during which most enter the job market and compete on the marriage market. Youth between the ages of fifteen and twenty-nine make up 29 percent of the population of Tunisia, 30 percent of the population of Egypt, 32 percent of the population of Algeria, and 34 percent of the population of Libya. They also make up the bulk of the unemployed (for example, in Egypt they make up 90 percent of the unemployed).[7]

Demography is not, of course, destiny, and frustrations about job or life prospects do not necessarily translate into rebellion. And youth has hardly been the only segment of Arab populations that has mobilized during the uprisings: in Tunisia and Egypt, labor played a major role; in Libya and Syria, parents protesting the way the state had dealt with their children sparked them. Nevertheless, by 2010 there was a cohort of youth throughout the Arab world with a significant set of grievances. Under the proper circumstances, this cohort was available to be mobilized for oppositional politics.

The third factor that has made regimes in the Arab world vulnerable has to do with the recent shock to the international food supply chain. The Arab Middle East is more dependent on aggregate food imports than any other region in the world. Egypt alone is the world's largest wheat importer. Since mid-2010, the world price of wheat has more than doubled, spiking in January 2011. Economists attribute this to a number of factors, from speculation to drought to more acreage in the United States and Europe devoted to growing corn for biofuel.[8]

But in addition to its dependence on food imports, there are two other reasons that skyrocketing food prices are a particular burden in the Arab world. First, the portion of household spending that goes to pay for food in the Arab world ranges as high as 63 percent in Morocco. Compare that to the average percentage of household spending that goes to pay for food in the United States: 7 percent—a figure that includes eating as entertainment (that is, dining outside the home).[9] The second reason the damage caused by skyrocketing food prices in the Arab world is particularly punishing is the neoliberal economic policies adopted by governments in the region. Pressure from the United States and the IMF has constrained governments from intervening into markets to fix prices and has forced governments to abandon across-the-board subsidies on food.

The final factor making regimes vulnerable is their brittleness. The years between the onset of the economic crisis of 2008 and the first uprising, in Tunisia, were not good ones for governments throughout the world. Governments found themselves caught between bankers and economists recommending austerity, on the one hand, and populations fearing the end of the welfare state they had come to know, on the other. While uprisings were spreading in the Arab world, governments fell in the United Kingdom, Greece, Ireland, Portugal, Spain, Iceland, Italy, and elsewhere, and were challenged in France and the United States. Throughout it all, not one government was overthrown, nor were political institutions uprooted. Blame fell on politicians and parties and the policies they pushed.

In the Arab world, popular representatives could not be turned out of office because there were no popular representatives. This is why populations throughout the region took to the streets as their first option. This also explains why the most common slogan during this period has been "Down with the *nizam* [regime]," not "Down with the government [*hukuma*]."

These four factors, then, made all regimes throughout the Arab world vulnerable to the sort of street protests we have witnessed since December 2010. They did not, of course, cause the uprisings. To attribute the uprisings to these factors or to any others overlooks a key variable—the human element—that determines whether an uprising will or will not occur. That being said, however, the remarkable fact remains that since December 2010 uprisings or protests of one sort or another broke out in all but possibly five of the twenty-two member states of the Arab League,[10] demonstrating that the term "Arab world" connotes more than a geographic expanse.

NATIONAL OUTCOMES

Once uprisings began to break out in the region, they took a number of forms. In the main, the uprisings that have broken out so far might be placed into four clusters.

The first cluster consists of Tunisia and Egypt, where militaries, siding with protesters and not with autocrats, eased the ouster of the latter from power. It is commonplace for observers to highlight the differences between Tunisia and Egypt. Tunisia is tinier in terms of both size and population, relatively wealthier, more urbanized, and more cosmopolitan than its neighbor to the east. Yet there is one thing that Tunisia and Egypt hold in common that is unique in the Arab world: both Tunisia and Egypt have long histories as autonomous, developmentally oriented states. Beginning in the nineteenth century, both experienced more than two centuries of continual state-building. As a result, there were functioning institutions autonomous from the government's executive branch in both. Most importantly, there was a functioning military that could step in under crisis conditions.

During the uprisings, the militaries of both states stepped in to preserve their privileges and essential parts of the *nizam*. To accomplish this, they ensured that the most provocative symbol of the regime—Ben Ali and his family in Tunisia, Mubarak and his in Egypt—was out of the way. Nevertheless, although the militaries initially took similar stands in Tunisia and Egypt, their subsequent actions diverged, again in accordance with their institutional histories. The Tunisian military had never seen action and was kept the smallest in the Arab world by Tunisia's two postindependent presidents, Habib Bourguiba and Zine al-Abidine Ben Ali. Both feared that a powerful military would threaten their hold on power. In contrast, the Egyptian military is the largest in the Arab world—about 450,000 active duty personnel—and is equipped with the best force-on-force hardware that $1.3 billion a year in military assistance from the United States can buy. It also controls a significant portion of the Egyptian economy (estimates run from 15 to 40 percent), with holdings in everything from real estate to manufacturing to agricultural production.[11] The Tunisian military thus went back to its barracks under popular pressure; the Egyptian military, anxious to preserve a political position commensurate with its size as well as its economic empire, has, a year and a half after it seized power, yet to do so.

The second cluster of states undergoing uprisings includes Yemen and Libya, where regimes fragmented, pitting the officers and soldiers, cabinet ministers, politicians, and diplomats who stood with the regime against those who joined the opposition. (Tribes and tribal confederations, upon which the regimes depended to compensate for institutional underdevelopment also divided into opposing camps.) The fragmentation of regimes in the two states is not surprising: in contrast to Tunisia and Egypt, both Yemen and Libya are poster children for what political scientists call "weak states." In weak states, governments and the bureaucracies upon which they depend are unable to assert their authority over the entirety of the territory they rule; nor are they able to extend their reach beneath the surface of society. It is partly for this reason that populations in weak states lack strong national identities. Such is the situation in both Yemen and Libya.

To a certain extent, the weakness of the Yemeni and Libyan states is a result of geography. Neither country has terrain that makes it easy to govern—Yemen because of the roughness of its terrain, Libya because of the expansiveness of its territory. To a certain extent, the weakness of the Yemeni and Libyan states is a result of their history (or lack thereof). Both states are relatively recent creations, artificially constructed from disparate elements. Yemen had been divided between an independent North Yemen and South Yemen until 1990. Contrasting social structures found in each Yemen reflect the legacies of formal imperialism in the south and the absence of formal imperialism in the north. The United Nations created an independent federated Libya in 1952 from the remnants of three former Italian colonies that had been kept separate until 1934. Even then, regional differences remained. Finally, the weakness of the Yemeni and Libyan states was a product of the ruling styles of their leaders: both Ali Abdullah Saleh of Yemen and Muammar al-Gadafi of Libya avoided establishing strong institutions in favor of a personalistic style of rule (justified in Gadafi's case by his Third Universal Theory as outlined in his *Green Book*).

With virtually no institutions that might maintain regime cohesion, the regimes in Yemen and Libya simply splintered when exposed to the pressure of uprisings. This also accounts for why the uprisings in both states necessarily became violent and drawn out. Unlike in Tunisia and Egypt, there was no unified army that could intervene, declare *its* commitment to nonviolence, and keep regime loyalists and regime opponents separated. On the other hand, there may be an upside to the disintegration of the regimes in the two countries. Because institutions in both Yemen and Libya were weak and are unlikely to survive the overthrow of the ruling clique, it is in these two countries that a better opportunity for revolutionary change exists than in Egypt, for example. This revolutionary change has so far been frustrated in Yemen, largely because of the interference of foreign powers, particularly the United

States and Saudi Arabia. Revolutionary change is under way in Libya, but as of this writing its direction is yet to be determined.

A third cluster of states includes Algeria, Syria, and Bahrain, where regimes maintained their cohesion against the uprisings. We might even say that in Algeria, Syria, and Bahrain regimes had no choice but to maintain their cohesion against uprisings. Thus, once uprisings broke out in these three states, there was little likelihood that one part of the ruling institution would turn on another, as happened in Tunisia or Egypt, or that the ruling institution would splinter, as happened in Libya and Yemen.

The reason for regime cohesion in Algeria differs from that in Bahrain and Syria. Since Algeria won independence in 1962, the state has been in the hands of the victorious National Liberation Front (FLN). The state apparatus of Algeria is both *of* and coextensive *with* the FLN, while the FLN itself consists of three parts: the army (which has been kingmaker), the president and the political leadership (those anointed by the military), and the party (the FLN's link to the public). This odd setup came about as a result of Algeria's peculiar history. Before 1962, there had never been an Algeria. Instead, the territory that is now Algeria had been three *départements* (provinces—not colonies) of France. During the Algerian war of independence, the FLN constructed an army, a trade union apparatus, a state apparatus that included various ministries, and legislative, executive, and judicial branches. Once the FLN proved victorious, it established the first independent Algerian state in history, and this apparatus became both the regime and the "representional" and mobilizational apparatus spawned by the regime.

In Syria and Bahrain rulers effectively "coup-proofed" their regimes by, among other things, exploiting ties of sect and kinship to build a close-knit, interdependent ruling group. In Syria this group consists of Bashar al-Assad, his extended family, and members of the minority Alawite community (which makes up about 11 percent of the population). Thus Maher al-Assad, President Assad's brother, is the head of the presidential guard, and General Assef Shawkat, Assad's brother-in-law, is deputy chief of staff. Neither can turn on the regime: if the regime goes, they go too. In addition, the regime has outsourced much of the repression to *ashbah* ("ghosts," sing.: *shabiha*)—Alawite hoodlums who hail from the Assad family's home region—who supplement the formal, overlapping security agencies. The *ashbah* have played a critical role during the uprising by "mopping up" pockets of resistance in neighborhoods previously softened up by bombardment—a task with which Sunni conscripts could not be trusted.[12]

Similarly, the core of the regime in Bahrain consists of members of the ruling Khalifa family who hold critical cabinet portfolios, from the office of prime minister and deputy prime minister to ministers of defense, foreign affairs, finance, and national security. The commander of the army and the commander of the royal guard are also family.[13] As in Syria, members of a minority community—Sunni Muslims, who make up an estimated 30 to 40 percent of the population—form the main pillar and primary constituency of the regime. The regime has counted on the Sunni community to circle its wagons in the regime's defense, although the recent uprising started out as intersectarian in nature (as happened in Syria, it took on more sectarian trappings as regime repression increased). And to assure a steady stream of Sunni recruits into the military and security apparatus, the regime has adopted a policy of "political naturalization"—that is, importing and naturalizing Sunnis from the rest of the Arab world who come to work for it.[14]

None of this is meant to imply that the uprisings in Algeria, Bahrain, and Syria would necessarily play themselves out in similar ways. They have not. The Algerian uprising never really gained traction. When the National Coordination for Change and Democracy called for a massive demonstration against the regime in Algiers in February 2011, approximately 30,000 riot police officers easily dispersed a crowd one-tenth that size.[15] The Bahraini uprising, on the other hand, did pose a serious challenge to the monarchy, but it was crushed with the help of outside intervention from Saudi Arabia and the United Arab Emirates. As in Algeria, however, anger has continued to roil under the surface, and sporadic protests and confrontations with the authorities have also continued. In contrast, as of this writing the Syrian uprising shows no sign of abating or diminishing. Instead, it has morphed into an increasingly tragic and violent affair. But while regime cohesion in Algeria, Bahrain, and Syria has had little bearing on the paths the uprisings have taken, it has restricted the possible outcomes for those uprisings to one of four alternatives: total victory for the regimes and their supporters, total victory for their opponents, prolonged stalemate, or the exhaustion of both.

The final cluster of states that have experienced uprisings consists of five of the seven remaining monarchies: Morocco, Jordan, Saudi Arabia, Kuwait, and Oman. Here the word "uprising" is a misnomer. With the exception of the uprising in Bahrain, *protests* in the Arab monarchies share two important characteristics that set them apart from *uprisings* in the Arab republics: they have been more limited in scope, and they have demanded reform of the *nizam*, not its overthrow.

It is not altogether clear why this discrepancy has been the case—or, for that matter, whether it will continue to be so. According to sociologist and political scientist Jack A. Goldstone, the reason the demand is for reform and not revolution is that monarchs have an ability that presidents—even presidents for life—do not have: they can retain executive power while ceding legislative power to an elected assembly and prime minister. As a result, the assembly and prime minister, not the monarch, become the focal point of popular anger when things go wrong.[16] King Abdullah of Jordan has been particularly adept at placing blame for the slow pace of reform on the shoulders of others: between the onset of the Arab uprisings and spring 2012, he went through four prime ministers.

Goldstone's argument has made quite a splash in the policymaking and academic communities, but it fails to convince. The model he provides more closely fits Jordan or Kuwait, which have operating parliaments, than, for example, Saudi Arabia, which is a wholly owned subsidiary of the House of Saud. As a matter of fact, save for the fact that Saudi protesters demanded reform of the Saudi regime rather than its complete replacement, Saudi Arabia might be removed from the monarchies category altogether and placed in the same category as Algeria, Syria, and Bahrain. As vulnerable as the Saudi regime has at various times appeared, ties of kinship and tribe suffuse it, inextricably binding the military and security apparatus with the royal family and religious establishment, which uses its position to lend the regime its veneer of legitimacy.[17] Finally, the exceptional case of Bahrain flies in the face of Goldstone's argument.

It is entirely possible in the future that it might be necessary to subdivide the monarchies into a number of categories that reflect uprisings that have not yet occurred. One of those divisions might prove to be between oil-rich and oil-poor states (that is, the Gulf monarchies versus Morocco and Jordan), because the former have deeper pockets with which to buy off their populations than the latter. Another possible division might separate those monarchies in which members of minority communities rule (Jordan, if it follows the path of Bahrain) from those in which members of majority communities rule.[18] Where the regime is in the hands of a minority community, that community might circle its wagons if its privileged position is threatened; on the other hand, rule by the majority community would obviously make it easier for the government to crush the opposition before an uprising reaches critical mass. A third possible fissure among monarchies might separate those in which the extended family is in control from those in which partial control has been ceded to allies or those who pose no threat to monarchic rule. If this fissure in fact opens up, it will partially salvage Goldstone's theory. Finally, events might compel us to differentiate between monarchies in which noncitizens make up a higher percentage of the inhabitants than citizens and those in which they do not (the United Arab Emirates, for example, where guest workers make up four-fifths of the population, as opposed to Saudi Arabia, for example, where they make up between one-quarter and one-third). Guest workers who face deportation and have no stake in the political process are less likely to rebel than citizens who do have a stake. Or maybe the monarchies other than Bahrain will remain relatively quiescent. One thing that should be evident by now is that uprisings such as those that have broken out since December 2010, their trajectories, and their long-term effects are unpredictable, except in retrospect.

It is for this reason that this chapter's assessment of the uprisings must remain provisional. As time goes on, events in one or more of the states discussed above, or in Iraq or Palestine, for example, may force us to rethink the entire wave of uprisings or the categorization of individual uprisings. This is, of course, to be expected. After all, what eighteenth-century Frenchman, reflecting on events a year and a half after the storming of the Bastille—an incident as electrifying for the French as Bouazizi's self-immolation was for Arabs—could have foreseen the execution of Louis XVI (still two years distant) or the reign of terror (two years, eight months distant), much less the event that, for many historians, closed the books on the French Revolution: the coronation of Napoleon as emperor of France (nine years distant)?

NOTES

1. See, for example, Jeff Jacoby, "The Arab Spring," *Boston Globe*, March 10, 2005, http://www.boston.com/news/globe/editorial_opinion/oped/articles/2005/03/10/the_arab_spring/, accessed April 21, 2012; and Charles Krauthammer, "The Arab Spring of 2005," *Seattle Times*, March 21, 2005, http://seattletimes.nwsource.com/html/opinion/2002214060_krauthammer21.html, accessed April 21, 2012.

2. See, inter alia, Naira Antoun, "Threads of Narrating the Arab Spring," Jadaliyya, March 25, 2012, http://www.jadaliyya.com/pages/index/4820/threads -of-narrating-the-arab-spring, accessed April 30, 2012; Rami G. Khouri, "Drop the Orientalist Term 'Arab Spring,'" Daily Star (Beirut), August 17, 2011, http://www.dailystar.com.lb/Opinion/Columnist/2011/Aug-17/Drop-the -Orientalist-term-Arab-Spring.ashx#axzz1tBZ5yacU, accessed April 19, 2012; and Tariq Ramadan, "Neither an Arab Spring nor Revolutions," http://www.tariq ramadan.com/spip.php?article11750&llang=fr&llang=fr, accessed April 19, 2012.

3. For further discussion, see James L. Gelvin, "Reassessing the Recent History of Political Islam in Light of the Arab Uprisings," forthcoming.

4. Joel Beinin, "Egypt at the Tipping Point?," *Foreign Policy*, January 31, 2011, http://mideast.foreignpolicy.com/posts/2011/01/31/egypt_at_the_tipping_point, accessed May 1, 2012.

5. See James L. Gelvin, "American Global Economic Policy and the Civic Order in the Middle East," in *Is There a Middle East?: The Evolution of a Geopolitical Concept*, ed. Michael Bonine, Abbas Amanat, and Michael Gasper (Palo Alto, CA: Stanford University Press, 2011), 191–206; and Steven Heydemann, "Social Pacts and the Persistence of Authoritarianism in the Middle East," in *Debating Arab Authoritarianism: Dynamics and Durability in Nondemocratic Regimes*, ed. Oliver Schlumberger (Palo Alto, CA: Stanford University Press, 2008), 21–38.

6. CIA, *The World Factbook 2009* (Washington, DC: Central Intelligence Agency, 2009), https://www.cia.gov/library/publications/the-world-factbook /rankorder/2172rank.html, accessed April 19, 2012.

7. See Farzaneh Roudi, "Youth Population and Employment in the Middle East and North Africa: Opportunity or Challenge" (New York: United Nations Secretariat, 2011), http://www.un.org/esa/population/meetings/egm-adolescents /p06_roudi.pdf, accessed April 19, 2012; and "Egypt Human Development Report 2010: Youth in Egypt: Building Our Future" (Cairo: Egyptian Institute of National Planning/United Nations Development Programme, 2010).

8. Elena Ianchovichina, Josef Loening, and Christina Wood, "How Vulnerable Are Arab Countries to Global Food Price Shocks?" (Washington, DC: World Bank, 2012), http://www-wds.worldbank.org/servlet/WDSContentServer /WDSP/IB/2012/03/29/000158349_20120329154735/Rendered/PDF/WPS 6018.pdf, accessed April 19, 2012.

9. http://www.rediff.com/business/slide-show/slide-show-1-8-reasons-why -food-prices-are-rising-globally/20111017.htm, accessed April 19, 2012; Business

Insider, "The Twenty-Five Countries That Will Be Screwed by a World Food Crisis," Wall Street Cheat Sheet, October 12, 2010, http://wallstcheatsheet.com /economy/the-25-countries-that-will-be-screwed-by-a-world-food-crisis.html, accessed April 19, 2012.

10. Technically, there are twenty-one member states of the Arab League, along with the Palestinian territories. Depending on the definition of protests or uprisings being used, the five in which it might reasonably be said that uprisings have not occurred are the Comoros, Lebanon, Somalia, Qatar, and the United Arab Emirates.

11. "Egypt Military's Economic Empire," al-Jazeera, February 15, 2012, http:// www.aljazeera.com/indepth/features/2012/02/2012215195912519142.html, accessed April 19, 2012; Stephen H. Gotowicki, "The Role of the Egyptian Military in Domestic Society," http://fmso.leavenworth.army.mil/documents/egypt /egypt.htm, accessed April 19, 2012.

12. Elizabeth A. Kennedy, "Syria Gunmen Used to Crush Protests," Huffington Post, May 16, 2011, http://www.huffingtonpost.com/2011/05/26 /syria-gunmen-protests_n_867550.html, accessed April 19, 2012; Nir Rosen, "The Tides of Mosques," al-Jazeera, October 2, 2011, http://www.aljazeera .com/indepth/features/2011/10/2011101143646274931.html, accessed April 26, 2012.

13. A complete list of cabinet ministers can be found at https://www.cia.gov /library/publications/world-leaders-1/world-leaders-b/bahrain.html, accessed April 26, 2012.

14. Omar al-Shehabi, "Demography and Bahrain's Unrest," Sada, March 16, 2011, http://carnegieendowment.org/2011/03/16/demography-and-bahrain -s-unrest/6b7y, accessed April 26, 2012.

15. Azzedine Layachi, "Algeria's Rebellion by Installments," MERIP Reports, March 12, 2011, http://www.merip.org/mero/mero031211, accessed April 26, 2012.

16. Jack A. Goldstone, "Understanding the Revolutions of 2011: Weakness and Resilience in Middle Eastern Autocracies," Foreign Affairs, May-June 2011, http://www.foreignaffairs.com/articles/67694/jack-a-goldstone/understanding -the-revolutions-of-2011, accessed April 26, 2012.

17. Rand senior analyst James T. Quinlivan has argued that the Saudi Arabian regime shares characteristics with Syria under Hafiz al-Assad and Iraq under Saddam Hussein. To this we might add Bahrain. See James T. Quinlivan, "Coup-

Proofing: Its Practice and Consequences in the Middle East," *International Security* 24 (Autumn 1999): 131–165.

18. Anywhere from three-fifths to three-quarters of the population of Jordan are Palestinians, as opposed to "East Bankers," who make up most of the remainder and have traditionally provided the main support for the throne.

About the Contributors

Julia Clancy-Smith is Professor of Modern North African, Middle Eastern, and Mediterranean History at the University of Arizona, Tucson. She is the author of *Mediterraneans: North Africa and Europe in an Age of Migration, c. 1800–1900* (University of California Press, 2011), which won two book awards, and *Rebel and Saint: Muslim Notables, Populist Protest, Colonial Encounters (Algeria and Tunisia, 1800–1904)* (University of California Press, 1997), which received three awards. She also coedited *Walls of Algiers: Narratives of the City Through Text and Image* (University of Washington Press, 2009).

Mary-Jane Deeb is the Chief of the African and Middle Eastern Division at the Library of Congress. She is the author of *Libya's Foreign Policy in North Africa* (Westview Press, 1991) and coauthor with M. K. Deeb of *Libya Since the Revolution: Aspects of Social and Political Development* (Praeger, 1982).

Robert O. Freedman is the Peggy Meyerhoff Pearlstone Professor of Political Science Emeritus at Baltimore Hebrew University and is currently Visiting Professor of Political Science at Johns Hopkins University, where he teaches courses on Russian foreign policy and on the Arab-Israeli conflict. Among his recent publications are *Russia, Iran, and the Nuclear Question: The Putin Record* (Strategic Studies Institute of the U.S. Army War College, 2006) and *Israel and the United States: Six Decades of US-Israeli Relations* (Westview Press, 2012).

James L. Gelvin is Professor of History at the University of California, Los Angeles. A specialist in the social/cultural history of the modern Middle East, he is the author/editor of five books, including *The Arab Uprisings: What Everyone Needs to Know* (Oxford University Press, 2012)and *The Modern Middle East: A History* (Oxford University Press, 2005), along with numerous articles and chapters in edited volumes.

Mark L. Haas is Associate Professor in the Political Science Department and the Graduate Center for Social and Public Policy at Duquesne University in Pittsburgh. He is the author of *The Clash of Ideologies: Middle Eastern Politics and American Security* (Oxford University Press, 2012); *The Ideological Origins of Great Power Politics, 1789–1989* (Cornell University Press, 2005); and coeditor with David W. Lesch of *The Middle East and the United States: History, Politics, and Ideologies* (Westview Press, 2012, 5th ed.).

David W. Lesch is Professor of Middle East History in the History Department at Trinity University in San Antonio, Texas. He has published twelve books. Among them are *Syria: The Fall of the House of Assad* (Yale University Press, 2012); *The New Lion of Damascus: Bashar al-Asad and Modern Syria* (Yale University Press, 2005); and *The Arab-Israeli Conflict: A History* (Oxford University Press, 2008).

Reza Marashi is Research Director at the National Iranian American Council. He formerly served in the Office of Iranian Affairs at the U.S. Department of State. His articles have appeared in the *New York Times, Foreign Policy, The Atlantic,* and *The National Interest,* among other publications.

Trita Parsi is the 2010 recipient of the Grawemeyer Award for Ideas Improving World Order. He is the Founder and President of the National Iranian American Council and the author of *Treacherous Alliance: The Secret Dealings of Iran, Israel, and the United States* (Yale University Press, 2007), the silver medal winner of the 2008 Arthur Ross Book Award from the Council on Foreign Relations, and *A Single Roll of the Dice: Obama's Diplomacy with Iran* (Yale University Press, 2012).

Ilan Peleg is the Charles A. Dana Professor of Government and Law at Lafayette College and an Adjunct Scholar at the Middle East Institute in Washington, DC. He is the author of *Israel's Palestinians: The Conflict Within* (Cambridge University Press, 2011, coauthored with Dov Waxman); *The Foreign*

Policy of George W. Bush (Westview Press, 2009); and *Democratizing the Hegemonic State: Political Transformation in the Age of Identity* (Cambridge University Press, 2007).

Jeremy Pressman is the Alan R. Bennett Honors Professor and Associate Professor in the Department of Political Science at the University of Connecticut. His publications include *Warring Friends: Alliance Restraint in International Politics* (Cornell University Press, 2008); and "Power Without Influence: The Bush Administration's Foreign Policy Failure in the Middle East," *International Security* 33, 4 (Spring 2009): 149–179. He is on Twitter @djpressman.

Bruce K. Rutherford is Associate Professor of Political Science at Colgate University and Director of the university's program in Middle Eastern Studies and Islamic Civilization. His publications include *Egypt After Mubarak: Liberalism, Islam, and Democracy in the Arab World* (Princeton University Press, 2008 and 2012); "What Do Egypt's Islamists Want? Moderate Islam and the Rise of Islamic Constitutionalism," *Middle East Journal* 60, 4 (Autumn 2006): 707–731; and "Surviving Under 'Rule by Law': Explaining Ideological Change in Egypt's Muslim Brotherhood," in *Constitutionalism, the Rule of Law, and the Politics of Administration in Egypt and Iran*, ed. Said Arjomand and Nathan Brown (State University of New York Press, forthcoming).

Curtis R. Ryan is Associate Professor of Political Science at Appalachian State University in North Carolina. He is the author of *Inter-Arab Alliances: Regime Security and Jordanian Foreign Policy* (University of Florida Press, 2009); and *Jordan in Transition: From Hussein to Abdullah* (Lynne Rienner, 2002).

Steve A. Yetiv is University Professor of Political Science at Old Dominion University. He is the author, most recently, of *Explaining Foreign Policy: U.S. Decision-Making in the Gulf Wars* (Johns Hopkins University Press, 2011, 2nd ed.); *The Petroleum Triangle: Oil, Globalization, and Terror* (Cornell University Press, 2011); and *Crude Awakenings: Global Oil Security and Amercian Foreign Policy* (Cornell University Press, 2004; 2010 paperback).

Index

influence of, 231–232
invasion of Iraq, 85, 139, 228–229, 241
and Iran, 139, 221
and Israel, 177–178, 180, 185–188, 189, 221
and Libya, 64–65, 68, 202, 220, 223, 226, 228, 229
Middle East and North Africa Incentive Fund, 228
Middle East Transitions (MET) office, 227–228
and Muslim Brotherhood, 230–231
and Russia, 197, 208, 212, 213
sale of F-15 fighters to Saudi Arabia, 104
security interests of, 220, 221, 222, 223, 224, 226
and status quo in Middle East, 137
and Syria, 209, 220, 225–226, 229–230
U.S.-Israeli-Saudi alliance, 136, 137, 141, 142, 143, 147, 224
See also under Egypt; Turkey
Ursan, Ali, 210
USAID. *See* United States: Agency for International Development

Values vs. economic/security interests, 223
Velayati, Ali-Akbar, 166
Viticulture, 20

Wahhab, Muhhamad bin Abd al-, 111
Walters, Barbara, 89–90
Wantchekon, Leonard, 101
War crimes, 73
Washington Post, 67, 73, 179
Water, 19

Waxman, Dov, 187
Weak states, 248
Wealth distribution, 85, 119, 245. *See also* Poverty
Welfare state, 98, 246
WikiLeaks, 16, 23, 81, 136
Wittes, Tamara, 221, 227
Women, 5, 70
  in Bahrain, 242
  in Egypt, 47, 48, 49, 50, 51, 52, 53, 225
  in Kuwait, 241
  in Saudi Arabia, 106, 241
  in Syria, 81
  in Tunisia, 15–16, 25–26
Wood, Reed, 230
World Bank (WB), 14, 18, 26, 228
World Trade Organization, 27
World Wars, 19

Yavuz, M. Hakan, 159
Yelisov, Archbishop Alexander, 210
Yeltsin, Boris, 196, 199
Yemen, 66, 68, 71, 82, 110, 125, 145, 191, 223, 224, 239, 240, 247–249
Young people, 15, 16, 22, 41, 59, 68, 69, 70, 76, 82, 89, 98
  in Algeria, 245
  in Egypt, 3, 164, 245
  in generational conflict, 75
  in Jordan, 122
  in Libya, 3, 245
  in Saudi Arabia, 107
  in Syria, 3, 81
  youth bulges, 3, 4, 17, 20, 81
Yugoslavia, 66

Ziadeh, Radwan, 205
Zuccotti Park in New York City, 27
Zuma, Jacob, 203–204